THE GRIM PHOENIX

THE GRIM PHOENIX

Reconstructing Thomas Pynchon

William M. Plater

 INDIANA UNIVERSITY PRESS
Bloomington & London

Manufactured in the United States of America

Library of Congress Cataloging in Publication Data

Plater, William M   1945–
The grim phoenix.

Bibliography: p.
Includes index.
1. Pynchon, Thomas—Criticism and interpretation.
I. Title.
PS3566.Y55Z79   1978   813'.5'4   77-12833
ISBN 0-253-32670-2   1 2 3 4 5 82 81 80 79 78

For Gail

CONTENTS

PREFACE

merely a scholarly quest after all, an adventure of the
mind . . .

V.

Thus far the most common element of Pynchon criticism is apology, or at least
an acknowledgment of its propriety. Far from affected pedantry, this self-
consciousness is a demand made on critics by the very nature of Pynchon's art
and, implicitly, by Pynchon himself in his absence and denial. To read Pynchon
is a scholarly quest, an adventure of the mind, even if our traditional tools and
attitudes have been turned toward mean ends as though we were so many
Stencils. Anyone who reads Pynchon feels the compulsion to talk about the
experience—if only as an antidote—because there is something eerie, uncertain,
about his work. There is a need, then, for criticism, for talking, apart from
scholarship, and it is with such a claim that this study is justified.

An almost instantaneous community of critics has grown up around Pynchon,
and the countless articles and monographs are good for the critics despite what
little comfort they may be to the object of their study. I am indebted to this
community in more ways than I can acknowledge or any longer recognize,
though the individuals whose works I have consulted are listed in the bibliography; I have not attempted to note the many points of agreement or disagreement
on the assumption that most of my readers will have been long familiar with the
principal arguments. Similarly, I have not felt obligated to include extensive
notes documenting Pynchon's many literary antecedents, such as his use of
allegory or the quest and travel motifs, since these will be rather obvious to the
readers interested in them.

I owe a greater debt to a number of authors whose works have greatly in-
fluenced my preconceptions and analyses. Some of these—Henry Adams, "Karl
Baedeker," Sigmund Freud, Werner Heisenberg, Abraham Moles, R. M. Rilke,
Erwin Schrödinger, Norbert Wiener, and Ludwig Wittgenstein—are obvious.

Others have been equally important though not as apparent: Roland Barthes, Norman O. Brown, Kenneth Burke, Walter Dornberger, Hugh Duncan, Gerald Holton, Neil Kleinman, Humberto Maturana, George Herbert Mead, Laurence Sterne, Colin Turbayne, and Heinz von Foerster. Conspicuously absent are a number of hermeneutic, new textual, or structuralist critics, in addition to Barthes and Moles, whose strategies offer a great deal for the analysis of Pynchon's fiction. While I have not chosen a structuralist approach, I have been conscious of common interests, which will be evident in the text.

I owe a personal debt to several individuals. Harold Walsh cheerfully shared his thoughtful readings of Pynchon. Cora Freeman and Kathy Schulz typed the manuscript. David Shwayder read portions of it and helped me understand why a philosopher might be disappointed. Nina Baym, James Hurt, Daniel Madjiak, Cary Nelson, and Edward Sullivan read the entire manuscript and without their help, I would still be out there in the great glass sphere with no way to get back, so at the mercy of language. Finally, I owe my greatest debt to Gail Maxwell, my wife; this book is for her.

ACKNOWLEDGMENTS

Grateful acknowledgment is given for permission to quote from the following works under copyright:

Henry Adams, *The Education of Henry Adams*, edited by Ernest Samuels (Boston: Houghton Mifflin Company, 1974). Copyright © 1973 by Houghton Mifflin Company. Reprinted by permission of the publisher.

Karl Baedeker, *Egypt* (1929), *Germany* (1936), and *Greece* (1894) (Leipsic: Karl Baedeker). All rights reserved by Karl Baedeker. Reprinted by permission of the publisher.

Abraham Moles, *Information Theory and Esthetic Perception*, translated by Joel E. Cohen (Urbana: University of Illinois Press, 1966). Copyright © 1966 by the Board of Trustees of the University of Illinois. Reprinted by permission of the publisher.

Thomas Pynchon, "A Journey Into the Mind of Watts," in *The New York Times Magazine*, 12 June 1966. Copyright © 1966 by The New York Times Company. Reprinted by permission of the publisher.

Thomas Pynchon, *V.* (New York: J. B. Lippincott Company, 1963). Copyright © 1961, 1963 by Thomas Pynchon. Reprinted by permission of J. B. Lippincott Company.

Thomas Pynchon, *The Crying of Lot 49* (New York: J. B. Lippincott, 1967). Copyright © 1965, 1966 by Thomas Pynchon. Reprinted by permission of J. B. Lippincott Company.

Thomas Pynchon, *Gravity's Rainbow* (New York: The Viking Press, 1973; London: Jonathan Cape Limited, 1973). Copyright © 1973 by Thomas Pynchon. Reprinted by permission of the Viking Press and Jonathan Cape Limited.

R. M. Rilke, *The Duino Elegies*, translated by Stephen Garmey and Jay Wilson (New York: Harper & Row, 1972), pp. 66, 67–68, 73. Copyright © 1972 by Stephen Garmey and Jay Wilson. Reprinted by permission of Harper & Row.

Max Weber, *The Protestant Ethic and the Spirit of Capitalism*, translated by Talcott Parsons (New York: Charles Scribner's Sons, 1958). Copyright © 1958 by Charles Scribner's Sons. Reprinted by permission of the publisher.

Norbert Wiener, *The Human Use of Human Beings* (Boston: Houghton Mifflin Company, 1967). Copyright © 1950, 1954 by Norbert Wiener. Reprinted by permission of the publisher.

Ludwig Wittgenstein, *Tractatus Logico-Philosophicus,* translated by D. F. Pears and B. F. McGuinness (New York: Humanities Press, 1966). Copyright © 1961 by Routledge & Kegan Paul Ltd. Reprinted by permission of Humanities Press, Inc., and Routledge & Kegan Paul Ltd.

Herbert Warren Wind, "The House of Baedeker," in *The New Yorker,* 22 September 1975. Copyright © 1975 by *The New Yorker.* Reprinted by permission of the publisher.

Introduction

Thus have we set down the true nature of *Atonement* or
Reconciliation with God; But as far as the *Dialogue's*
Atonement, it is nothing else, but a *vain, idle, imaginary*
and *illusory* thing, a *mere fiction,* which he having fancied and framed out to himself would fain obtrude
upon others, without the least color of testimony from
the Word of God. . . .

From Nicholas Chewney's 1656 critical study
of William Pynchon's dialogue,
The Meritorius Price of Our Redemption.

Over three hundred years after William Pynchon's alleged gross
errors and heresies were confuted by critics, Thomas Pynchon began
to frame his own mere fictions and, like his ancestor, to seek in exile
a personal mode of survival. Critics have treated the later Pynchon
more kindly, but the problems of representing and surviving one's
own world are remarkably unchanged; testimony from the word
remains the central dilemma of reconciliation with God or, in his
absence, perceptible forces of destiny. This book originated nearly
five years ago when I first began to consider Thomas Pynchon's use
of language both as the subject of his fiction and as the relational
process between the individual and his community, more specifically
the author and his reader. My particular interest focused on metaphor as a system of transformation—a form of aesthetic seduction
favoring imagination rather than reason—in which the limits of language are exploited as revelation. Pynchon's ability to make manifest
a reality that cannot merely be described with language offers a

preternatural landscape where experience survives speech as intent, where we do become lost in the way time is passing and images of uncertainty replace things that had names, faces, histories. In Pynchon there is a density of experience that forces the reader into his or her private resources—memories, anxieties, imaginings, and, inevitably, facts. These scraps of certainty, finally, impinge on imagination and recall the reality that is coordinate with language. Pynchon leaves us between fictions, imprisoned in language, and we must reconcile our multiple truths with whatever testimony we can summon.

This book is one reconciliation. It is also a self-confessed betrayal, which claims no other justification than the necessity of reaching some kind of accommodation with language and all it proposes. Faced with a world as complex as Pynchon's, I have sought accommodation in considering several basic themes: the idea of the closed system and entropy as social phenomena, the way in which illusion and reality are aspects of form, the interrelationships of life and death, and the way in which order and "connectedness" are fictions of necessity as well as convenience. By identifying these few subjects, I do not imply that Pynchon is circumscribed or defined by them; rather, they are points of departure for considering multiple themes, characters, and contexts. Nor do I imply that Pynchon's fiction contains such discrete categories. In addition to exploring Pynchon's multiplexity, this study demonstrates that all thematic categories intersect. Pynchon makes his world comprehensible by showing how various things are related, how there are parallel existences, and, possibly, how there is reconciliation.

As a consequence, I have investigated single situations or episodes from several perspectives as a means of illustrating diverse themes. There is repetition to be certain, but it is by repetition and recapitulation that Pynchon advances his own art. While he does not repeat himself tiresomely, Pynchon continues to develop the same ideas, dilemmas, and even characters in successive stories. There is evidence of this everywhere and I have attempted to suggest the way in which

Pynchon's skill and sophistication have evolved from his first stories to *Gravity's Rainbow*. More importantly, I have tried to suggest that this continuity from novel to novel is simultaneously a record of the works' achievement and the effective integration of form with content. One of Pynchon's recurring metaphors is the accumulation of debris into layered deposits, each of which is itself transformed by successive additions. Pynchon's fiction may be viewed from a similar perspective: stories and novels are continuous but layered; each new layer modifies the way we perceive those that came before; and past layers are the foundation for each new one. *Gravity's Rainbow* abandons nothing that came before it, but its own density has compressed, combined, and transmuted the perceptions of earlier works into a wholly new substance—one of the most impressive works of fiction of this century.

The continuity of Pynchon's fiction is obvious in the recurrence of motifs such as the quest, the preoccupation with death, repeated use of scientific models, or even the reappearance of characters. However, the constant element that dominates Pynchon's fiction—and by implication this study—is a sense of duality, paired opposites. The most important of numerous dualities is the familiar thermodynamic situation of entropy and the disintegration of order into disorder. Pynchon explored this theme in his first published story and each subsequent work. It occurs in many guises and situations, but it is always the condition within which each plot unfolds. The notion of establishing and maintaining order suggests the dualities of human skill as opposed to chance, the deliberate creation of illusion to mask or alter reality, the struggle of life against death, and the effort to communicate and relate at the expense of originality and individuality. Phrased in only a slightly different way, Pynchon presents two simultaneous and alternate worlds: the world as it simply is and the world that civilization has created with its collective inventions and clever designs. The world as it is presents a frightening prospect: entropy increases, accident and chance are everywhere, and nothing is certain. This is a world described by Boltzmann and Gibbs's

probabilities, Einstein's relativity, and Heisenberg's uncertainty relations—modes of definition that suggest that our knowledge of the
world is always partial and never quite as certain as it appears to be,
that it depends on perceptions and contingencies. In contrast, the
world created by illusions of order, finite certainty, history, and
predictable futures is not only more familiar but preferred. It is recognizable everywhere in governments, corporations, schools, media,
religion, and criticism. These two worlds exist in a perpetual tension
of chaos and order, complexity and simplicity, chance and control.

The conflict between the need to order and control events, people,
even the physical world, and the continual rediscovery of uncertainties and probabilities structures Pynchon's fiction. Though it is his
principal theme, this tension cannot be stated or even described; it
must be shown. The primary purpose of this study, therefore, is to
explore this conflict and to suggest ways of thinking about the world
Pynchon reveals. Leni Pökler of *Gravity's Rainbow* is one of the few
characters in all his stories and novels to recognize the effects of
control, though even she cannot articulate her feelings directly. Her
difficulties exemplify the problem of showing rather than describing
and help account for the organization of this book. She is unable to
explain herself to her husband: "Not produce, . . . not cause. It all
goes along together. Parallel, not series. Metaphor. Signs and symptoms. Mapping on to different coordinate systems, I don't know . . ."
There is repetition but not a series, continuity without cause and
effect.

The title of this book has been drawn from one of Pynchon's
metaphors not only to suggest the basic theme of man's attempt to
control uncertainties and probabilities, but also to insist that metaphor is perhaps the only way we can perceive and describe our world,
whether we be scientists or poets, suburban housewives or soldiers.
The metaphor is Leni Pökler's. She invented it in the quiet darkness
of her bedroom to tell her husband what world she had seen. Her
metaphor may seem strange, but as will become evident it describes
—as best language can—the world we all inhabit this twentieth cen-

tury: "It moves slowly, so slowly and so far away . . . but it will burst out. It is the grim phoenix which creates its own holocaust . . . *deliberate resurrection.* Staged. Under control. No grace, no interventions by God. . . ." Though the passage of the grim phoenix may describe Western civilization in its course toward a technological inevitability and the promise of another new age, its flight is an illusion. The earth itself and the universe of things change always—without redemption, without resurrection, and without escape. If any atonement is possible among this world's preterite, it may be only what Pig Bodine calls that physical grace to keep it all going, even if only temporarily through accommodation, metaphor, illusion. Atonement, finally, may be a last testimony from the word of man.

THE GRIM PHOENIX

1 All That Is the Case

> Gibbs' innovation was to consider not one world, but
> all the worlds which are possible answers to a limited
> set of questions concerning our environment. His cen-
> tral notion concerned the extent to which answers that
> we may give to questions about one set of worlds are
> probable among a larger set of worlds. Beyond this,
> Gibbs had a theory that this probability tended natu-
> rally to increase as the universe grows older. The mea-
> sure of this probability is called entropy, and the
> characteristic tendency of entropy is to increase.
>
> Norbert Wiener,
> *The Human Use of Human Beings*

PRELIMINARIES

"The world," begins Wittgenstein's *Tractatus Logico-Philosophicus*, "is
all that is the case. The world is the totality of facts, not of things."[1]
With the speculative imagination of a theoretical physicist, Thomas
Pynchon examines the philosophical world as if it were a closed
system in which facts, rather than molecules, are distributed according to the laws of thermodynamics. The result is a series of seven
stories, three novels, and an essay, in which forces and processes are
more important than people, in which organizations and structures
are more the manifestation of hope than of conviction, and in which
the ability and opportunity to communicate are measures only of
how little there is to be said. In taking the closed system as a metaphor for the world, Pynchon considers a number of cases, each of

which shares Wittgenstein's and the physicist's view of a closed system: an isolation defined by boundaries that enclose a totality and an organization that tends increasingly toward chaos. The metaphor belongs to both epistemology and physics, but through the assimilation of Pynchon's imagination it becomes the environment of his fiction.

Having studied physics as well as literature at Cornell University, Pynchon has more than a casual knowledge of thermodynamics and scientific descriptions of the closed system. The education of Thomas Pynchon may, in fact, account for many of the coincidences and accidents that play such an important part in his fiction. Inescapably, Pynchon's novels both parody and affirm the idea of *The Education of Henry Adams.* Clausius, Maxwell, and Boltzmann would have been familiar names to any engineering student, while the recent works of Claude Shannon and Norbert Wiener were imaginatively captivating in the 1950s. At Cornell various things came together for Pynchon. In addition to cultivating an enthusiasm for both thermodynamics and cybernetics, he undoubtedly was affected by the philosophy department, which, under Norman Malcolm's leadership, placed heavy emphasis on Wittgenstein (the philosopher had lectured at Cornell several years before Pynchon's arrival and his influence was still strong). By coincidence, Maxwell and Boltzmann were among Wittgenstein's favorite scientific authors, and the philosopher had anonymously given financial support to Rainer Maria Rilke, whose poetry also affected Pynchon. Without question Pynchon was influenced by Vladimir Nabokov, whom he had as a teacher, but the influence was certainly greater after publication of Nabokov's novels. Though dynamic, Nabokov was a remote teacher with little personal contact with his students; Pynchon probably attended Nabokov's large lecture course, which surveyed the Russian novel. These sources provided Pynchon with all the materials he needed to construct his own image of the world as a system isolated within the limits of language. Too well trained to ignore the confluence of science, philosophy, history, and literature, Pynchon took advantage

of such loosely connected relationships to find therein his own metaphor of the closed system. What actually conspired in its creation is
a matter for conjecture. What it contains is a matter for exploration.

If Pynchon views the world as a closed system, then the measure
of its condition is entropy—a term, introduced in 1854 by the physicist Rudolph Clausius, that increasingly attracted the attention of
creative writers of both fiction and history and has in recent decades
been overworked. In Pynchon's fiction, entropy literally measures
the disorganization of a closed system. Pynchon is unusual, too, in
using the concepts not in isolation but in their cultural contexts, of
which science is only one aspect. Closed systems recur so often in his
fiction that they require a series of inferences to make each metaphor
both fresh and consistent. Entropy, for example, measures not only
a system's disorganization but also its capacity to change. Pynchon
is syncretic. One level of meaning makes his metaphor literal and the
other makes it figurative.

Though we can never be certain how much history Pynchon
knows, the cultural context of entropy does enter his fiction in a
loosely connected chain of people stretching from Clausius and James
Clerk Maxwell to Ludwig Boltzmann, Henry Adams, Ludwig Wittgenstein, and Claude Shannon—each of whom enlarges our understanding of the term. Pynchon draws on these sources selectively,
playing his readers' knowledge against their own ignorance, much as
if his fiction were a closed system tending toward equilibrium, with
the responsibility for organization falling partly to the reader. Most
of Pynchon's principal closed systems will be sorted out subsequently. However, the one that subsumes all others is the world, and
it is moving in only one direction—toward death. This irreversible
transformation recurs in each microcosm. One of Pynchon's few
believable characters, the sailor Mehemet from the novel *V.*, states
the case with succinct familiarity: "You're old . . . I am old, the world
is old; but the world changes always; we, only so far. It's no secret,
what sort of change this is. Both the world and we . . . began to die
from the moment of birth."[2]

In turning to science for his metaphor of entropy, Pynchon is able to give his representation of the world a feeling of precision and accuracy, as if he were observing some cosmic experiment. However, it is from Henry Adams that he gets help in applying the principles of science to the human condition. *The Education of Henry Adams* is not just a source; the book takes on an identity of its own, moving just beneath the narrative surface, yet clearly evident in a character like Herbert Stencil. Adams says of himself "he never invented his facts; they were furnished him by the only authorities he could find."[3] Among them, of course, are Clausius, Maxwell, and their contemporaries. The *Education* gives Pynchon an intact historical system that has already accommodated science. In his chapter on the "Grammar of Science" Adams worries about the scientific outlook for the twentieth century while suddenly discovering that "after sixty or seventy years of growing astonishment, the mind wakes to find itself looking blankly into the void of death." Adams's view authenticates the application of entropy to time:

> Satisfied, the future generation could scarcely think itself, for even when the mind existed in a universe of its own creation, it had never been quite at ease. As far as one ventured to interpret actual science, the mind had thus far adjusted itself by an infinite series of infinitely delicate adjustments forced on it by the infinite motion of an infinite chaos of motion; dragged at one moment into the unknowable and unthinkable, then trying to scramble back within its senses and to bar the chaos out, but always assimilating bits of it, until at last, in 1900, a new avalanche of unknown forces had fallen on it, which required new mental powers to control. If this view was correct, the mind could gain nothing by flight or by fight; it must merge in its supersensual multiverse, or succumb to it. (460–61)

The infinite chaos of motion is another way of describing the entropy of the world's closed system: both we and the world begin to die from the moment of birth. Adams provides Pynchon these basics: the exaltation of information, unknown forces, mental powers of control, succumbing to the supersensual multiverse, and an increasing chaos.

Pynchon's fiction turns Adams's generalities into particulars and embellishes them imaginatively.

In the *Education* Pynchon finds more than a mechanism for translating physics into history. He also finds that the perspective necessary for seeing whole systems must lie outside the system itself. Adams's repeated wish to escape the void he had discovered signals a self-consciousness about being trapped in it. Yet a novelist cannot so easily betray his presence. Adams's scientific model shapes his view of the world, which "differed in nothing essential from the kinetic theory of a perfect gas"(455). He discovers that the only unity is the system itself—science—but that within the system there is only multiplicity and chaos. Adams's perspective integrates the second law of thermodynamics with history and suggests a similar model for the novelist:

> He found himself in a land where no one had ever penetrated before; where order was an accidental relation obnoxious to nature; artificial compulsion imposed on motion; against which every free energy of the universe revolted; and which, being merely occasional, resolved itself back into anarchy at last. He could not deny that the law of the new multiverse explained much that had been most obscure, . . . but the staggering problem was the outlook ahead into the despotism of artificial order which nature abhorred. (457–58)

It will take Pynchon almost six hundred thousand words to make Adams's statement sufficiently complex and chaotic, enabling his encyclopedic fiction to become experience.

Pynchon augments Adams with Wittgenstein's *Tractatus Logico-Philosophicus,* published midway between the *Education* and Pynchon's birth. Serving Pynchon as science served Adams, the *Tractatus* provides still another representation of the world as a closed system.[4] Since fiction is not philosophy, Pynchon does not have to use the *Tractatus* consistently. Instead, it becomes a paradigm implying much that Pynchon need not say. The *Tractatus* appears in Pynchon's fiction in a variety of references to closed systems—groups of people, the world itself, even systems of belief. Pynchon manipulates the reader's knowledge of the *Tractatus* to extend the implications of each situation. The initial proposition that "the world is all that is the case" and the subsequent eight major propositions define a philosophically "closed" system. Thus, the tract models the conditions involved in trying to describe such a system. For example, Wittgenstein declares, "If I know an object I also know all its possible occurrences in states of affairs. (Every one of these possibilities must be part of the nature of the object.) A new possibility cannot be discovered later"(9). In creating a fictional world, Pynchon shows all possible occurrences in states of affairs, their interrelationships, causes, and effects, at the same time he shows that the entire system is arbitrary, subject to observation. The world observed, as Wittgenstein notes, has its particular limits: "The world is *my* world: this is manifest in the fact that the limits of *language* (of that language which alone I understand) mean the limits of *my* world. The world and life are one. I am my world. (The microcosm)"(115–17).

Pynchon presses at the edge of the knowable world with his language. Indeed, the world he creates is precisely the same as his language, but its cultural referentiality is determined by the limits of the individual readers' information. The closed system—Wittgenstein's philosophical world or Pynchon's fictional world—is all that language is capable of stating as the case. If the second law of thermodynamics were applied to language, then entropy might be a measure of its banality, its tendency toward an equilibrium of thought. However, it is the order of language—its ability to impose structure and meaning on experience—that makes it valuable for representing the world. In Wittgenstein's view:

> Everything that can be thought at all can be thought clearly. Everything that can be put into words can be put clearly.
> Propositions can represent the whole of reality, but they cannot represent what they must have in common with reality in order to be able to represent it—logical form.
> In order to be able to represent logical form, we should have to be

able to station ourselves with propositions somewhere outside logic, that is to say outside the world. (51)

Because the connections between elements of Pynchon's system are necessarily random and changeable to some degree, he can appear to station himself outside the world of his creation and observe what Henry Adams referred to as "the despotism of artificial order which nature abhorred." He may watch the creatures of his imagination struggle against entropy, but he does not represent what his world has in common with the readers' reality. Rather, he lets his readers infer their own world; "what *can* be shown, *cannot* be said"(51), notes Wittgenstein.

PYNCHON: IN THE ROOM

As the world is a closed system, so is its representation. Pynchon's representation began in 1959 with the publication of a short story "Mortality and Mercy in Vienna." In succession he published "Lowlands" and "Entropy" in 1960, "Under the Rose" in 1961, *V.* in 1963, "The Secret Integration" in 1964, "The World (This One), The Flesh (Mrs. Oedipa Maas), and The Testament of Pierce Inverarity" in 1965, "The Shrink Flips," *The Crying of Lot 49,* and "A Journey into the Mind of Watts" in 1966, and *Gravity's Rainbow* in 1973. Through these works, Pynchon reveals the world that he sees from the isolation of his room. It is a world of people and places, but they are incidental to systems and forces. In early works, the forces are simply those of entropy—decay, decadence, and death. Later they are elaborated by time, history, information, the despotism of an artificial order. The early stories tend to speak about entropy. As Pynchon's skill develops, the novels reveal, but they do not speak.

The image of the artist alone in his room is a familiar one, almost mandatory for any contemporary writer suspected of self-conscious narration. Pynchon does not disappoint his readers. His first novel provides a stereotype so clearly drawn that no one can miss the point. Fausto Maijstral is a poet and he is alone in his room:

> It takes, unhappily, no more than a desk and writing supplies to turn any room into a confessional. This may have nothing to do with the acts we have committed, or the humours we do go in and out of. It may be only the room—a cube—having no persuasive powers of its own. The room simply is. To occupy it, and find a metaphor there for memory, is our own fault. (284)

To occupy the room is to accept the closed system as the environment of fiction and entropy as the metaphor for memory. What is a story if it is not a digression? While Fausto is not the only storyteller in Pynchon's world, he is the only one who self-consciously talks about his craft. It would be a mistake to regard Fausto as a stand-in for Pynchon, but it would be a greater mistake not to recognize Pynchon's closed world in Fausto's room. The poet's confession may be as much Pynchon's playful apology for his earlier narrative voice as it is Fausto's. "Shakespeare and T. S. Eliot ruined us all"(288) may be Fausto's lament, but the reference to Pynchon's own earlier "Mortality and Mercy in Vienna" and "Low-lands" is unmistakable. After *V.* there is no question that Pynchon will create his own world and enlarge the worlds of his predecessors. Wittgenstein's "The world is *my* world" approximates Pynchon's own relationship with the world he observes.

Pynchon finds a metaphor for memory in Wittgenstein's totality of facts. As Fausto observes, "the facts are history, and only men have histories. The facts call up emotional responses, which no inert room has ever showed us"(285). As Pynchon knows from Adams, a closed system—whether room or world—is not inert but is an infinite chaos of motion, the object of increasing entropy. To create a world and to represent it, he is obligated to impose upon the multiverse of facts some artificial order. The only order at his disposal within the isolation of the room is a memory of his experiences, whatever he can reclaim from the past. As Fausto recognizes, however, he must pay a price for giving up his own memory to the printed page: "So we do sell our souls: paying them away to history in little installments. It isn't so much to pay for eyes clear enough to see past the fiction of continuity, the fiction of cause and effect, the fiction of a humanized history endowed with 'reason' "(286). In order to create a world that reveals the world as a closed system, Pynchon is willing to pay the price of a public identity (which critics create in little installments) in return for the reality of his fiction. Pynchon's own silence and exile give credence to Wittgenstein's observation that:

> Whatever we see could be other than it is.
> Whatever we can describe at all could be other than it is.
> There is no *a priori* order of things.
> Here it can be seen that solipsism, when its implications are followed out strictly, coincides with pure realism. The self of solipsism shrinks to a point without extension, and there remains the reality coordinated with it. (117)

Wittgenstein's concept of the self as "the limit of the world—not a part of it"(119) offers Pynchon a useful image for describing the writer's role in fiction. The only reality coordinated with Pynchon's self, or memory, is the world created in his fiction. This world is not confined to any one story or novel, but is revealed at various points in time and space in each of them. Together, they constitute the limits of Pynchon's world and a system within which facts rather than molecules are distributed. If we imagine the second law of thermodynamics applied to this system, we may find that Pynchon has disappeared; shrunken to a point without dimension, he has become his own Maxwell's demon, sorting out facts and concentrating them in the favored pockets of creation that become his stories and novels. His world may be solipsistic, a fault of memory, but as the narrator of *Gravity's Rainbow* reminds the reader at Pynchon's most advanced stage of creation: "You had thought of solipsism, and imagined the structure to be populated—on your level—by only, terribly, one. No count on any other levels. But it proves to be not quite that lonely. Sparse, yes, but a good deal better than solitary."[5]

If Pynchon's fictional world is a closed system, then it must be subject to entropy; and yet fiction is nothing more than language— a system of logic and order, even if the implicit order is not always obvious in its manifestations. How can order represent chaos? According to Wittgenstein's *Tractatus,* sentences are pictures of reality, and as pictures they must have the same form as the reality they represent. The apparent contradiction is perhaps resolved by Adams, who realizes that as chaos increases, the demand for the illusion of order increases as well. In Pynchon reality lies hidden beneath the inherent logic of language. Fausto gives up the psychological self for eyes clear enough to see past logic and order. The reader, however, is in much the same position as the heroine of Pynchon's second novel. Oedipa Maas is confronted with the fact of her own limited vision:

> She could, at this stage of things, recognize signals like that, as the epileptic is said to—an odor, color, pure piercing grace note announcing his seizure. Afterward it is only this signal, really dross, this secular announcement, and never what is revealed during the attack, that he remembers. Oedipa wondered whether, at the end of this (if it were supposed to end), she too might not be left with only compiled memories of clues, announcements, intimations, but never the central truth itself, which must somehow each time be too bright for her memory to hold; which must always blaze out, destroying its own message irreversibly, leaving an overexposed blank when the ordinary world came back.[6]

In its dependence on an artificial order, the "ordinary world" can accommodate institutionalized violence but not a permanent intrusion of chaos; and only those who have given up any claim to this world retain vision clear enough to see past illusion—paranoids, schizophrenics, writers isolated in their memories.

With his scientific background, Pynchon is particularly conscious of the role of the observer. Fausto claims eyes clear enough to see, for example, and Oedipa wonders about the central truth. Observation, whether visual or metaphorical, is a special problem for those within a closed system. The most distinguishing characteristic of Fausto's room is that it is "sealed against the present." Regardless of how much he may claim to see within memory, constancy of purpose will not permit him to see beyond it. Wittgenstein declares that for us to see what our closed system has in common with its representation we would have to station ourselves outside the system. If Pynchon's closed system actually represented the world, he too would have to be stationed outside it. But Pynchon does not represent; he creates a world and thereby poses the problem of observation for the reader, who, like Oedipa, must wonder about the central truth. This transferral is not only amusing, it is functional. It removes Pynchon's fiction from the merely interesting to the entrapping. While the engineer might invite us to look beyond his model to the mechanism itself, the novelist will not permit us to escape the limits of his metaphor. As an observer, the reader is enclosed within Pynchon's fictional world by his relationship with it.

Pynchon's intrusion into his readers' complacency makes his artifice real. Moreover, his craft is as much that of an engineer as a novelist. The revolution worked on science by the likes of Clausius, Maxwell, Boltzmann, and Gibbs resulted in "a shift in the point of view of physics in which the world as it actually exists is replaced in some sense or other by the world as it happens to be observed,"[7] as Norbert Wiener remarks in *The Human Use of Human Beings*, a book that undoubtedly gave added significance to Pynchon's classroom encounters with physics. It was Boltzmann and Gibbs whose theories expanded Maxwell's concept of probability distributions to a statistical analogue of entropy and made the world a function of observation as well as disintegration. This was in part the "law of the new multiverse," which led Henry Adams to conclude that "Chaos was the law of nature; Order was the dream of man"(451). In Adams's view, "the historian must not try to know what is truth, if he values his honesty; for, if he cares for his truths, he is certain to falsify his facts"(457). Similarly, Wittgenstein, for whom the world was the totality of facts, could conclude that "whatever we see could be other than it is. Whatever we can describe at all could be other than it is." Clearly, Maxwell, Boltzmann, Gibbs, Adams, Wittgenstein, and Wiener are not addressing each other, nor are their interests and terminologies coincidental. However, they observe the same world—though the perspectives vary—and reach remarkably similar conclusions. Pynchon more or less successfully integrates these views into a useful, if not entirely accurate, system of reference, which adds veracity to his fiction at the same time it tempts the less scrupulous reader to forego his own perception for that of someone else—all in the interest of imposing order on the increasing entropy of the world that simply is.

Within Pynchon's fictional world there are two orders of observation: that of characters such as Fausto and Oedipa, whose world is limited to the fiction itself, and that of the reader, who looks at their world from outside it but who is also enclosed by his or her relationship with that world. The respective problems of observation are similar. In his second story, "Low-lands," Pynchon details the problems of observation through Dennis Flange, who worries about telling a sea story:

> . . . it is all right to listen to but not to tell stories about that sea, because you and the truth of a true lie were thrown sometime way back into a curious contiguity and as long as you are passive you can remain aware of the truth's extent but the minute you become active you are somehow, if not violating a convention outright, at least screwing up the perspective of things, much as anyone observing subatomic particles changes the works, data and odds, by the act of observing.[8]

The act of observing, the manipulation of data, and participation in the world being described are as much the acts of a person who would live in the world as they are of a person who would write about it. The choice appears to be one of involvement or disengagement, and in Pynchon's stories we can see characters exercising their rights of choice. The gesture may be futile because there always lurks the question of what difference a choice makes, whether the truth even matters—screwed up or not. The problem is obviously important to Pynchon since he continually returns to it; as the next chapter will show, it is one of his preoccupations. In terms of the closed system, however, observation defines the relationship of each character to the world he inhabits and, similarly, of each reader to Pynchon's creation. In *V.*, for example, Fausto observes from the confines of his room that "it is the 'role' of the poet, this 20th Century. To lie" (305). At the same time, the explorer Hugh Godolphin has become circumscribed by the word "Vheissu" and his recollection of the place: "it was not what I saw or believed I saw that in the end is important. It is what I thought. What truth I came to"(190). In situations that the reader can observe, Pynchon allows his world to reveal what it has in common with the reader's own world, all the time recalling Wittgenstein's proposition that whatever we can see or describe could be other than it is.

To ensure that the reader does not miss the connection, Pynchon includes an important detail in *V.* that relates the metaphor of entropy, Wittgenstein's representation of the world, and the reader's relationship with Pynchon's creation: it "shows" the despotism of artificial order. An engineer, Kurt Mondaugen works within the closed system of communication, in which maximum entropy is a state of maximum information and minimum order, in which noise is associated with disorder but is actually differentiated from a signal only by the intent of the sender or the desire of the receiver. Although Pynchon does not literally integrate the information theory of Claude Shannon and the philosophical system of the *Tractatus,* he uses their intersection to show that the only order is artificial order. "Surrounded by decadence," or social chaos, Mondaugen moniters "sferics"—atmospheric radio disturbances, noise in the system that may be a reflection of increasing entropy but that certainly has something to do with the earth's magnetic field. While Mondaugen examines sferics for possible meaning, one of the decadents, a soldier named Weissmann, discovers the logic and order of the apparently meaningless clicks and whistles that seem to come from beyond the earth:

"The remainder of the message," Weissmann continued, "now reads: DIEWELTISTALLESWASDERFALLIST."

"The world is all that the case is," Mondaugen said. "I've heard that somewhere before." A smile began to spread. "Weissmann, for shame. Resign your commission, you're in the wrong line of work. You'd make a fine engineer: you've been finagling." (258-59)

Although the full significance of the message will not become clear until Mondaugen and Weissmann reappear in *Gravity's Rainbow,* Pynchon serves early notice that Flange's fears are real. The only thing that you can do with the totality of facts is finagle.

The only thing the reader can do with the facts of Pynchon's novels is try to impose some order on all the clicks and whistles, all the noise. That Pynchon intends to enclose his readers within his fiction is obvious. In *V.* and *The Crying of Lot 49* he uses mystery-story plots, laid tantalizingly close to the surface, to involve his readers in the search for clues. In *V.,* for example, Pynchon mocks the reader for becoming involved in the search for V.'s identity: "If we've not already guessed, 'the woman' is, again, the lady V. of Stencil's mad time-search. No one knew her name in Paris"(382). Of course the order-seeking reader did—without having to be told. In *The Crying of Lot 49,* as in *V.,* Pynchon allows the reader to see more of his world than any one of his characters can. The effect is not only to lure the reader into the characters' searches for meaning, but to catch the reader off guard and remind him that he has been finagling. In *Gravity's Rainbow,* Pynchon is more direct; this novel, unlike the earlier ones, does not have an obvious plot, but is almost chaotic—noise or sferics—which demands that the reader impose his own meaning. There is no choice. The order-seeking reader must either play Weissmann to the novel's disorder, or succumb to it. Even readers toughened by the random fiction of Joyce or Beckett are tempted by the clues to order. And Pynchon is less gentle with the entrapped reader than in earlier works. Without pretense of any sort, the narrator can say, "you will want cause and effect. All right"(663), and then give it knowing full well that that is precisely what the reader wants. Or he is capable of listing a series of towns and suggesting possible reasons for having done so, only to remark: "Well, you're *wrong*, champ. . . . Ha, ha! Caught *you* with your hand in your pants!" (695–96). Among the hundreds of examples showing the reader that he has been caught finagling, Pynchon has his most fun with readers who discover his use of archetypes—like the closed system—and think they have found the key to his code: ". . . oh you hear some of these new hires, the seersucker crowd come in the first day, 'Wow! Hey—that's th-th' *Tree o' Creation!* Huh? Ain't it! Je-eepers!' but they calm down fast enough, pick up the reflexes for Intent to Gawk, you know self-criticism's an amazing technique, it shouldn't work but it does" (411).

Among the several strategies Pynchon employs for involving his readers in his fictional world, one of the most effective is his use of detail and fact. Not only do these facts bring the readers' act of observing to the level of consciousness, but they force the readers to sort out referents and referring fictions. Names, places, events, scientific principles, chemical compounds spill over from Pynchon's fiction into the readers' own reality. The more curious may track down sources and references, but even the most casual reader must begin to ponder the limits of the totality of facts. They range from isolated details of *V.*, such as the measurements of Botticelli's *The Birth of Venus*, to the orchestrated details of *Gravity's Rainbow*, such as the role of Shell Oil in World War II. Regardless of complexity or specific function, each of these facts has the same purpose—which the narrator of *V.* alludes to after giving a list of the mass deaths that occurred from July 1 to August 28, 1956: "Look in any yearly Almanac, under 'Disasters'—which is where the figures above come from"(271). The impact of Pynchon's system of fiction depends largely on the congruence, or at least overlap, of his created world with that of his readers. The potential intrusion of reference works —almanacs, science texts, histories, even specific books like the *Tractatus*—continually reminds readers of their observational relationship. Like many other contemporary novelists, Pynchon will not permit his readers the luxury of suspended belief—he reminds us that we are reading a text. But Pynchon is not content with forcing mere self-awareness on the reader; he insists on inflicting the awareness of all that is the case.

Pynchon reinforces literary techniques with cinemagraphic forms. In the stories and in *V.* he employs devices common to both forms, such as flashbacks or manipulations of the audience's sense of time, without any discoverable intent to associate the two media. However, by the time Pynchon writes "A Journey into the Mind of Watts" and *The Crying of Lot 49* he is certainly aware of the implications of cinemagraphic form for the novel. By altering the mode and self-consciousness of observation, cinema (and television) further blurs the distinctions between illusion and reality. In its economy of description, for example, cinema can make illusion, dream, or fantasy both present and objective on the screen, while the novel can only imply another level of illusion. Further, cinema enacts a perpetual present in representing the sequential order of time. Cinema has no past, no future, and no reality except in the viewer's memory. While cinema may be a function of observation, the relationship of the observer with his object demands participation in creating the world he observes. With directness and efficiency, film accomplishes the same objectives as the use of facts and details—with their invitation to consult reference works—in the novel.

Clearly fascinated by the implications of cinema for the novel, Pynchon writes *The Crying of Lot 49* almost as if it were a movie; it has a tightly controlled plot based on the highly successful mystery-movie formula, an economy of dialogue, plausible fantasy, and characters that are at least imaginable. One of these is Mr. Thoth, a ninety-one-year-old man whom Oedipa Maas interrupts from a dream about his grandfather. When Oedipa asks him about his dream, he points at the television and says the dream was mixed up with a Porky Pig cartoon: "It comes into your dreams, you know. Filthy machine"(66). From a man who bears the name of the Egyptian god of wisdom and the inventor of hieroglyphics, this pronouncement is more than an innocuous detail. It is also a reflection of Pynchon's increased awareness of the impact of visual media. In an earlier episode, he is more direct, not only outlining the capacity of film to make fantasy appear objectively real but also suggesting that the reality of film lies outside the normal time sequence. A lawyer named Metzger explains his reality to Oedipa:

"But our beauty lies," explained Metzger, "in this extended capacity for convolution. A lawyer in a courtroom, in front of any jury, becomes an actor, right? Raymond Burr is an actor, impersonating a lawyer, who in front of a jury becomes an actor. Me, I'm a former actor who became a lawyer. They've done the pilot film of a TV series, in fact, based loosely on my career, starring my friend Manny Di Presso, a one-time lawyer who quit his firm to become an actor. Who in this pilot plays me, an actor become a lawyer reverting periodically to being an actor. The film is in an air-conditioned vault at one of the Hollywood studios, light can't fatigue it, it can be repeated endlessly." (20)

While having fun at the expense of novelists of exhaustion, Pynchon nonetheless accurately portrays the capacity of film to disorient the viewer's sense of reality. In a *New York Times Magazine* article about Watts written four months after *The Crying of Lot 49* was published, Pynchon makes the same point in a more serious vein: "For Los Angeles, more than any other city, belongs to the mass media. What is known around the nation as the L. A. Scene exists chiefly as images on a screen or TV tube. . . ."[9]

In *Gravity's Rainbow* Gerhardt von Göll makes a movie of fantasy for the Allied propaganda machine depicting Africans in positions of high responsibility in Hitler's Aryan army. When he discovers that there is a Schwarzkommando, he believes that his movie has created reality and he offers to do the same for a group of Argentine anarchists who wish to bring their romantic hero, Martín Fierro, into reality. With more than a faint resemblance to Erich von Stroheim or Fritz Lang, von Göll proclaims, "It is my mission . . . to sow in the Zone seeds of reality. The historical moment demands this, and I can only be its servant. My images, somehow, have been chosen for incarnation. What I can do for the Schwarzkommando I can do for your dream of pampas and sky"(388). Similarly, Pynchon's readers can never be quite certain at what level the story that they are reading takes place—it may be only the narrator's account of another of von Göll's films, or a dream the narrator is waiting for the reader to bring into reality. Pynchon reinforces this possible confusion with the coincidental conception of Bianca and Ilse, one on each side of the screen. Bianca is actually conceived during the filming of a rape scene, a scene that excites Pökler when he sees it and stimulates him to recreate the rape in his own bedroom. Ilse mirrors Bianca, who is born of fantasy. The narrator of *Gravity's Rainbow*, however, reminds his readers that they too are complicit: "She favors you, most of all. You'll never get to see her. So somebody has to tell you"(472). Pynchon allows for the possibility of his readers' creating their own personal mental pictures in the privacy of their own rooms, safely out of the sight of other moviegoers, thus fusing movie and novel, at least for the moment.

Pynchon ends *Gravity's Rainbow* with a final reminder:

> The screen is a dim page spread before us, white and silent. The film has broken, or a projector bulb has burned out. It was difficult even for us, old fans who've always been at the movies (haven't we?) to tell which before the darkness swept in. The last image was too immediate for any eye to register. (760)

Each section of the novel is populated with movie stars (remember the Kenosha Kid?) and countless extras; but there is no movie without the readers' projections. Whether in a poet's lonely room, a movie theater, or the pages of a novel, we are always enclosed in a system of our own observation and creation. Driblette, the director of *The Courier's Tragedy* in *The Crying of Lot 49*, speaks for all of us: "I'm the projector at the planetarium, all the closed little universe visible in the circle of that stage is coming out of my mouth, eyes, sometimes other orifices also"(56). Oedipa Maas thinks she ought to "try to be

what Driblette was, the dark machine in the centre of the planetarium"(58), and asks of herself the essential question: "*Shall I project
a world?*"[10] Whether the observer is a cameraman looking through
his lens or an author looking through his metaphors for memory, the
world exists only as it happens to be observed. Its projection is
always enclosed—whether within a planetarium as expansive as the
universe or a universe as small as a room—and at the center is the
self.

THE SELF

In the *Tractatus* Wittgenstein equates the world with the self: "The
philosophical self is not the human being, not the human body, or
the human soul, with which psychology deals, but rather the meta-
physical subject, the limit of the world—not a part of it"(119). Despite Norbert Wiener's contention that the human body is not an
isolated system, there is a sense in which the self, for which the body
is a container, is closed within its projection of a world. The world
as it is and as it is created come together in the self, in the "I" and
eye of the observer. From his earliest stories to *Gravity's Rainbow*
Pynchon explores the self that is all that is the case. Among his more
fascinating exhibits are Herbert Stencil, V., Benny Profane, Fausto,
and Pig Bodine of *V.*; Pierce Inverarity, Mucho and Oedipa Maas of
The Crying of Lot 49; and Edward Pointsman, Blicero, and Tyrone
Slothrop of *Gravity's Rainbow.* In the variety and complexity of their
projections, these characters begin to suggest the limits of the world,
and the isolation of the self.

By choice or necessity, Herbert Stencil's self-identity is defined by
his mad time-search for V. As the novel's narrator explains, other
"people read what news they wanted to and each accordingly built
his own rathouse of history's rags and straws," but Stencil is more
conscious of his role:

He only felt (he said "by instinct") when a bit of information was useful, when not: when a lead ought to be abandoned, when hounded to the inevitable looped trail. Naturally about drives as intellectualized as Stencil's there can be no question of instinct: the obsession was acquired, surely, but where along the line, how in the world? Unless he was as he insisted purely the century's man, something which does not exist in nature. (209)

The looped trail is Stencil's personal Ouroboros—the cosmic serpent swallowing its own tail, or in Stencil's case—tale. Within this self-projected world, Stencil attempts to order the totality of facts about V. into a meaningful structure, as if he were a historian. For him, identity is a matter of bookkeeping—an external projection rather than the product of emotions. Despite his disguises, Stencil is none other than the fulfillment of Henry Adams's prophecy—and at least partially a parody of Adams himself. If chaos is the law of nature, then Stencil's dream of order is the only mechanism available to preserve the illusion of his identity. Adams speaks of "the theory of history to be imposed by science on the generation born after 1900" (459)—coincidentally the year of Stencil's birth. Although it would be simple "to call him contemporary man in search of an identity" (209), Stencil creates an identity by continually revising his theory of V.'s history. His searches take him through sewers, the diaries of his father, interviews with people who might have known V., memories, history. On Malta, when he seems to be on the verge of perceiving the ultimate V-structure, he refuses the possibility because the end of the search would leave him with only the chaos of nature and the irreversible process of entropy.

If Stencil's identity coincides with the looped trail of his search for V., then the history of V. gives an indication of who he is—like the vapor trail a high speed particle leaves in a cloud chamber. V., however, is problematic. Not only does she assume various guises—Victoria, Vera, Veronica—but she is presented to the reader second and third-hand through Stencil's V-structure and through the narrator, who has his own fun with the reader's gullibility. As far as the narrator is concerned, her identity and Stencil's coincidences are merely data that he can manipulate for the purpose of involving the reader in his own self-conscious V-structure—a technique that may drive the humorless reader away, but that guarantees the persistent reader's involvement.

V. qualifies as the novelist's personification of Henry Adams's theory of history and as the mechanized twentieth-century equivalent of Adams's Virgin or Venus:

> Symbol or energy, the Virgin had acted as the greatest force the Western world ever felt, and had drawn man's activities to herself more strongly than any other power, natural or supernatural, had ever done; the historian's business was to follow the track of the energy; to find where it came from and where it went to; its complex source and shifting channels; its values, equivalents, conversions. (388–89)

In the world that is all that is the case, the Virgin-Venus is interchangeable with a less remote symbol: "... to Adams the dynamo became a symbol of infinity.... Among the thousand symbols of ultimate energy, the dynamo was not so human as some, but it was the most expressive"(380). Pynchon has fused the Virgin-Venus with the dynamo into the single V., a remarkably scattered concept that can be represented adequately by no known single word, but only by an initial that means everything and nothing. In this one act, Pynchon has brought off a feat that will in a sense dominate all the works that come after. The identity of V. requires the reader's consideration of the whole range of possibilities, one so large that the entire novel is required to present them. *V.* is V.: a symbol without reference—except that supplied by Stencil and the narrator ... or the reader.

The identity of V., therefore, is a model of the world as it is seen rather than as it exists. In addition to V.'s symbolic character ("v" is also a symbol for "variant reading" as well as the logical relationship "or" in the *Tractatus*), she has a personal character that is revealed both by the narrator's finagling and by Stencil's coincidences. The reader has ample reason to see V. as a person accumulating a series of identities from her initial appearance as the young girl Victoria Wren to her death as the Bad Priest. The V. that is a summation of these subidentities has meaning, however, only within a structure imposed upon her random appearances—Stencil's V-structure or the reader's own. Within Wittgenstein's logical system, *V.* may be regarded as a picture of V. Both the novel and V. are closed systems, the limits of which are the separate selves of the various observers.

Pynchon, however, detects still another possibility for revealing the self as a closed system. If V. is a totality of facts that Stencil can collect and assemble into a history, and if facts, according to Wittgenstein's propositions 2 and 2.01, are states of affairs that are in turn combinations of things, Pynchon can take Wittgenstein literally and also allow V. to represent a combination of inanimate things. At this point, Wittgenstein's philosophy and Adams's history merge in the identity of V. As she becomes a "state of affairs" in her various intrigues, she increasingly becomes an object, a mechanized Virgin-Venus: "Victoria was being gradually replaced by V.; something entirely different, for which the young century had as yet no name" (386). V. becomes a symbol of the world's closed system, with its increasing disorder and tendency toward an inanimate stasis, at the same time she is herself literally a closed system in which entropy is a measure of decadence. The identity of V. begins to merge with the world during her episode in Paris with Mélanie l'Heuremaudit (accursed hour), amid a group of amateur decadents whose abstractions V. will embody: "A decadence . . . is a falling-away from what is human, and the further we fall the less human we become. Because we are less human, we foist off the humanity we have lost on inanimate objects and abstract theories"(380). The new century's Venus, V. deals away her humanity for a more powerful force, the one that Adams predicted would fall upon the world after 1900. As we watch Stencil attempting to impose order on this chaos, we can also see V., like Stencil, fusing identity and observation into a single act, but in her case one aimed at disintegration and fragmentation. V. consummates Mélanie's mirrored fetish by becoming her double, a voyeur: "As for V., she recognized—perhaps aware of her own progression toward inanimateness—the fetish of Mélanie and the fetish of herself to be one. As all inanimate objects, to one victimized by them, are alike"(385). In this act V. becomes both subject and object. Enclosed within her own mirrored room, the only world she can project is the one she sees. As objects V. and Mélanie can combine only in states of affairs, a relationship. After Mélanie is crucified during the performance of Porcépic's ballet, having "neglected to add to herself the one inanimate object that would have saved her"(389), V. is capable only of a succession of identities tending increasingly toward equilibrium and death. During her last appearance as the Bad Priest, V. makes Pynchon's metaphor of Adams's Virgin-dynamo and the closed system literal as she is reduced into various inanimate parts by the children of Malta in a grisly Eucharist of the century's new goddess: wig, artificial foot, dentures, navel stone, glass eye. Fausto wonders if the disassembly might go on forever: "Surely her arms and breasts could be detached; the skin of her legs be peeled away to reveal some intricate understructure of silver openwork. Perhaps the trunk itself contained other wonders: intestines of parti-coloured silk, gay balloon-lungs, a rococo heart"(322). In death, the only sounds she makes are cries—"so unlike human or even animal sound that they might have been only the wind blowing past any dead reed"(322). V. may not be so human as some of Pynchon's characters, but among all the possible ways of representing the effects of isolation on the self, she is the most expressive in her death.

Benny Profane's identity differs in its particulars, but he too is an isolated system. He feels the force unleashed by the Virgin-dynamo: "To Profane, alone in the street, it would always seem maybe he was looking for something too to make the fact of his own disassembly plausible as that of any machine"(30). Profane fears this potential disassembly so much that he keeps himself in constant motion to minimize the possibility of his reaching a point of equilibrium. His motion, however, is that of the yo-yo—itself a kind of machine that moves without going anywhere, a dynamo that does no work. The limits of his world are determined by the length of the string that binds Profane to his own self: "If you look from the side at a planet swinging around in its orbit, split the sun with a mirror and imagine a string, it all looks like a yo-yo. The point furthest from the sun is called aphelion. The point furthest from the yo-yo hand is called, by analogy, apocheir"(26). Profane moves up and down the East coast of America, in and out of work, under and on top of the street that is his life, with and without the entanglements of people. While the street may suggest an alternative to the enclosure of the room, Profane knows that every street is the same and that it has only one path —an orbit with a fixed apocheir. Left on Malta by Stencil at the novel's end, Profane admits the limits of the street to one who shares it with him:

> "The experience, the experience. Haven't you learned?"
> Profane didn't have to think long. "No," he said, "offhand I'd say I haven't learned a goddamn thing." (428)

In the street, experiences are always the same; they are just randomly distributed. Profane has not learned; he has only gathered information about his experiences, but he cannot act on it. Unable to organize himself or his experiences, Profane is an object amid the chaos of the world, at the mercy of fortune.

Profane is not merely passive. He may function as an unwitting secular agent of the Virgin-dynamo. Profane is a schlemihl who takes and never gives. He refuses every opportunity to order or structure events. The movement that sustains Profane is the same at work in the world's closed system, where energy is constantly diffused from areas of high to areas of low concentration until equilibrium is achieved. He takes humanity from Rachel, Paola, and Fina to maintain the illusion of his own movement and his own identity, depleting them a little with each encounter. It is Profane who by accident confirms Stencil's sense that events are ordered into an ominous logic when he delivers an account of Father Fairing's sewer parish only seconds after Stencil remarks that V.'s emissaries "haunt this century's streets"(423). V.'s force and Profane's accident intersect at a crucial point in Stencil's V-structure. Though both are aspects of the same closed system, Profane, without even recognizing his role, diminishes Stencil's humanity even more by forcing him to affirm the pretense of his search. To Stencil's mind, Profane's soul is possessed by the devil V., but to himself he is only sick, drunk, or more likely both. Lacking the illusion of a closed room, Profane seems to live only in the timeless present—the interface of exchanges of energies: "as if all his homes were temporary and even they, inanimate, still wandering as he: for motion is relative . . ."(427).

Pig Bodine, a companion of Benny Profane's, has a similar identity and function, but he has mastered the technique so well that he takes in more energy than Profane. Bodine shows a remarkable capacity to survive entropy as he moves efficiently through most of Pynchon's stories and novels, always present but not quite a presence. Coming from Bodine, the question "what do you think of Sartre's thesis that we are all impersonating an identity?"(118) is ridiculous until we consider that Bodine may know a great deal about the impersonation of an identity. In his continuity and his ability to survive, Pig may be a new guide to the world in the grip of entropy. Although this is a subject for subsequent discussion, it is worth noting that in the gentle chaos before patriarchal order was established the pig was a consort of the Venus-Virgin, a sacrificial symbol of death and rebirth. In the new world where the goddess is V. and order has given way to chaos, Bodine may be an equivalent to Maxwell's demon, at the interface of energy and information, negotiating exchanges in return for an uncertain existence. There are others of Bodine's sort—perhaps Fausto, Oedipa Maas, or Tyrone Slothrop, for example—who occupy a different position in Pynchon's world.

Stencil, V., and Profane are Pynchon's first fully developed characters; they are, superficially, the prototypes of subsequent inhabitants of his world. As Pynchon's skill increases, the complexity and subtlety of characterization reflect less a change in the author's view of the world than an awareness of his own cunning. These variations, however, are important because it is from them that we can infer our own reality. With *The Crying of Lot 49,* Pynchon leaves, at least temporarily, the puppetry and plotfulness of *V.* for a media-induced realism familiar to all inhabitants of the late twentieth century.

Pierce Inverarity is another V. The testament he leaves behind is more than a will; it is a statement of belief and the evidence of his existence—a series of clues to his identity, which Oedipa Maas is charged with embodying into whatever abstract theory she can impose on all the detritus of his life: "she read over the will more closely. If it was really Pierce's attempt to leave an organized something behind after his own annihilation, then it was part of her duty, wasn't it, to bestow life on what had persisted, to try to be what Driblette was, the dark machine in the centre of the planetarium, to bring the estate into pulsing stelliferous Meaning, all in a soaring dome around her?"(58). Inverarity exists only in bits and pieces. Even in life the only identity he possessed was that imposed upon him by the observer. To Oedipa, he had been a failed "knight of deliverance" (11), unable to help her escape from the imprisoning tower of her own consciousness of the world: "she had noticed the absence of an intensity, as if watching a movie, just perceptibly out of focus, that the projectionist refused to fix"(10). To the anarchist Jesús Arrabal, he is the embodiment of organization, order, and control: "An anarchist miracle. . . . He is too exactly and without flaw the thing we fight. In Mexico the privilegiado is always, to a finite percentage, redeemed—one of the people. Unmiraculous. But your friend, unless he's joking, is as terrifying to me as a Virgin appearing to an Indian" (89). Which is, of course, exactly what he is—this novel's V. In the end, Oedipa must see the identity of Inverarity as continuous with time, a finite existence "assumed back into the American continuity of crust and mantle"(133). But he may be more. He may be an abstraction that, if she could only fit the pieces together, might impose an order on the chaos of clues and events around her, might explain the forces that seem to be in control of the world. In life,

Inverarity was defined by his "need to possess, to alter the land, to bring new skylines, personal antagonisms, growth rates into being" (134). She had to consider the possibility, however, that this identity did not end with his body's disintegration but had become a force itself, with an existence of its own:

> Or he might even have tried to survive death, as a paranoia; as a pure conspiracy against someone he loved. Would that breed of perversity prove at last too keen to be stunned even by death, had a plot finally been devised too elaborate for the dark Angel to hold at once, in his humorless vice-president's head, all the possibilities of? Had something slipped through and Inverarity by that much beaten death? (134)

If the coincidences are real, Oedipa has not encountered Inverarity's history, but something more appalling. Like V., Inverarity has lost his humanity to the inanimate—factories, corporations, housing developments—and his identity to the equilibrium of events.

Mucho Maas is horrified by his perception of the closed system in others, by their loss of humanity to the inanimate objects of their respective worlds. As a car dealer, Mucho sees nothing but "endless, convoluted incest"(5) between the self and its projection; his customers trade automotive projections of lives, not cars. Having given up the car lot to become a radio announcer, he becomes a disembodied voice rather than a disembodied process. He discovers LSD, "the bridge inward"(7), and his projection of the world begins to mirror the closed system of his own self. His boss remarks to Oedipa: "they're calling him the Brothers N. He's losing his identity. . . . He enters a staff meeting and the room is suddenly full of people, you know? He's a walking assembly of man"(104). Unlike Stencil, or the earlier Mucho, whose identity is a single projection, he has merged with the supersensual chaos, a totality of facts in which all the individual parts can be seen.

The inverse of Inverarity, Mucho can disassemble systems. With an identity that has become one with a world tending toward equilibrium, he claims that he can "listen to anything and take it apart again.

Spectrum analysis, in my head. I can break down chords, and timbres, and words too into all the basic frequencies and harmonics, with all their different loudnesses, and listen to them, each pure tone, but all at once"(105–106). Mucho goes one step further than V. and Mélanie in their attempts to bring their collective self into conformance with the world they perceive:

> Everybody who says the same words is the same person if the spectra are the same only they happen differently in time, you dig? But the time is arbitrary. You pick your zero point anywhere you want, that way you can shuffle each person's time line sideways till they all coincide. (106)

In Mucho's projection of the world, equilibrium has been reached; all the parts of the system are the same, energy has been diffused: "You're an antenna, sending your pattern out across a million lives a night, and they're your lives too"(107).

After seven years of silence, Pynchon offers still another, more complex, version of the self's closed system. The central characters in *Gravity's Rainbow* are forces like gravity and entropy; they are, for the most part, unseen and unnamed, but they control the novel and its human characters. With only token help from the likes of Tyrone Slothrop, the reader alone must sort out clues, impose a structure on the facts stated or implied. However, Pynchon develops a character trait only hinted at in V. and Inverarity: control. Both V. and Inverarity sought to order and structure events and things, and in the process they achieved their own disintegration—the despotism of an artificial order that nature abhorred, as Henry Adams would say. To the extent that *Gravity's Rainbow* is *about* anything, it is about the interaction of the forces of nature with the efforts of men to create their artificial orders and to impose them on nature. Identity, as a consequence, is usually only an extension of the despotism of order into the lives and thoughts of the more or less human agents of the meta-cartels and a global military-industrial complex.

Of all the possible cases, Edward Pointsman is the most obvious, and most interesting, example. In Pointsman there is perfect congruity between abstract theory and his own identity: the outside and inside brought into conformity. Thinking of a recently deceased fellow-Pavlovian, Pointsman "feels patterns on his cortex going dark, settling to sleep forever, parts of whoever he's been now losing all definition, reverting to dumb chemistry . . ."(141). The lapse into disintegration, however, is temporary. For Pointsman, the world is nothing more than stimulus and response, cause and effect. Recalling Adams's Venus-Virgin and Pynchon's version of the Venus-turned-dynamo, Pointsman—like a scientific Stencil—looks for his own equivalent of V.: Pavlov's lectures "came to him at age 28 like a mandate from the submontane Venus he could not resist: to abandon Harley Street for a journey more and more deviant, deliciously on, into a labyrinth of conditioned-reflex work . . ."(88). Pointsman's entire identity is derived from his desire to prove that his view of the world is accurate. He wishes to pick up where Pavlov left off,"at the very threshold of putting these things on an experimental basis" (90). The "things" are Pavlov's belief that "all the diseases of the mind could be explained, eventually, by the ultraparadoxical phase, the pathologically inert points on the cortex, the confusion of ideas of the opposite"(90). He can see his own self in no other terms than the patterns of his cortex, a process concomitant with his proving his theory with experiments on Tyrone Slothrop, whom he sees as a "bit of Psychology's own childhood, yes pure history, inert, encysted"(168). With Slothrop available to prove his theory, his fear of failure is "defined inversely, by horror, by ways all hopes might yet be defeated and he find only his death, that dumb, empty joke, at the end of this Pavlovian's Progress"(169). Slothrop holds the key to the embodiment of his theory and to a confirmation of his own identity; his fears of chaos and a thermodynamic death are put off by the possibilities locked inside Slothrop: "But now with Slothrop in it—sudden angel, thermodynamic surprise, whatever he is . . . will it change now?"(143). Pointsman and his world are one and the same. The crypto-Pointsman has become the only Pointsman and, he will discover, the labyrinth is a closed system no larger than himself.

TIME AND HISTORY

In *V.* Willem van Wijk, a minor bureaucrat, tries to explain his function to the young Kurt Mondaugen:

> "We are, perhaps, the lead weights of a fantastic clock, necessary to keep it in motion, to keep an ordered sense of history and time prevailing against chaos. Very well! Let a few of them melt. Let the clock tell false time for a while. But the weights will be reforged, and rehung, and if there doesn't happen to be one there in the shape or name of Willem van Wijk to make it run right again, so much the worse for me." (216)

In *Gravity's Rainbow,* over 16,000 revolutions of his own clock later, the same Kurt Mondaugen updates the concept:

> "Personal density," Kurt Mondaugen in his Peenemünde office not too many steps away from here, enunciating the Law which will one day bear his name, "is directly proportional to temporal bandwidth."
> "Temporal bandwidth" is the width of your present, your *now*. It is the familiar "Δt" considered as a dependent variable. The more you dwell in the past and in the future, the thicker your bandwidth, the more solid your persona. But the narrower your sense of Now, the more tenuous you are. It may get to where you're having trouble remembering what you were doing five minutes ago.... (509)

In Pynchon's fiction, a clock is more than a metaphor. The face, arms, and hands of a clock may have lost their metaphorical qualities through familiarity. Pynchon, however, not only reminds us of the metaphor, but also suggests that the relationship of a clock with a body may be similar to that of time with identity. Both the clock and the body are the visible manifestations of more complex abstractions. As the clock-body metaphor becomes literal, time and identity become indistinguishable and merge onto the same axis. The greater the sense of time, the more definite the identity.

Nowhere is this principle more clear than in Herbert Stencil, whose life is pure movement, like a clock, directed toward the search for V. in a series of endless cycles and repetitions. Stencil's identity is congruent with the passage of time: "he began to discover that sleep was taking up time which could be spent active. His random movements before the war had given way to a great single movement from inertness to—if not vitality, then at least activity"(44). The search for V. was a matter of "forcible dislocation of personality into a past he didn't remember and had no right in, save the right of imaginative anxiety or historical care, which is recognized by no one"(51). Although a parody of Henry Adams, Stencil's "mad time-search" shows how history orders time. As a sampling of Adams's own words reveals, the association is intentional:

> Historians undertake to arrange sequences,—called stories, or histories —assuming in silence a relation of cause and effect.... he insisted on a relation of sequence, and if he could not reach it by one method, he would try as many methods as science knew. Satisfied that the sequence of men led to nothing and that the sequence of their society could lead no further, while the mere sequence of time was artificial, and the sequence of thought was chaos, he turned at last to the sequence of force.... (382)

On Malta, when he comes close to a sequence of events that would explain V., Stencil fears that his search—and his own animateness— will be over if he accepts the death of the Bad Priest as the end of V. In this case the past would have returned full circle to the present, leaving Stencil without a future. Unwilling to face this possibility, Stencil instead considers that perhaps he "has never encountered history at all, but something far more appalling"(423–24).

Appropriately, Stencil's father—on Malta in 1919—has a similar encounter with something more appalling than history. Under the tutelage of the sailor Mehemet, he comes to realize that time tends toward death, that if the world is a closed system, then it can only decay into a universal chaos of timelessness. Like his son, he shies away from the vision clear enough to see past "the fiction of a humanized history endowed with 'reason,' " choosing instead to humanize the sight, to reduce it to personal history:

> "But then: suppose Sidney Stencil has remained constant after all—suppose instead sometime between 1859 and 1919, the world contracted a disease which no one ever took the trouble to diagnose because the symptoms were too subtle—blending in with the events of history, no different one by one but altogether—fatal. This is how the public, you know, see the late war. As a new and rare disease which has now been cured and conquered for ever."
>
> "Is old age a disease?" Mehemet asked. "The body slows down, machines wear out, planets falter and loop, sun and stars gutter and smoke. Why say a disease? Only to bring it down to a size you can look at and feel comfortable?" (433)

The vision will be repeated many times in the world of Pynchon's novels. It will vary as the cast of characters varies, but throughout, time is seen in its decay toward timelessness and history is seen as the proof of sequence and order, assumptions made ridiculous by the buffoonery of a Herbert Stencil or almost plausible by the reflections of a Sidney Stencil. The senior Stencil offers a rational explanation for the life his son would parody:

> "If there is any political moral to be found in this world," Stencil once wrote in his journal, "it is that we carry on the business of this century with an intolerable double vision. Right and Left; the hothouse and the street. The Right can only live and work hermetically, in the hothouse of the past, while outside the Left prosecute their affairs in the streets by manipulated mob violence. And cannot live but in the dreamscape of the future.
>
> "What of the real present, the men-of-no-politics, the once-respectable Golden Mean? Obsolete; in any case, lost sight of. In a West of such extremes we can expect, at the very least, a highly 'alienated' populace within not many more years." (440)

The highly alienated populace, presumably, would be alienated from time itself, people with narrow bandwidths, as Kurt Mondaugen would say, growing more tenuous all the time. Sidney Stencil, so near the beginning of the new age predicted by Adams, overlooks the more frightening prospect of making life conform to the process of time in favor of life's endowing time with some sort of meaning— or history. He is frightened by V. because "riot was her element, as surely as this dark room, almost creeping with amassed objects. The street and the hothouse; in V. were resolved, by some magic, the two extremes"(459). Her temporal bandwidth is a fusion of past and future. V. is not subject to time. She does not have the history for which Stencil junior so vainly searches. V. *is* history, time itself.

For most people, the eye is the instrument of perceiving events that are then ordered into history. Time is an observational artifact. V., however, takes a shortcut. Speaking with Mondaugen during the siege of Foppl's villa, V. in the guise of Vera Meroving notices Mondaugen's curiosity about her artificial eye and

> obligingly removed the eye and held it out to him in the hollow of her hand. A bubble blown translucent, its "white" would show up when in the socket as a half-lit sea green. A fine network of nearly microscopic fractures covered its surface. Inside were the delicately-wrought wheels, springs, rachets, of a watch, wound by a gold key which Fräulein Meroving wore on a slender chain round her neck. Darker green and flecks of gold had been fused into twelve vaguely zodiacal shapes, placed annular on the surface of the bubble to represent the iris and also the face of the watch. (219)

She looks upon the world with the "evil eye of time"(363), as one person remembers her. Seeing others through the face of a clock, she becomes pure history, manipulating the events of life to conform to some elaborate vision known only to her but encountered by Stencil and others. Still a man of the nineteenth century, Sidney Stencil knows only that V. is frightening. Hoping that he will never be called upon to explain what he really thinks she is, Stencil ponders the repetition of Situations, the sequence of events: "The inert universe may have a quality we can call logic. But logic is a human attribute after all; so even at that it's a misnomer. What are real are the cross-purposes"(455). The cross-purposes, of course, are related to V. and the closed world of time made personal. With V.—as with the Situation—Sidney Stencil recognizes that time loses all meaning: "No history, all history at once . . ."(456). Nearing the end of his life with these observations, Stencil has modified his theory of objective reality. During the Vheissu Situation, he could be satisfied that "the only consolation he drew from the present chaos was that his theory managed to explain it"(174). On Malta in 1919, the Situation and V. are one and the same: "For it came to that, finally: an alienation from time, much as Malta itself was alienated from any history in which cause precedes effect"(460).

In *The Crying of Lot 49*, Pierce Inverarity, like V., may have tried to escape time's inevitable decay by replacing his humanity with companies and stocks instead of V.'s more literal prostheses. Inverarity, by design or effect, extends through time beyond the boundaries of death, at least for Oedipa: "Though she could never again call back any image of the dead man to dress up, pose, talk to and make answer, neither would she lose a new compassion for the cul-de-sac he'd tried to find a way out of, for the enigma his efforts had created"(134). The enigma, Inverarity's testament, is the same enigma of V.: a code with infinite reference, but somehow a key to all the events that overwhelm Oedipa. What is at stake is not the execution of Inverarity's will, but something more fundamental: an understanding of whether events are ordered into an ominous logic that is history imposed on the contingency of events or whether all possibility for order is steadily decreasing, thereby making the efforts to find and maintain order all the more necessary. In Inverarity there is the same integration of the hothouse and the street that Stencil found so frightening, but Inverarity is more plausible in his resolution of the past and the present. In Mondaugen's terms, Inverarity possesses a broad personal bandwidth. He brings the American Protestant ethic into the twentieth century and merges the Calvinist impulses toward order and control with the businessman's necessity of stringing corporations together as if they were chapters in his life's history. Oedipa's effort to unravel Inverarity's will depends on her being able to uncover the history of the Tristero. In both Inverarity and the Tristero, Oedipa has to discover whether there is some history, some meaningful organization of time, or whether there is only the illusion of history beneath which some other "dark history slithered unseen"(122). The distinction is suggested by the Scurvhamites, for whom nothing "ever happened by accident, Creation was a vast, intricate machine. But one part of it, the Scurvhamite part, ran off the will of God, its prime mover. The rest ran off some opposite Principle, something blind, soulless; a brute automatism that led to eternal death"(116). It is this brute Other, which kept one half of the universe "running like clockwork"(117), that is manifested in V. and Inverarity. They are Newtonian time, running with great efficiency, manipulating the lives and events of other people, but subject still to the entropy of any closed system. The clockwork of V. is dismantled —as if the mainspring finally wound down and could not hold all the pieces together in some organized whole—while the testament of Pierce Inverarity fades and merges into the history of America. In his death Inverarity seeks to become the cause for the future's effect: a simultaneous past and present, life and death, fixed in the present moment.

In *Gravity's Rainbow* Herbert Stencil has his counterpart in the likes of Edward Pointsman and General Pudding, men made ridiculous by their insistent belief in a humanized history endowed with reason, by their beliefs that they can understand and give shape to the events of the world. The Pavlovian Pointsman is shocked by one of his colleagues' belief in contingency:

> How can Mexico play, so at his ease, with these symbols of randomness and fright? Innocent as a child, perhaps unaware—perhaps—that in his play he wrecks the elegant rooms of history, threatens the idea of cause and effect itself. What if Mexico's whole *generation* have

turned out like this? Will Postwar be nothing but "events," newly created one moment to the next? No links? Is it the end of history? (56)

On the lighter side of Pointsman is General Pudding, who "was brought up to believe in a literal Chain of Command, as clergymen of earlier centuries believed in the Chain of Being. The newer geometries confuse him"(77). In his retirement, Pudding sets out to write a book entitled *Things That Can Happen in European Politics*, which he begins by speculating what would happen if Ramsey MacDonald should die: "By the time he went through resulting party alignments and possible permutations of cabinet posts, Ramsey MacDonald had died. 'Never make it,' he found himself muttering at the beginning of each day's work—'it's changing out from under me. Oh, Dodgy —very dodgy' "(77). In Pudding's hands cause and effect theories of history become as silly as Herbert Stencil's attempt to recreate the history of his father's past.

V. and Inverarity have their counterpart as well, only Pynchon has expanded his representation of the Nameless Other—elaborated the theme to make it even more terrifying. In Mondaugen's scheme Blicero is a man with a personal density, a bandwidth, so great that it seems to be gravity itself. In *V.* Blicero—at that time he is still Weissmann—meets Mondaugen at Foppl's villa in 1922 and predicts "someday we'll need you . . . for something or other, I'm sure. Specialized and limited as you are, you fellows will be valuable"(224). Particularly conscious of time after his conversation with van Wijk, Mondaugen becomes one of the best observers and reporters of the phenomenon Blicero represents. In 1922, the year Einstein received the Nobel Prize for his general theory of relativity, Blicero is still tied to the clockwork nameless Other, not yet the principle of the twentieth century that Henry Adams predicted and feared. At Foppl's villa, Mondaugen sees Weissmann and the others reliving the excitement of 1904 with such conviction that the past and the present become indistinguishable.[11] Weissmann, however, goes even beyond this "Now" in his assumption of a future that will include using

Mondaugen: "Yes. You are my man. The young people especially, Mondaugen, because you see—I know this won't be repeated—we could be getting it back"(225). Mondaugen's mistaken assumption that Weissmann is referring merely to Germany's prewar empire and dreams of conquest causes him to burst into laughter. Weissmann, of course, has some greater scheme in mind—nothing less than getting back the past, bringing it into congruence with the future. After leaving Weissmann and Foppl's villa, Mondaugen goes into the bush to live with the Hereros. In *Gravity's Rainbow*, we learn that in this isolation he developed his theory of time:

> In his electro-mysticism, the triode was as basic as the cross in Christianity. Think of the ego, the self that suffers a personal history bound to time, as the grid. The deeper and true Self is the flow between cathode and plate. The constant, pure flow. Signals—sense-data, feelings, memories relocating—are put onto the grid and modulate the flow. We live lives that are waveforms constantly changing with time, now positive, now negative. Only at moments of great serenity is it possible to find the pure, the informationless state of signal zero. (404)

With the scientist's understanding of entropy, Mondaugen is unable to accept a cause and effect, sequential system of time and history. Rather, like Henry Adams, he recognizes the need for an illusion of order and sequence with which men can explain their existences (the grid) and accepts the actual facts of chaos and flux (the constantly changing waveforms mapped onto the grid). In effect, Mondaugen has updated van Wijk's Newtonian clock with his own Einsteinian timepiece. This transition from V. to Blicero, from a Newtonian to a relativistic framework, is one of the most significant developments in Pynchon's fiction.

When Weissmann first appears in *Gravity's Rainbow*, he has already bridged the time void between the living and the dead. His realm is described by a medium during a seance: "It's control. All these things arise from one difficulty: control. For the first time it was *inside*, do you see. The control is put inside. No more need to suffer passively under 'outside forces' . . ." (30). He is no longer subjected to entropy, but has merged with it. Blicero has superseded the Scurvhamite Other. Like V., he has become time itself in all its decadence. But Blicero, fully a creature of the twentieth century, has achieved a space-time equivalence that was not possible before relativity theory added a fourth dimension to the universe. His is "the comfort of a closed place, where everyone is in complete agreement about Death"(299). Margherita Erdmann can recognize Blicero as the post-Newtonian Other who, like his predecessor V., has "no humanity left in its eyes: that had faded out, day after day, and been replaced by gray furrows, red veins in patterns that weren't human"(486). V.'s eye was replaced with a watch. Blicero's eyes become a map of the world—a world in which time has become spatialized:

> "he was seeing the world now in *mythical regions:* they had their maps, real mountains, rivers, and colors. It was not Germany he moved through. It was his own space. But he was taking *us* along with him! . . . the chances for our annihilation, delicious never knowing when it would come down because the space and time were Blicero's own." (486)

In Blicero's region there is no distinction between illusion and reality, past and present; he has made time his own in an effort to transcend his own death—the end of personal time—and the entropy of the universe.

His instrument, with the help of Mondaugen and others, is the Rocket: ". . . in the dynamic space of the living Rocket, the double integral has a different meaning. To integrate here is to operate on a rate of change so that time falls away: change is stilled. . . . 'Meters per second' will integrate to 'meters.' The moving vehicle is frozen, in space, to become architecture, and timeless. It was never launched. It will never fall"(301). The Rocket at Brennschluss is controlled by a pendulum—the familiar tick of time, the movement of gravity. Brennschluss: "a point in space, a point hung precise as the point where burning must end, never launched, never to fall. And what is

the specific shape whose center of gravity is the Brennschluss Point?"
(302) For Blicero, the shape is his special rocket 00000, the vehicle
for his complete and ultimate control of the eternal time that coincides with Brennschluss. The Rocket is a complex symbol drawn
from a variety of sources, Zeno's arrow, for example. Although the
entropy of time proceeds in only one direction—from present to
future—and is, therefore, asymmetrical—the notion of going back in
time is not only imaginable but suggests a means of controlling time
if its direction could be reversed or perhaps arrested. Blicero's rocket
not only conforms to the requirements of spatialized time—"the
distance along the flight path" (301)—but seeks "that backward
symmetry again"(301).[12]

It is not just individuals who try to control time, to impose their
own history on the events of the world. In *V.* the Whole Sick Crew
is a community sharing a sense of exhausted time—run-down, deca-
dent, like the art they produce and the forms of life they imitate; their
parties represent the whole community's sense of time: "The party,
as if it were inanimate after all, unwound like a clock's mainspring
toward the edges of the chocolate room, seeking some easing of its
own tension, some equilibrium"(41). Also in *V.,* during the siege
party of 1922, the same sort of decadence controls those trapped
within Foppl's villa; not only is there a physical and spiritual decadence, but time itself is confused as the party merges with von
Trotha's death campaign of 1904—"as the siege party progressed it
became more and more difficult to make the distinction"(223)—and
with the decadence that infests all of Europe—"a constantly rising
curve, taking human depravity as ordinate"(225). In *The Crying of Lot
49* there are similar communities, such as the Scurvhamites already
mentioned, or the Peter Pinguid Society, which attempts to make the
facts fit its view of history and to make its view of history account
for the world they see—a novel approach to cause and effect. The
Inamorati Anonymous seek the same control.

In *Gravity's Rainbow* the Hereros, victims of von Trotha, have been
transplanted from *V.* and the Southwest Protectorate to Germany

and the service of the Rocket. Although they seek a similar end, they are divided among themselves. Those who have elected tribal death are the Empty Ones and they promise "a day when the last Zone-Herero will die, a final zero to a collective history fully lived"(318). The others, like Enzian, seek the same practical end, but "what Enzian wants to create will have no history. It will never need a design change. Time, as time is known to the other nations, will wither away inside this new one" (318–19). Enzian and his followers see in the Rocket a symbol for a new beginning outside time and outside history. To them, "the Rocket was an entire system *won,* away from the feminine darkness, held against the entropies of lovable but scatter-brained Mother Nature"(324). Of course this system of belief was taught to Enzian, and the others in turn, by Blicero, who is the equivalent of V.—a union of Venus, or Mother Nature, and the machine. Enzian intends to launch himself toward the past: ". . . it is a return, this voyage"(327). The Rocket is not only a modern-day replacement for Mother Nature, but is the symbol of the fusion of past and present. Enzian desperately believes that the Rocket—the special Rocket 00001—offers some means for defying the entropy of time, "but it is *their* time, *their* space, and he still expects, naïvely, outcomes the white continuum grew past hoping for centuries ago" (326). Although Enzian has mastered only the form and not the substance of Blicero's instructions, he believes that the Hereros "have learned to stand outside . . . history and watch it, without feeling too much"(362). Both the Empty Ones and Enzian know that history is only a way of describing how people and groups of people die. They may be able to watch history, but they cannot escape it. The difference between tribal suicide and Rocket 00001 is only a matter of names, of history.

Another group sharing similar assumptions with the Hereros is the Argentine anarchists, who also had their introduction in *V.*—at least implicitly—through the Gaucho, an Argentine cowboy. A man of action, the Gaucho sought history in the streets, the present. His successors in *Gravity's Rainbow* share the Gaucho's desire to create history, but they would rewrite it, using the filmmaker von Göll to create an illusionary history that could be substituted for the official history and be based on the romantic hero and anarchist saint Martín Fierro, himself a gaucho. Like the Gaucho of *V.*, the anarchists are paradoxical; they look forward to the chaos that accompanies the disintegration of time, but their image of the desired future is drawn from a hothouse memory of the past: "nostalgia is like seasickness: only the hope of dying from it is keeping them alive"(384). They too hope to fuse the past and the future, placing their faith in von Göll's promise to their leader Squalidozzi: "I can take down your fences and your labyrinth walls, I can lead you back to the Garden you hardly remember . . ."(388). With a nod toward Jorge Luis Borges, Pynchon has von Göll propose an entropic view of history by removing James Clerk Maxwell's sorting gate, his fence. Von Göll's madness is infectious: "It seemed what they had been waiting for. 'Africans!' . . . 'What if it's true? What if we've really come back, back to the way it was before the continents drifted apart?' . . . 'Back to Gondwanaland. . . . When Rio de la Plata was just opposite South-West Africa . . .' "(388). The vision is enough to convince von Göll that his is a messianic mission: "The historical moment demands this, and I can only be its servant"(388). At the same moment that one of the anarchists wonders whether Martín Fierro's soul will "survive the mechanics of . . . light and sound," she notices that "above and beyond her the Zodiac glides, a north-hemisphere array she never saw in Argentina, smooth as an hour-hand"(388). Regardless of where they are and what illusions of history the anarchists may harbor, they are all enclosed within the system of time that is smoothly, steadily winding down to an anarchy, the undifferentiated chaos of no time. The dream of a rewritten history will be dismantled.

Through incidents such as those summarized above, Pynchon shows that history is all that is the experience of time. In Stencil, *V.*, Inverarity, Pointsman, Blicero, and the others there is an obvious tendency toward determinism and control, manipulation rather than accident. In *V.* Pynchon explicitly draws upon Machiavelli to estab-

lish a basic dichotomy between virtù and fortune, which he continues to exploit throughout his novels. As a prototype, for example, V.
represents an ultimate manifestation of human intervention and control dedicated to increasing the world's disorder and decadence; in
subsequent novels, the model is perfected and enlarged. Yet V.'s own
disintegration and disassembly are the result of an accident, the
unfortunate fall of a beam during a bombing. By integrating the
Machiavellian dichotomy with Henry Adams's view of a world of
increasing entropy, Pynchon generates a tension between control and
order on one hand and accident and chaos on the other. History, of
course, must plot events on the grid of these two axes and the reader
is left to resolve Pynchon's ambiguities.

Although Pynchon uses Adams and Machiavelli to establish the
tension between human control and accident, he certainly has Wittgenstein in mind as well, according to whom everything outside logic
is accident. Proposition 2.0121 in part says, "It would seem to be a
sort of accident, if it turned out that a situation would fit a thing that
could already exist entirely on its own. If things can occur in states
of affairs, this possibility must be in them from the beginning."
Within Wittgenstein's system, there is only an accidental relationship between volition and what happens in the world. Through
Sidney Stencil, Pynchon introduces a similar concept:

> He had decided long ago that no Situation had any objective reality:
> it only existed in the minds of those who happened to be in on it at
> any specific moment. Since these several minds tended to form a sum
> total or complex more mongrel than homogeneous, The Situation must
> necessarily appear to a single observer much like a diagram in four
> dimensions to an eye conditioned to seeing its world in only three.
> (174)

Time, of course, is the fourth dimension. Stencil spends a lifetime
applying his theory to time, explaining the chaos he sees before him.
Near his own death, he remarks to himself that "The Situation is
always bigger than you, Sidney. It has like God its own logic and its

own justification for being, and the best you can do is cope"(455). His life amid the constant distractions of the Situation, and the inescapable tradition of Western man permit only one form of logic: "History there was the record of an evolution. One-way and ongoing"(452). As he leaves Malta, a place "where all history seemed simultaneously present"(452), convinced of the logic of time's inevitable progress, he is destroyed by a chance waterspout lasting no more than fifteen minutes. "For all that happens and is the case is accidental," Wittgenstein says in proposition 6.41.

Regardless of what theories men may impose on the unwinding of time, regardless of the histories they may invent to explain what they see, accident has the last say. A similar fate awaits Driblette in *The Crying of Lot 49,* who, like Stencil, projects his own world order and who walks, presumably, into the sea after the last performance of his play: "Had *he* even known why? No one could begin to trace it. A hundred hangups, permuted, combined—sex, money, illness, despair with the history of his time and place, who knew"(121). In *Gravity's Rainbow* Edward Pointsman, who seeks to overcome his anxieties about the "End of History" by controlling the lives and histories of others and who lives by the maxim, "History is not woven by innocent hands" (277), is undone in his master plan for controlling Tyrone Slothrop by an accident, by Major Marvy's being mistaken for Slothrop. As one of Pointsman's victims of controlled history, Slothrop sees a particularly apt image of the Pointsmans, Inveraritys, or Stencils of the world:

> Oh, the hand of a terrible croupier is that touch on the sleeves of his dreams: all in his life of what has looked free or random, is discovered to've been under some Control, all the time, the same as a fixed roulette wheel—where only destinations are important, attention is to long-term statistics, not individuals: and where the House always does, of course, keep turning a profit. . . . (209)

The crooked roulette wheel is a controlled wheel of fortune, or just another version of Maxwell's closed system, in which a demon opens and shuts a gate to let selected molecules into the favored chamber.

His system intact, drawing upon his sources as capriciously as is convenient, Pynchon takes energy for his machinery of time and history from the disintegrating tension between order and chaos, much as a time clock based on atomic decay. While most characters are revealed in their futile attempts to resist a universe running down by their own fictions of control and history, a few appear to have accommodated themselves to the inevitable. The equivalent of entropy's equilibrium in time is death, or a timelessness. It may also be "the informationless state of signal zero" that is suggested in Mondaugen's electromysticism, in which the cathode and the plate are order and chaos. Through several characters, particularly Fausto Maijstral, Oedipa Maas, and Tyrone Slothrop, Pynchon raises the possibility of the efficacy of signal zero.

At this point it may be valuable to reflect briefly on the sources that Pynchon implies in his novels. Although his treatment of time and history grows more complex with each novel and he incorporates an increasing number of references, the system remains essentially constant; the direction of time is always related to entropy, and history is always an attempt to impose order on time. The relationship of entropy to time—popularized with Sir Arthur Eddington's 1929 conceptualization that increasing entropy gives the direction of "time's arrow"—has been more readily accepted in both scientific and philosophic circles since publication of Boltzmann's H-Theorem. Boltzmann's formulation provides a definition of entropy that is more general than its thermodynamic definition (it can accommodate thermodynamic surprises and fluctuations) and that suggests a parallel between the past-to-future direction of time and the succession of different physical states of a system (the progression of time and entropy are thus measurable). This is the background not only for V.'s disintegration, but also for most of the contemporary explorations of the meaning of time, including the correlation of relativity theory with thermodynamics. Although *Gravity's Rainbow* incorporates a number of specific references in this context—Minkowski's four-dimensional geometry, Gödel's rocket, Einstein's general theory of relativity, Jung's synchronistic events, to name only a few—Pynchon's basic views were formulated in *V.* and did not change, but only grew more complex.

Relativity theory and quantum theory provide Pynchon with two specific concepts, in addition to the direction of time, that are characteristic of the alternative represented by Fausto, Oedipa, and Slothrop. Although the formal and precise derivation would require extensive explanation, it is obvious that Pynchon draws upon relativity theory and quantum physics to establish the relativity of the observer. Quantum physics, for example, does not specify how the world is, but instead gives the result of observation by an observer; thus two descriptions may be both valid and different. Change, or time lapse, as Gödel suggested in his article on the relationship of relativity theory with philosophy, is an appearance due to our special mode of perception as a result of the relativization of simultaneity. In short, time changes with motion relative to an observer and in accord with the assumptions the observer makes about his motion. This characteristic is vital to an understanding of Fausto, Oedipa, and Slothrop because they, unlike most characters, are self-conscious about their respective roles as observers and possess, perhaps intuitively, a sense of the relativity of their own motion through time.

The second scientific concept Pynchon incorporates is derived from relativity's impact on the present. The present moment was formerly spatialized at the zero point on an axis in which the past was represented by negative numbers and the future by positive numbers; the present was a cosmic now, universal, simultaneous and instantaneous. With the acceptance of relativity, the present moment became localized—an accidental and changing perspective within the timeless, four-dimensioned, relativistic universe. The present could no longer be the simple point of demarcation between a linear past and future; instead there must be a trichotomy of past, future, and elsewhere, in which the present moment of time is arbitrary and observer-dependent. While other characters maintain the fiction of a present separating past from future on a single continuum, the present for Fausto, Oedipa, and Slothrop is arbitrary and timeless, located as it is within the "elsewhere" of other observers. When viewed with this referential background, the triode of Mondaugen's electro-mysticism is more than metaphorical. In the standard representation of relativistic time, the double cone of past and future is prescribed by *signals* travelling inward to and outward from a zero point with the speed of light. "Signal zero" is the arbitrary present. The "grid" of Mondaugen's system is the illusion of history: "Think of the ego, the self that suffers a personal history bound to time, as the grid." This, in turn, is a reformulation of Hugo Bergmann's point that "now is a temporal mode of experiencing ego," which he expressed in *Der Kampf um das Kausalgesetz in der jungsten Physik* in 1929. Despite its simplicity, Mondaugen's concept of "lives that are waveforms constantly changing with time" approximates a relativistic construct—transformed perhaps, but intact. Within this system, Fausto is little more than a self-conscious observer; Oedipa, in her encounter with the alcoholic sailor, goes one step further in her confrontation with the time differential; and Slothrop takes the final step in merging with the relativistic present, becoming signal zero. As with other characters in *V.,* Fausto is more a representation of ideas than a human being, one of many similarities between Fausto and his artistic counterpart in Thomas Mann's *Doctor Faustus,* a work that may have influenced Pynchon in a variety of ways, not the least of which is the mingling of fictional events and people with those of "history" and myth. Inherently allegoric, Fausto's position approximates that of an author who recognizes that the world, its inhabitants, and their verbal representations are all closed systems. In his confessions Fausto describes the metamorphosis of self in terms of his awareness of time and his consciousness of history, both his own and that of Malta. As he reflects on his movement through time he recognizes another name for entropy:

Decadence, decadence. What is it? Only a clear movement toward death or, preferably, non-humanity. As Fausto II and III, like their island, became more inanimate, they moved closer to the time when like any dead leaf or fragment of metal they'd be finally subject to the laws of physics. All the time pretending it was a great struggle between the laws of man and the laws of God. (301)

As he progresses through his successive identities, Fausto learns life's single lesson: "that there is more accident to it than a man can ever admit to in a lifetime and stay sane"(300). With more than a casual allusion to Goethe's Faust, Fausto learns that the illusion of a humanized history is a necessary precondition for civilization; the effort of men to control history is the same as the attempt to control reality. An ironic Faust, Fausto sees the world in its entirety and understands that there is no cure for death, regardless of what histories we may contrive. Since life itself is an allegory in which history and death are joined only momentarily and arbitrarily, the function of his self-conscious art is to insist on their separation. After watching the dismantling of V., Fausto can imagine a certain timelessness, or still-point, in the history and ordered time of others, but no escape from death. Goethe's Faust is saved by a choir of angels; Fausto is beyond salvation because he sees past the illusions of a humanized God into the inevitable final entropy of time. V.'s fate is his own, as it is the world's.

Goethe's Faust, toward the end of Part II, attempts to reclaim land from the sea to found an ideal society; in Fausto's version, Malta was once attached to Africa, but "since then the sea has steadily crept in" (301). This bit of rock still above the sea becomes for Fausto a symbol of the point he claims for himself in time and his own ideal society. As he explains to Herbert Stencil, his role is confined to that of watching, dominated by a certain passiveness: "The characteristic stillness, perhaps, of the rock. Inertia. I'd come back—no, in—come in to the rock as far as I would"(419). Fausto chooses not to participate in the illusions of time—the histories of the men who have occupied Malta—but will be only like the rock itself. Unlike Faust's child, who is drowned by its desperate mother, Fausto's child not only lives but comes to occupy the still point that Fausto can only imagine in his capacity as a metaphor-maker. During the siege of Malta, Paola was left to the very old—the past—and the very young —the future. In his confessions to Paola, Fausto writes: "Did the two forces neutralize and leave you on the lonely promontory between two worlds? . . . If so you stand at an enviable vantage: you're still that four-year-old belligerent with history in defilade. The present Fausto can look nowhere but back on the separate stages of his own history. No continuity. No logic"(310). In between past and future, Paola is part of neither.

In the process of executing Inverarity's will Oedipa Maas discovers the history of the Tristero. Sensitized, she sees the illusion of history, with its ordering of events into a humanized logic, as a choice between the clumsy, overt manipulation of the Penguid society and the highly efficient control of Inverarity or the Tristero. Uncertain of the Tristero's relationship with Inverarity, she comes to see it as "time's ghost," through which "power, omniscience, implacable malice, attributes of what they'd thought to be a historical principle, a Zeitgeist, are carried over to the now human enemy"(124). Oedipa is trapped between a past someone else has created and a cause-and-effect future that she will inherit depending on her responses to the past she discovers. The possible pasts and the predictable futures neutralize each other as they did for Paola. Oedipa is left only with her consciousness of the entropy of time, which she encounters with the innocent help of an old sailor. Despite dissimilarities of appearance, the sailor delivers the same message to Oedipa that Mehemet gives to Stencil and that seaman Bodine will give to Slothrop:

"dt," God help this old tattooed man, meant also a time differential, a vanishingly small instant in which change had to be confronted at last for what it was, where it could no longer disguise itself as something innocuous like an average rate; where velocity dwelled in the projectile though the projectile be frozen in midflight, where death

dwelled in the cell though the cell be looked in on at its most quick. . . .
But nothing she knew of would preserve them, or him. (95–96)

The only result of time is death. At the end of the novel, Oedipa
makes a deliberate choice to refuse the symmetrical choices before
her; in essence, she refuses both the history that would explain the
Tristero and the one that would exclude it. The only thing she ac-
knowledges is the inevitability of death: "either an accommodation
reached, in some kind of dignity, with the Angel of Death, or only
death and the daily, tedious preparations for it"(136–37). After that
there is only the "waiting for a symmetry of choices to break down,
to go skew. She had heard all about excluded middles; they were bad
shit, to be avoided; and how had it ever happened here, with the
chances once so good for diversity?"(136). Like Fausto, Oedipa can
look nowhere but back on the stages of her own history. But Oedipa
can find no comfort in the fact of her own self-consciousness, in her
knowledge that the riddle of life in space and time lies outside space
and time.

   Tyrone Slothrop finally comes to occupy the promontory outside
the worlds of past and future that Fausto and Oedipa only imagine.
In the postwar chaos of the Zone he encounters his past and his
future simultaneously just as he encounters the attempts of others—
Pointsman, Katje, Jamf, Blicero, and the nameless They—to impose
their controlled history on him. He confronts change for what it is
and as a result steps into the void that lies outside past and future
—the relativistic Elsewhere. Slothrop's past is Calvinist, part of that
New England stock that was dedicated to imposing a new order and
meaning onto the chaos of a land without history. In the Zone,
Slothrop's personal past and his ancestors' puritan cult of death transcend the ominous logic of time to confront him with his own
present. As a rocket falls on London he thinks of his Berkshire past:
"slender church steeples poised up and down all these autumn hill-
sides, white rockets about to fire, only seconds of countdown away,
rose windows taking in Sunday light, elevating and washing the faces

above the pulpits defining grace, swearing *this is how it does happen—
yes the great bright hand reaching out of the cloud . . ."*(29). In his search
for the Schwarzgerät and Rocket 00000, Slothrop discovers that the
Rocket has "a life of its own"(301) and that its life, as mentioned
earlier, is synonymous with death. The Rocket-State cosmology,
however, has its own equivalent of grace.

The future crashes into Slothrop's present in his vision of a
Raketen-Stadt, a "City of the Future"(674), that reorders time. In it,
Slothrop must rescue the Radiant Hour,

> which has been abstracted from the day's 24 by colleagues of the
> Father, for sinister reasons of their own. Travel here gets complicated
> —a system of buildings that move, by right angles, along the grooves
> of the Raketen-Stadt's street-grid. . . . Chess. Your objective is not the
> King—there is no King—but momentary targets such as the Radiant
> Hour. (674)

The Radiant Hour, of course, is the hour of dawn, an hour of sacrifice
and death; the grid is that self which suffers a personal history bound
to time; and the Raketen-Stadt itself exists in Minkowski's four-
dimensional space-time. In a series of complex and interrelated images, Pynchon shows Slothrop, in a special time Zone, struggling
with the fusion of past and future into a present he cannot understand. On Mondaugen's scale, Slothrop's personal density shrinks
toward nothing. However, his present is not a fixed point, the universal instant of the Newtonian continuum, but instead the relativistic
arbitrary now of the isolated observer. While Fausto and Oedipa had
the comfort of a psychological present, Slothrop begins to lose even
this. As he descends into the Germans' underground rocket factory,
Slothrop comes to realize that

> it is hard down here in the Mittelwerke to live in the present for very
> long. . . . our flesh doesn't sweat and pimple here for the domestic
> mysteries, the attic horror of What Might Have Happened so much as
> for our knowledge of what likely *did happen* . . . it was always easy, in
> open and lonely places, to be visited by Panic wilderness fear, but these

are the urban fantods here, that come to get you when you are lost or isolate inside the way time is passing, when there is no more History, no time-traveling capsule to find your way back to, only the lateness and the absence that fill a great railway shed after the capital has been evacuated, and the goat-god's city cousins wait for you at the edges of the light, playing the tunes they always played, but more audible now, because everything else has gone away or fallen silent . . . barn-swallow souls, fashioned of brown twilight, rise toward the white ceilings . . . they are unique to the Zone, they answer to the new Uncertainty. Ghosts used to be either likenesses of the dead or wraiths of the living. But here in the Zone categories have been blurred badly. The status of the name you miss, love, and search for now has grown ambiguous and remote, but this is even more than the bureaucracy of mass absence—some still live, some have died, but many, many have forgotten which they are. Their likenesses will not serve. Down here are only wrappings left in the light, in the dark: images of the Uncer-tainty. . . . (303)

Increasingly conscious of his tenuous position in time, Slothrop, like Fausto and Oedipa, sees himself only as a series of past identities; it is a high price, but he is no longer the victim of history and the time-control of others: "Past Slothrops, say averaging one a day, ten thousand of them, some more powerful than others, had been going over every sundown to the furious host"(624). Slothrop welcomes, or at least accepts, the entropy of time, the equilibrium of seconds and years: an undifferentiated chaos of time. Thus freed from history, he can "listen in to traffic from the Other Side, hearing about the future (no serial time over there: events are all there in the same eternal moment and so certain messages don't always 'make sense' back here: they lack historical structure, they sound fanciful, or in-sane)"(624). Slothrop begins to fade as his personal density de-creases, his personal bandwidth gets smaller, and his sense of a distinct Now approaches signal zero. In the uncertainty and am-biguity of the Zone (a zone without reference to Greenwich) Slothrop achieves timelessness—not the frozen point of a fused past and fu-ture that Blicero seeks, but the timelessness outside of time. Seaman Pig Bodine is the last to let him fade: "He's looking straight at

Slothrop (being one of the few who can still see Slothrop as any sort of integral creature any more. Most of the others gave up long ago trying to hold him together, even as a concept—'It's just got too remote' 's what they usually say)"(740). In one of their last meetings Bodine gives Slothrop a shirt soaked in John Dillinger's dying blood and tells him "Yeah, what we need isn't right reasons, but just that *grace*. The physical grace to keep it working"(741). From the puritan grace flowing from the blood of Christ to Bodine's grace, from the doctrines of election and absolute control to the doctrine of signal zero and chaos, Slothrop has been transformed.

Slothrop's disintegration has multiple significances, each of which depends on the perspective of the observer. At least one thing is certain: Slothrop not only confronts change for what it is, but also succumbs to the entropy of time. Within the post-Boltzmann probabilistic view of the world, Slothrop has a microscopic state with its own position and motion at each instant; he also has a macroscopic state that involves his relative position in regard to entropy. At the end of *Gravity's Rainbow,* reports of Slothrop's state are conjectured. One of the "standard histories," that of Microcosmists, is reported in the *Wall Street Journal:* "he was a genuine, point-for-point microcosm"(738). Secrets "to preserve against centrifugal History" (737) are given out by various groups, each with their own perspective. Although the source is not identified, there is at least one macroscopic theory: "There is also the story about Tyrone Slothrop, who was sent into the Zone to be present at his own assembly—perhaps, heavily paranoid voices have whispered, *his time's assembly*—and there ought to be a punch line to it, but there isn't. The plan went wrong. He is being broken down instead, and scattered"(738). It is this macroscopic state that places Slothrop within the closed system of time.

Unlike Blicero's Rocket—whose parabolic path in a microscopic state at Brennschluss holds the promise of freezing time against entropy at an instant of motion—Slothrop's career follows the pattern of average entropy as a function of time. It follows the same parabolic curve as the Rocket, but reaches infinity— maximum entropy—at its apex and never falls. As one of his historians explains, the Rocket was only a fiction for Slothrop ". . . to help him deny what he could not possibly admit: that he might be in love, in sexual love, with his, and his race's, death. . . . a fascinating combination of crude poet and psychic cripple . . ."(738). Time and entropy are irrelevant to the Slothrop whose delta t is infinity rather than an instant. Although he is subject to whatever history or identity others, including critics, may wish to create for him, Slothrop's Tarot points only to mediocrity: "(not only in his life but also, heh, heh, in his chroniclers too, yes yes nothing like getting the 3 of Pentacles upside down covering the significator on the second try to send you to the tube . . . and try to forget the whole thing)" (738). The Three of Pentacles predicts mediocrity in workmanship, commonplace ideas. Slothrop's apparent last card is the Hanged Man reversed: a false prophecy. There is no hope in the pattern of Slothrop's life. It is commonplace and inevitable. But history increases even as time runs down.

THE IDEA ITSELF

Presented as a multiform metaphorical structure that defines the limits of Pynchon's fictional world, the closed system may be seen everywhere in his novels and stories. We feel entropy increasing as we are lured further into Pynchon's deliberate uncertainties. That the form of Pynchon's fiction may in fact be an example of the entropy of information theory—where equiprobability permits maximum choice in constructing a message—demonstrates the metaphor's pervasiveness at the level of the reader's own experience. However, the idea of the closed system is more than a frame for the way we read —and Pynchon writes—his fiction. His characters are aware of the closed system in their own world; thus we can see them involved with the very problems that occupy us. Fausto, with his self-conscious stammerings about his room and his metaphors, is a prime example; other characters encounter manifestations of the closed system—particularly information theory and the mapping of physical space—without the luxury of reflection.

The thermodynamic and informational uses of the closed system, embellished with Adams's metaphorical construct, are at the center of Pynchon's third story, "Entropy." The significance of the story grows, in retrospect, as an aesthetic source and a preface for the novels that follow. In contrast to their uncertainties, this work is almost proverbial in its clarity and simplicity. "Entropy" actually comprises two separate stories, united by the theme of the title. Callisto, who is obsessed with the fact that the temperature has remained a constant thirty-seven degrees for three days, turns his apartment into a hothouse in an effort to escape the thermal death he knows must be occurring outside his personal closed system. At the same time, he imitates Henry Adams in applying thermodynamics metaphorically to the social system. He predicts "a heat-death for his culture in which ideas, like heat-energy, would no longer be transferred, since each point in it would ultimately have the same quantity of energy; and intellectual motion would, accordingly, cease."[13] Callisto anticipates Herbert Stencil and lays the groundwork for all of Pynchon's subsequent works.

The lease-breaking party at Meatball Mulligan's apartment, a floor beneath Callisto's hothouse, shares the characteristics of Adamsian historical decadence that Callisto fears; it is an early version of the "street" that later appears in Sidney Stencil's analogy. Most of the people attending the party are government workers, all of whom have something to do with processing information, directly or indirectly. Thus we encounter a high degree not only of social entropy, but also of information entropy, a facet of the closed system only hinted at in previous discussions. One of the representative party-goers tells his host that he and his wife have broken up over an argument about information theory and whether or not human behavior is more machinelike than vice versa: "Ambiguity. Redundance. Irrelevance, even. Leakage. All this is noise. Noise screws up your signal, makes for disorganization in the circuit"(285). At the same time the Duke di Angelis quartet performs in "the airless void" (290) by thinking music rather than playing it; although members of the group can end their song together, they have other problems, such as thinking different songs or different keys. The noise and silent music of Mulligan's party has its parallel in Callisto's apartment, where Aubade—a term for both a morning concert and, ironically, catcalling—lives in her own isolated world of sound, "a howling darkness of discordancy" (280). In her the two closed systems and two entropies intersect: "arabesques of order competing fugally with the improvised discords of the party downstairs, which peaked sometimes in cusps and ogees of noise. That precious signal-to-noise ratio, whose delicate balance required every calorie of her strength, seesawed inside the small tenuous skull as she watched Callisto . . ."(287).

The party disintegrates into fights and arguments: noise that "reached a sustained, ungodly crescendo"(291). Noise, of course, is any undesirable signal in information theory and corresponds to disorder in the way that a signal corresponds to order. The party is overcome by entropy. Mulligan anticipates Oedipa Maas, however, when he realizes that he must either isolate himself from the chaos of the party by hiding in a closet or restore order among the guests. He rejects the closet because "he did not feature being alone"(291) and tries to calm his guests one by one. Upstairs, Callisto (whose name possibly refers to Fernando de Rojas's frustrated lover of *La Celestina*) is startled by the noise into an awareness that he has not saved his bird by warming it, lovingly, with the heat of his body: "Almost as if I were communicating life to him, or a sense of life. What has happened? Has the transfer of heat ceased to work?" (292). Entropy increases despite the efforts of a Mulligan or a Callisto. It is Aubade—unable to maintain the signal-to-noise ratio—who goes in silence to break the window with her bare hands, to accelerate the equilibrium when ". . . the hovering, curious dominant of their separate lives should resolve into a tonic of darkness and the final absence of all motion"(292). The metaphors merge in Aubade's symbolic gesture. Pynchon will explore the ratio of signal-to-noise in all of his subsequent works. As already noted, the efforts of Herbert Stencil to organize and energize his life by ordering information about V. are an elaboration of the themes of "Entropy."

In *The Crying of Lot 49*, Pynchon unites the entropy of Mulligan's party, Callisto's shattered hothouse, and Adams's historical vision with his own experiments in *V.* to achieve a remarkably compact metaphor in Nefastis's Machine. The young engineer Stanley Koteks explains Maxwell's demon to Oedipa Maas, noting that the demon gets "something for nothing, causing perpetual motion," to which she responds ironically: "Sorting isn't work? . . . Tell them down at the post office, you'll find yourself in a mailbag headed for Fairbanks, Alaska . . ."(62). Intuitively, Oedipa raises the principal objection to Maxwell's concept. Nefastis, however, offers his own version of Leo Szilard's 1929 theory that the demon reacts to information about individual molecules and converts this information into negative entropy. From Nefastis Oedipa gathers that there are ". . . two distinct kinds of this entropy. One having to do with heat-engines, the other to do with communication. The equation for one, back in the '30's, had looked very like the equation for the other"(77). The concept of the demon is all standard fare except that Nefastis goes one step further: "Communication is the key. . . . The Demon passes his data on to the sensitive, and the sensitive must reply in kind" (77). In Nefastis's machine, the sensitive feed in information and the demon feeds out some "staggering set of energies"(77). Presumably, Nefastis can use his machine to counteract the effects of entropy on time, the equilibrium of history.

Nefastis's own decadence is, of course, the best example of the failure of his machine. In expressing his preference for sexual intercourse in front of the TV while the news is on, Nefastis demonstrates that his machine is irrelevant to him since the prepackaged information of the news report is what gives him his sexual energies. Information and energy have already reached an equilibrium in him, a conclusion supported by the implication that Nefastis has already merged with a television image of himself as he chases after Oedipa "in a hippy-dippy, oh-go-ahead-then-chick fashion he had doubtless learned from watching the TV also"(79). While Nefastis's machine fails at the purpose for which it was intended, it serves as a metaphor for the entire novel. Oedipa is a modified Maxwell's demon, sorting out the clues of Inverarity's will as if they were molecules, trying to differentiate between the reality and the illusion of the Tristero as if to sort her information into some order. As Fausto before her in his own closed room tries to sort the past from the present, Oedipa knows she is in between two worlds, receiving information about both, but not able to sort the faster-moving molecules from the slower.

In *Gravity's Rainbow* entropy has dissipated into a general system that Pynchon no longer needs to identify or insert as a scientific metaphor. Tyrone Slothrop is another version of Maxwell's demon. He tries to gain information of all sorts, but especially information related to Imipolex G, the particular result of a molecular discovery that Pynchon also relates to Maxwell's demon. Friedrich August Kekulé von Stradonitz had a dream that led him to discover the shape of the benzene ring and thus lay the foundation for synthetic compounds and aromatic chemistry. Kekulé was influenced by his professor of chemistry to change his field from architecture to chemistry:

Liebig himself seems to have occupied the role of a gate, or sorting-demon such as his younger contemporary Clerk Maxwell once proposed, helping to concentrate energy into one favored room of the Creation at the expense of everything else (later witnesses have suggested that Clerk Maxwell intended his Demon not so much as a convenience in discussing a thermodynamic idea as a parable about the *actual existence* of personnel like Liebig. . . . (411)

In his quest for information about one of the molecules that was the result of Kekulé's dream, Slothrop becomes a demon himself, losing his own bodily substance as he gathers more and more information until he finally disappears.

Early in his quest, Slothrop learns the nature of his function from Semyavin, one of the Zone's own people. When Slothrop tells him he is interested in information, Semyavin responds with a tragic sigh: "Information. What's wrong with dope and women? Is it any wonder the world's gone insane, with information come to be the only real medium of exchange?". In a moment he adds, "It'll get easier. Someday it'll be done by machine. Information machines. You are the wave of the future"(258). Of course Pynchon has already led Oedipa into the belly of the computer, but then *Gravity's Rainbow* is set in 1945 and not the 1960s. Slothrop becomes increasingly aware—as does the reader—that the Zone after the war is only another form of combat in which the stakes are information—about everything from the V-2 and its special variants to drugs and secret identities. Everyone seeks information about something; as Slothrop discovers, "everyone promises ya somethin' fer nothin', right? yes now oddly enough, that's the main objection engineers and scientists have always had to the idea of [lowering his voice] perpetual motion or as we like to call it Entropy Management . . ."(260). It does not take Slothrop long to learn what Entropy Management is or that he is being managed by others for the purpose of finding out information; too late in the game, he thinks of his relationship with Katje Borgesius: "He wants to preserve what he can of her from Their several entropies, from Their softsoaping and Their money: maybe he thinks that if he can do it for her he can also do it for himself . . ."(302). Before Katje ever meets Slothrop she wonders "if there's a real conversion factor between information and lives"(105). Within the closed system of the world, lives are being sorted instead of molecules. As Slothrop fades from the world he becomes signal zero, perhaps through a process of converting information to energy. In terms slightly reminiscent of Nefastis's machine, Slothrop's last words of the novel come at the end of a fantasy where distinctions between space and time, information and energy, have already begun to break down. He may be giving us a clue to what signal zero is like, or to where he has gone:

> A-and who sez it's a dream, huh? M-maybe *it exists.* Maybe there *is* a Machine to take us away, take us completely, suck us out through the electrodes out of the skull 'n' into the Machine and live there forever with all the other souls it's got stored there. *It* could decide who it would suck out, a-and when. . . . *We* can live forever, in a clean, honest, purified Electroworld—(699)

In such a world Aubade and Slothrop might meet.

The idea of the closed system takes other forms within Pynchon's fiction. Among them are the mechanical explanations of the world, such as Pointsman's conditioned responses, theories of heroic love from Mafia Winsome, spectra analysis from Mucho Maas, microcosms, and dialectics of good and evil. The ocular proof that the world is a closed space, however, is the fact that it can be mapped. A map defines boundaries, sets limits, establishes some sort of coordinate system onto which a finite world can be transposed.

Streets and the grid-coordinate system totally dominate Benny Profane; he has no reality beyond the map-made-street: "a single abstracted Street"(2). The desire to complete the map of the world, to fill in all blank spaces, drives Hugh Godolphin to Vheissu: "Contour lines and fathom-markings, cross-hatchings and colors where before there were only blank spaces on the map. All for the Empire" (156). When Oedipa Maas first arrives in San Narciso she sees it as a printed circuit, another kind of map for the electroworld: "The ordered swirl of houses and streets, from this high angle, sprang at her now with the same unexpected, astonishing clarity as the circuit card had"(13). Earlier, she had seen the entire world in another kind of map: " . . . all the other buildings and creatures, all the waves, ships and forests of the earth were contained in this tapestry, and the tapestry was the world"(10). By the time the novel ends, she has discovered that maps order space as history orders time; understanding the illusion of such order, she sees that San Narciso "had no boundaries. No one knew yet how to draw them"(134).

In *Gravity's Rainbow* maps play an even more important role. Early in the novel Tyrone Slothrop is not only bound by maps, but his identity as far as others are concerned is coordinated with the map that plots his sexual exploits: "Slothrop began work on this map last autumn, about the time he started going out to look at rocket-bomb disasters for ACHTUNG—having evidently the time, in his travels among places of death, to devote to girl-chasing"(19). To others, however, the map is more: "It's the map that spooks them all, the map Slothrop's been keeping on his girls. The stars fall in a Poisson distribution, just like the rocket strikes on Roger Mexico's map of the Robot Blitz"(85). And there is still another aspect of the same map according to Thomas Gwenhidwy: "I've been keep-ing my *own* map? Plot-ting da-ta from the maternity wards. The ba-bies born during this Blitz are al-so fol-lowing a Poisson distribution, you see"(173). London is seen entirely in terms of the rocket blitz, but its map is more than the limits of space and time: it is the map of love, death, and birth, all following the same Poisson distribution. Again, Pynchon brings the various aspects of the closed system together in a single image, in this case a statistical version of the familiar cycle of endless transformation, the self-consuming serpent. It may also be the narrator's own Poisson d'avril.

Slothrop's map-consciousness, however, undergoes an evolution similar to that of Oedipa. In the Zone things are different. Prewar boundaries and fixed positions have lost all meaning in the postwar scramble to establish a new map. The Zone is an interval between histories—a figurative zero point where new alignments of time and space are possible: "Separations are proceeding. Each alternative

Zone speeds away from all the others, in fated acceleration, red-shifting, fleeing the Center"(519). It is a time that requires the occupants of the Zone to learn "new maps of Earth: and as travel in the Interior becomes more common, as the maps grow another dimension, so must we . . ."(321). The Zone is as much a state of mind as it is the chaotic state of Europe; the Interior of both is newly open to those who have been on the outside of time. However, the Zone is a temporary moment for most people because soon "the new map of the occupation goes into effect"(328) as the Powers decide "how to cut up Germany"(370). While Slothrop wanders in search of the Schwarzgerät, he learns not only that there are no fixed boundaries, but also that all the normal coordinate points have been abandoned. The only map that exists is the one he projects, like Oedipa Maas wondering if she should project a world. Relative, arbitrary, and changing, his fantasy is as real as anything. Slothrop's four dimensional Raketen-Stadt may be closer to a true description of the world than any map of occupation, especially for the state of mind. In a sense, Slothrop does not really disintegrate; instead, he remains in the Zone, with his own coordinate system, as others are pulled back into the history of occupation and the coordinates of the new power axis. Bracketed by histories and maps, the Zone for a brief time is free from the pull of entropy, the tug towards death; it is no more than a minor fluctuation accounted for in Boltzmann's formulae.

Pynchon has created a fiction that shows as well as speaks about the closed system, and he has created a philosophically complete world, one that is all that is the case. He has been deliberate, precise, relentless. The world he shows us is frightening; there can be no more fundamentally pessimistic view. Even his stories and novels seem to draw energy from readers as they struggle with a signal-to-noise ratio, study the verbal landscape as a map. If there is a return for energy lost, it most probably comes as information gained, perhaps as knowledge about a closed system as seen from outside it. If this is the case, the narrator of *Gravity's Rainbow* summarizes our knowledge in what is undoubtedly Pynchon's single most conclusive passage. In correlating the actions of individuals with processes and observable conditions, he incorporates the reader in his definition of the human condition:

> Kekulé dreams the Great Serpent holding its own tail in its mouth, the dreaming Serpent which surrounds the World. But the meanness, the cynicism with which this dream is to be used. The Serpent that announces, "The World is a closed thing, cyclical, resonant, eternally-returning," is to be delivered into a system whose only aim is to *violate* the Cycle. Taking and not giving back, demanding that "productivity" and "earnings" keep on increasing with time, the System removing from the rest of the World these vast quantities of energy to keep its own tiny desperate fraction showing a profit: and not only most of humanity—most of the World, animal, vegetable and mineral, is laid waste in the process. The System may or may not understand that it's only buying time. And that time is an artificial resource to begin with, of no value to anyone or anything but the System, which sooner or later must crash to its death, when its addiction to energy has become more than the rest of the World can supply, dragging with it innocent souls all along the chain of life. Living inside the System is like riding across the country in a bus driven by a maniac bent on suicide. . . .
> (412)

In both Eastern and Western mythology the Cosmic Serpent represents a perpetual cycle of transformation, death into life.[14] However, Clausius also coined the term "entropy" from a Greek word for "transformation." By a coincidence not unlike the reconciliation of heat and information in Nefastis's machine, the Great Serpent offers the illusion of return at the same time it cloaks the real action. After the transformation of depletion, there is "no return, no salvation, no Cycle"(413). The world, its systems and bureaucracies, its people are betrayed by their own corporate cleverness. Knowledge has enabled man both to change the world and to understand what he has done. The biblical serpent came to the still-perfect garden as a giver of knowledge, trading information for eternity. Now a new serpent has come "to our ruinous garden, already too fouled, too crowded to qualify as any locus of innocence—unless innocence be our age's neutral, our silent passing into the machineries of indifference—something that Kekulé's Serpent had come to—not to destroy, but to define to us the loss of . . ."(413). As they document the vicissitude of the closed system, Pynchon's stories and novels also define a loss —to us as well as to his characters.

2 Baedeker Land

The purpose of Baedeker's Handbooks is to supply
travellers, in a handy form, aided by ample provision
of maps, with information based on personal observation and experience. They save the reader time, money,
and many an annoyance; reliable and impartial, they
relieve him of the necessity for verbal inquiries and of
dependence on advertisement folders and the like. The
mass of detail they contain is intended to help the
traveller to formulate his plans and sketch out possible
tours; it is certainly not meant to lead him into a senseless hustle through all the "sights" of the country.

from the preface of
Baedeker's 1936 *Germany*

TRAVELING INTO FOREIGN PARTS

If the closed system is the environment of Pynchon's fiction, then the
ruined garden is its landscape. Space is evidence. It testifies to the fact
of depletion and the work of entropy. Thus *Gravity's Rainbow* begins
with a final trip, an evacuation of London: "Underfoot crunches the
oldest of city dirt, last crystallizations of all the city had denied,
threatened, lied to its children. Each has been hearing a voice, one he
thought was talking only to him, say, 'You didn't really believe you'd
be saved. Come, we all know who we are by now. No one was ever
going to take the trouble to save *you*, old fellow . . .' " (4). God cursed
the ground and admonished Adam and his seed to eat of the earth
in sorrow. Moreover, God reminded Adam that he had been made of

dust and to dust he would return. Man and the earth were made one. His fate irrevocably tied to the world, man set forth from the Garden as a perpetual tourist, doomed ever to travel its surface as a stranger with no other home. The only imaginable destination is a memory, the dream of somewhere lost.

V., Profane, Fausto, the two Stencils, Inverarity, Oedipa Maas, Tyrone Slothrop, Blicero, and Enzian are all wanderers searching for information that will make their world a little less alien. The nature of their interaction with the land distinguishes Pynchon's fiction, elevates it from the intellectually curious to the artistically significant. Like Adam, these characters recognize a difference between the lost Garden and the ruined garden outside. Pynchon identifies Western man's territory more in terms of knowledge than scene. In short, the earth itself has become the vehicle of metaphor, important more for its descriptive value than its actuality. In harmony with the modern sensibility that extends from Machiavelli to Laurence Sterne and Lord Byron, through Herman Melville and Henry James to the present, Pynchon shows that reality becomes apparent only to the degree of its artificiality. It is a distinction essential to his works. Landscape, then, exists as much because of maps as because of rivers, mountains, or cities. It is what is imagined as well as seen.

In the world Pynchon offers his readers, Baedeker Land is another name for landscape, reality made perceptible by the artful representation of knowledge. From the time Karl Baedeker published his first guidebook in 1839 until the First World War, the name Baedeker grew synonymous with "travel guide" and it came to represent the standard in authenticity, reliability, and completeness. By 1880 the influence of Baedeker was so great that art had overtaken reality and begun literally to shape the world to the guidebooks' representation. Herbert Wind cites an illustrative anecdote in his 1975 *New Yorker* profile of the house of Baedeker:

> The key figure in one [story] that Karl Baedeker likes to tell is Kaiser Wilhelm I of Germany, whose preferred residence was his small palace

on Unter den Linden. One day in 1880, when he was talking to a visitor in an upstairs drawing room, Wilhelm, noting that it was almost noon, abruptly excused himself and hurried to a large corner window just in time to observe the changing of the guard in the avenue below. On returning to his visitor, he explained, "It's written in Baedeker that I watch the changing of the guard from that window, and the people have come to expect it."[1]

The power of Baedeker to shape, even create, experience is undeniable. In Pynchon's hands, however, this power of Baedeker stands as a symbol of man's knowledge of the world, a world known only by its representation. Baedeker selects the details of place for emphasis, creates a hierarchy of asterisks, and ignores most of what passes as reality for those who host the world's tourists.

With Kekulé's dream Pynchon takes Baedeker into a larger realm of tourism. His transition from the dream to a metaphor of travel— "Living inside the System is like riding across the country in a bus driven by a maniac bent on suicide"(412)—is deliberate, for Kekulé's dream did nothing less for synthetic reality than Baedeker did for tourism:

> Young ex-architect Kekulé went looking among the molecules of the time for the hidden shapes he knew were there, shapes he did not like to think of as real physical structures, but as "rational formulas," showing the relationships that went on in "metamorphoses," his quaint 19th-century way of saying "chemical reactions." But he could visualize. He *saw* the four bonds of carbon, lying in a tetrahedron— he *showed* how carbon atoms could link up, one to another, into long chains. . . . But he was stumped when he got to benzene. He knew there were six carbon atoms with a hydrogen attached to each one— but he could not see the shape. Not until the dream: until he was made to see it, so that others might be seduced by its physical beauty, and begin to think of it as a blueprint, a basis for new compounds, new arrangements. . . . (411–12)

The ability to visualize and to recognize shape is the essence of tourism, particularly if the "recognized shape" becomes a blueprint or a map. By coincidence, another Kekulé shared the architect-chemist's ability to visualize. Fritz Baedeker, who ruled the publishing house in its most glorious days, selected as one of his experts on shape Reinhard Kekulé von Stradonitz, who wrote the introductions on art for the Greek and Italian Baedeker editions of the late nineteenth century. With disquieting similarity to Friedrich August, Reinhard talks of all places and all times while introducing his readers to art in the 1894 Baedeker on Greece: "the various periods, the different schools, each within its own limits, show growth, blossom, and decay. Nor is decay always death. . . . it is sometimes only a transformation, producing new but not less marvelous forms as embodiments of the reviving conceptions of the mind."[2] Or as the Serpent whispered to Friedrich, "*They can be changed,* and new molecules assembled from the debris of the given . . . "(413).

Pynchon establishes the role of Baedeker in the third chapter of *V.* A refined version of "Under the Rose" published two years earlier, the chapter reveals some of the principles of tourism that will be taken for granted in later works. It includes eight sections narrated by "natives" of Alexandria and Cairo who observe European tourists interacting with a Baedeker landscape rather than Egypt itself. More accurately, these observers—merely part of a "landscape's feature" (52)—fantasize roles and plots for people who masquerade as tourists. They juxtapose their own illusions with Baedeker illusions: "There's no organized effort about it but there remains a grand joke on all visitors to Baedeker's world: the permanent residents are actually humans in disguise"(66). Thus freed, the permanent residents can occupy the same space and yet live in a different world as long as they do not violate the illusion of their disguises: "In Baedeker land one doesn't often run across imposters. Duplicity is against the law . . ."(63).

Pynchon allows the explorer Hugh Godolphin, a scientific tourist, to see past the illusions and beneath the skin of one place. The vision haunts and then destroys him. After telling Victoria Wren about Vheissu he looks at the tourists of Florence gaping at the Campanile and feels "isolated from a human community—even a common humanity . . ."(168). Later he reflects on the difference between his visit to Vheissu as an explorer and his discovery of what lay beneath its surface; he recognizes the shape of the grand joke of Baedeker Land:

"It was quite real; not like the vague hints they had given me before. I say 'they had given.' I think they left it there for me. Why? Perhaps for some alien, not-quite-human reason that I can never comprehend. Perhaps only to see what I would do. A mockery, you see: a mockery of life, planted where everything but Hugh Godolphin was inanimate. With of course the implication . . . It did tell me the truth about them. If Eden was the creation of God, God only knows what evil created Vheissu. The skin which had wrinkled through my nightmares was all there had ever been. Vheissu itself, a gaudy dream. Of what the Antarctic in this world is closest to: a dream of annihilation."(189–90)

The evil that created Vheissu is, of course, man; Vheissu is another name for the world—all surface and illusion to disguise the dust and waste of the ruined garden. If the serpent's knowledge of life and death—a dream of annihilation—leads to a wasteland, then man's creation is illusion—a gaudy dream. Only when the dreams are juxtaposed can we perceive that they are different.

Pynchon reserves his summative definition of Baedeker Land to describe the world V. abandons for a more perfect consummation of reality and the inanimate: " . . . a world if not created then at least described to its fullest by Karl Baedeker of Leipzig. This is a curious country, populated only by a breed called 'tourists.' Its landscape is one of inanimate monuments and buildings. . . . More than this it is two-dimensional, as is the Street, as are the pages and maps of those little red handbooks"(384). Tourists the world over constitute their own class: a metaphor for a population sprung from Adam's knowledge of death. Having known the garden and the dust, Adam established the principle of tourism, which Baedeker transformed into a science. Perception, what one is told he can see, distinguishes man from God. The two Kekulés understood the principle. Friedrich, predisposed toward architecture, discovered the benzene ring precisely because he could visualize its shape; he expected to see a ring. Reinhard could see nothing but shapes in the course of man's history. Both provide preliminary information for the guidebook all tourists have committed to the collective unconscious. A classless society itself, tourists know only the world that is organized, systematized, assimilated, and predicted by the unspoken conspiracy of consensus. As the narrator of *V.* explains:

> Tourism thus is supranational, like the Catholic Church, and perhaps the most absolute communion we know on earth: for be its members American, German, Italian, whatever, the Tour Eiffel, Pyramids, and Campanile all evoke identical responses from them; their Bible is clearly written and does not admit of private interpretation; they share the same landscapes, suffer the same inconveniences; live by the same pellucid time-scale. They are the Street's own.(384)

A tour is a journey into foreign parts, a movement in sequence. The word tour, with derivatives such as tourify, touristdom, touristry, touristic, and tourize, comes from a Greek word that denotes a tool for describing a circle: the serpent coils. A tour implies a return to the beginning, but that too is part of the illusion. The tour we are all on, like the bus ride, violates the cycle: "over your own seat, where there ought to be an advertising plaque, is instead a quote from Rilke: 'Once, only once . . . ' "(413).

THE TOUR

Pynchon offers a number of tours of Baedeker Land. Each is exotic, some are dangerous, and all rate an asterisk or two. There is an alligator hunt in the sewers of New York, a clandestine visit to the Uffizi, a bus ride through the midnight streets of San Francisco, a balloon trip over the Harz mountains, a desert trek to the Kirghiz Light, and a boat ride along the Oder. There are, literally, hundreds of tours through Europe, North America, Africa, and Central Asia. They are great, imcomprehensible movements reduced to a human scale. As one character in *Gravity's Rainbow* wonders, "What if we're all Jews, you see? all scattered like seeds? still flying outward from the primal fist so long ago"(170). Pynchon's preoccupation with the idea of the tour is as important to his fiction as the closed system. It is an idea little changed by the centuries and technologies that have intervened since Herodotus wrote the first great travelogue or, for that matter, since Adam set forth from the Garden. Despite its adoption as a literary motif by every generation of novelists from Fielding, Sterne, and Swift through Henry James, Henry Adams, and James Joyce, it retains a novelty and excitement. But for Pynchon, the tour is more than a literary artifact; it defines man's spatial and human relationship with his environment and serves as evidence of a person's continuing existence. Perhaps Herbert Stencil is typical: "His random movements . . . had given way to a great single movement from inertness to—if not vitality, then at least activity"(44).

Not all spatial movement is reducible to a single form. But the idea of the tour is essential because it is the reference against which all individual movements can be measured. A stranger, the tourist typically has no direct knowledge of the place he visits. If he has any knowledge at all it is preconceived and designed to help him see the country from the vantage of some arbitrarily selected, but generalized, point of reference, such as a Baedeker guidebook. The conception of a place and the place itself may be congruent, but more likely they are merely similar. Since the tourist cannot adopt the natives' point of view, he must either recreate the place in its image or he must reconcile illusion and new knowledge. Regardless of his degree of consciousness, the tourist is confronted with illusion in a way that he is not in his native land. While most tourists attribute their anxiety and displacement to the physical fact of their location, some understand that perception rather than the place is the source of alienation. This latter condition of tourism offers Pynchon a model for the way in which his characters can discover their world—a world not merely of places, things, and customs, but of ideas, forces, and dreams. They become self-conscious of their tours and see travel as process in addition to progress. The tour can take place anywhere because once the tourist confronts the discrepancy between illusion and observation, even one's own home can become alien territory and he a stranger in it. The tour is more than the simple act of travel. It is travel for its own sake and is therefore solipsistic; no one can take a tour for someone else. Herbert Stencil's explanation of his own situation has such eloquence that it speaks for all abstracted tourists:

> This place, this island: all his life he's done nothing but hop from island to island. Is that a reason? Does there have to be a reason? Shall he tell you: he works for no Whitehall, none conceivable unless, ha, ha, the network of white halls in his own brain: these featureless corridors he keeps swept and correct for occasional visiting agents. Envoys from the zones of human crucified, the fabled districts of human love. But in whose employ? Not his own: it would be lunacy, the lunacy of any self-appointed prophet. . . . (42)

Thus distinguished from travel in general, the tour possesses a number of characteristics that suggest that its self-contained form coincides with the closed system; as the world is increasingly overcome by entropy, the tour may be the only travel possible. Pynchon is clearly fascinated by the consequences of this possibility and attempts to show that the continental plan, group flight, and chartered bus may be all that is available to the hero in contemporary society. The once noble quest is reduced to tour, complete with guides, maps, schedules, and the sense that numberless others have been this way before. At least since *Childe Harold's Pilgrimage* it has been routinized and economized: the stages of perilous journey, struggle, and exaltation have been telescoped into a single act of sight-seeing. The enemy has become impersonal and diffuse—a force, a secret, or a corporate conglomerate. Since the beast cannot be identified or engaged and the hero cannot distinguish himself, there is nothing left but to travel and to search for information about the enemy.

There are any number of reasons for Pynchon to select information as the new medium of quest and tour: it is sequential and cumulative; it must be searched out; it implies a conclusion or resolution; it may be preconceived and then redefined by observation; it may be imagined or real; it has consequences. It is also this century's most important commodity and exists as its own territory, free from geography and national boundaries. And yet information has no value apart from those who seek it and, potentially, use it. Stencil searches for information about V.; Oedipa searches for information about the Tristero; Slothrop searches for information about the Schwarzgerät. None of these characters searches for the object itself because finding it would cancel the tour. Knowledge about the object offers fewer risks. As a prototype for subsequent searchers, Herbert Stencil summarizes the problem:

> Finding her: what then? Only that what love there was to Stencil had become directed entirely inward, toward this acquired sense of animateness. Having found this he could hardly release it, it was too dear. To sustain it he had to hunt V.; but if he should find her, where else would there be to go but back into half-consciousness? He tried not to think, therefore, about any end to the search. Approach and avoid. (44)

Stencil is Pynchon's first fully developed tourist. Although the principal character of *V.*, he is nonetheless conspicuously absent most of the time. Instead of Stencil, there is his track—a record of where he has been, clues he has pursued. Both Stencil and his name are maps of a landscape. After spending forty-four years of his life as an itinerant somnambulist Stencil discovers his career in 1945 while leafing through his father's journals, "bound in half-calf and warped by the humid air of many European cities"(43). These books become the younger Stencil's personalized Baedeker for retracing his father's steps, which he does methodically in his search for information about V. By December 1955 the tour has led Stencil to New York and a plastic surgeon transparently named Schoenmaker—a person who specializes in making reality conform to illusion and dream. The novel's account of Stencil's tour of New York is minimal and indirect: he attends a party at Fergus Mixolydian's; lounges about Bongo-Shaftsbury's apartment; chats with the chief alligator exterminator of New York; prowls the East Side sewers in disguise; sips coffee in a Hungarian coffee shop; interviews Dudley Eigenvalue, D.D.S.; is introduced to Bloody Chiclitz, president of Yoyodyne; drinks beer with Kurt Mondaugen; reads the confessions of Fausto Maijstral; gets drunk with Benny Profane at the Forked Yew; gets drunk again with Profane at the Rusty Spoon; breaks into Eigenvalue's office to steal a pair of false teeth; watches the sun rise over Central Park; makes a quick trip to Washington, D.C.; pays another visit to Eigenvalue; and attends a bon voyage party before departing for Malta.

While not typical tourist fare, each of Stencil's adventures is part of a chain of events in his search for V. More importantly, most of these are the occasion for commentary on the historical V-structure. Further, these sixteen encounters, plus his visit to Malta, provide the limited narrative scaffolding for the novel. Despite the fact that Herbert Stencil is shown seeing very little and speaking to few, his activities provide a structure precisely by offering the opportunity for guidebook entries. Tourism is less a matter of place than its perception. Stencil utters slightly more than one hundred words to Eigenvalue, for example, but these result in fifty-five pages of a reconstructed Florence of 1899; less than three paragraphs describing Stencil's meeting with Kurt Mondaugen develops into forty-eight pages of 1922 Africa.

Only in his first encounter with Eigenvalue and his drunken adventure with Profane does Stencil speak more than a few words during the New York leg of his journey. The importance of these two incidents is thus magnified. When Stencil suggests to the dentist that they "both drop pretense"(139), he is not referring to the pretense of his search but rather the "pretense" that there is no search. Eigenvalue's response suggests that he recognizes the distinction: "In a world such as you inhabit, Mr. Stencil, any cluster of phenomena can be a conspiracy. So no doubt your suspicion is correct. Buy why consult me? Why not the Encyclopedia Britannica? It knows more than I about any phenomena you should ever have interest in" (140). When pretense is dropped, the information that Stencil seeks becomes conventionally encyclopedic—that is, both comprehensive enough to construct a world and common enough for general reference. Like the details of any tourist guide, the facts that Stencil accumulates correspond to the V-structure in direct proportion to his preconceived perceptions, "merely a scholarly quest after all . . ." (50). However, Stencil confesses to Profane that he searches after V. perhaps only because he needs "a mystery, any sense of pursuit to keep active a borderline metabolism"(362). His greatest fear is the chance that reality might overtake, and immobilize, illusion. Before reciting his history of V. for Profane, Stencil explains his reluctance to visit Malta: "But he stayed off Malta. He had pieces of thread: clues. Young Stencil has been in all her cities, chased her down till faulty memories or vanished buildings defeated him. All her cities but Valletta. His father died in Valletta. He tried to tell himself meeting V. and dying were separate and unconnected for Sidney" (362). Valletta may have a reality of its own that will not submit to Stencil's preconception. He prefers to live in a fantasy world made up of reconstructed places and people; as he tells Eigenvalue, "Florence only a few summers ago had seemed crowded with the same tourists as at the turn of the century"(141). Places are less important to Stencil as sights than as vistas on the past, the reconstructed facts of his father's guidebook. He can walk the streets of the same New York City with Profane, but they are in different worlds. New York has no reality of its own and he is permitted the luxury of seeing it in terms of his own V-structure. Valletta is the only clue that might coincide with an actual place in Stencil's world. It scares him because it is unknown territory. He does not know what he is expected to see since it is the place of his father's death—the last entry in Sidney's journal and potentially the journey's end.

Stencil on Malta is a different person. His search there is nervous, alive with a sense of the place itself. One night he seeks out Fausto Maijstral and, huddled over tea, juxtaposes Sidney Stencil's past with his own present: "She cannot be dead . . . . One feels her in the city" (421). He goes on to tell Fausto of his fear that action will overtake movement and observation unmask perception:

> "Did you know, he's devised a prayer. Walking about this city, to be said in rhythm to his footsteps. Fortune, may Stencil be steady enough not to fasten on one of these poor ruins at his own random or at any least hint from Maijstral. Let him not roam out all Gothic some night with lantern and shovel to exhume an hallucination, and be found by the authorities mud-streaked and mad, and tossing meaningless clay about."(421)

Stencil, "who seemed more unaware each day (under questioning) of what was happening in the rest of the world"(421), is very close to ending his tour by the prospect of his illusion's becoming real. Crisis arrives for Stencil in the coincidence of Father Fairing's having been V.'s confessor and the New York sewer priest. Overcome by a sense of "ominous logic," or an external control over his movement, which seems to direct all his clues and his search for information, Stencil seeks Fausto's help when he discovers that Profane, whom he brought to Malta to help protect him from the place, fits into the design. Fausto tells Stencil that there is no cure for the condition of tourism. He must choose the world he will live in:

> Maijstral opened the window and stepped out on the balcony. Valletta by nightlight looked totally uninhabited. "No," Maijstral said, "you wouldn't get what you wanted. What—if it were your world—would be necessary. One would have to exorcise the city, the island, every ship's crew on that Mediterranean. The continents, the world. Or the western part," as an afterthought. "We are western men."(424)

In his final spoken words of the novel, Stencil asks the one question left him: "Is it really his own extermination he's after?" Fausto makes the only possible reply. Gesturing toward Valletta, he says,

"Ask her. . . . Ask the rock"(425). Valletta simply is, but Stencil must perceive her as the end of his search or as another of his endless clues; in so doing, he determines his future. Herbert Stencil is not the reflective tourist that his father was on Malta, but the elder Stencil's observations help explain what his son chose to avoid: "So at peace was Valletta that with the least distance she would deteriorate to mere spectacle. She ceased to exist as anything quick or pulsed, and was assumed again into the textual stillness of her own history" (446). The son can accept only spectacle, distance, and the textual stillness of his scholarly quest. He is unable to learn anything from his father's visit, but perhaps he was never told. Valletta had its magic for Sidney; it made him, at least, understand that there are, in fact, two orders of being:

> But the low wall surrounding the place drew his attention. Normally insensitive to the artistic or Baedeker aspect of any city he visited, Stencil was now ready to succumb to the feathery tentacles of a nostalgia which urged him gently back toward childhood; a childhood of gingerbread witches, enchanted parks, fantasy country. It was a dream-wall, swirling and curlicuing now in the light of a quarter moon, seeming no more solid than the decorative voids—some almost like leaves or petals, some almost like bodily organs not quite human—which pierced its streaked and cobbled substance. (447)

For Herbert there are only the decorative voids. The last trace of him before he disappears into one void is a note of farewell. He decides in favor of the tour and leaves Malta for Stockholm where he hopes a Mme. Viola can tell him about V.'s glass eye: "It will do for the frayed end of another clue"(425). Rather than engage the enemy in battle as demanded in a less mundane quest, Stencil climbs back on board the bus.

Stencil's tour is obviously more complex than this abbreviated account suggests, but there is very little of him present in the novel, despite his centrality. Most of the novel is digression that partially decorates the void of Stencil's existence. Together, various characters complete the picture of Baedeker Land. As the senior Stencil concludes on one occasion, tourism " . . . is a kind of communion" (443). Although he is comparing mob violence with tourism, his analysis applies equally well to both in its suggestion of the subversive roles image and illusion play for young Stencil, or even entire populations: "By its special magic a large number of lonely souls, however heterogeneous, can share the common property of opposition to what is. And like an epidemic or earthquake the politics of the street can overtake even the most stable-appearing of governments; like death it cuts through and gathers in all ranks of society" (443). Fantasy—whether personal like Stencil's or public like Hitler's —can and does replace whatever happens to be passing as reality.

The significance of Malta as a place and as an image is established by Fausto's confession. It is this information to which Herbert Stencil and the reader respond. Malta represents nothing less than the polarity of life and death. But it is no different from any other place that a tourist might encounter. Only its perception is significant, as Fausto explains, for he has explored Malta "as a kind of tourist" (304):

And was it not Valletta? During the raids everything civilian and with a soul was underground. Others were too busy to "observe." The city was left to itself; except for stragglers like Fausto, who felt nothing more than an unvoiced affinity and were enough like the city not to change the truth of the "impressions" by the act of receiving them. A city uninhabited is different. Different from what a "normal" observer, straggling in the dark—the occasional dark—would see. It is a universal sin among the false-animate or unimaginative to refuse to let well enough alone. Their compulsion to gather together, their pathological fear of loneliness extends on past the threshold of sleep; so that when they turn the corner, as we all must, as we all have done and do—some more often than others—to find ourselves on the street . . . You know the street I mean, child. The street of the 20th Century, at whose far end or turning—we hope—is some sense of home or safety. But no guarantees. A street we are put at the wrong end of, for reasons best known to the agents who put us there. If there are agents. But a street we must walk.(303)

Malta is crucial for Stencil because it is a place where illusion and reality meet, and he must choose between perceptions of his life's search. We cannot be certain of Stencil's choice, only that he chooses. The fact that he continues his search in pursuit of a flimsy clue suggests that he has recognized the tour and the world for what they are; at least the tour affirms the pretense of life. Malta is crucial to Fausto for precisely the same reasons, even though he is a native. He looks at Malta as if he were a tourist and confronts the same problem of illusion and reality, its surface and the truth beneath, as Stencil: "But the desert, or a row of false shop fronts; a slag pile, a forge where the fires are banked, these and the street and the dreamer, only an inconsequential shadow himself in the landscape, partaking of the soullessness of these other masses and shadows; this is 20th Century nightmare"(303). With a precision and density not found elsewhere in Pynchon's fiction, Fausto specifies how three elements of the tour —the place as it exists, the metaphorical street or the tour of life we must all take, and the dreamer—combine to isolate the tourist in a landscape that coexists with (but is not the same as) the land itself. Regardless of what perversities may accompany a particular illusion, the image of a place has its own form of reality. Fausto later explains the function of illusion:

> Proving perhaps that virility on Malta did not depend on mobility. They were all, as Fausto was first to admit, labourers not adventurers. Malta, and her inhabitants, stood like an immovable rock in the river Fortune, now at war's flood. The same motives which cause us to populate a dream-street also cause us to apply to a rock human qualities like "invincibility," "tenacity," "perseverance," etc. More than metaphor, it is delusion. But on the strength of this delusion Malta survived.(305)

There are others besides Fausto who help fill the void of Stencil's absence. In addition to the journal characters brought to life by memory and Stencil's retelling, Benny Profane and Pig Bodine are tourists as well. While their interactions with Stencil help provide the novel's content, their movements further define the tour as a universal form. Bodine is a sailor and Profane is a sailor turned yo-yo. Bodine is a bawdy, sketchily drawn character who fades in and out of Pynchon's fiction as a sailor might visit a port. In his continuity from "Low-lands" to *Gravity's Rainbow* he is certainly one of Pynchon's most intriguing characters—the abstracted universal sailor—but it is Profane who typifies the tourist: "Some of us are afraid of dying; others of human loneliness. Profane was afraid of land or seascapes like this, where nothing else lived but himself. It seemed he was always walking into one: turn a corner in the street, open a door to a weather-deck and there he'd be, in alien country"(12). He discriminates among sights while Bodine does not. Since leaving the navy Profane "had been road-laboring and when there wasn't work just traveling, up and down the east coast like a yo-yo"(2). Profane's relationship with the "single abstracted Street"(2) is the profane manifestation of Fausto's metaphor; almost identical words are used to describe Profane: "This was all there was to dream; all there ever was: the Street"(31). He typifies the tourist at the most trivial level, touches the reader with a recognizable familiarity. Profane demonstrates that we are all tourists, even at home. His yo-yoing on a Lexington Avenue local is one occasion for the narrator to provide a guidebook commentary:

> The shuttle after morning rush hour is nearly empty, like a littered beach after tourists have all gone home. In the hours between nine and noon the permanent residents come creeping back up their strand, shy and tentative. Since sunup all manner of affluent have filled the limits of that world with a sense of summer and life; now sleeping bums and old ladies on relief, who have been there all along unnoticed, re-establish a kind of property right, and the coming on of a falling season.(28)

Profane is as conscious of tourism as the narrator. At the Feast of San' Ercole dei Rinoceronti in New York's Little Italy, his companions urge him to approach a group of girls because he speaks "guinea," to which Profane ironically responds, "It isn't like it was a foreign country"(126). On a subway from Brooklyn to Manhattan, Profane recognizes himself in a sleeping bum—one of the permanent residents—who, he thinks, must be dreaming his own submarine country; it is another version of Fausto's dream: "If under the street and under the sea are the same then he was king of both"; but he thinks of himself "not like a king . . . more like a schlemihl, a follower"(199). Profane even senses the same control of his trip that haunts Stencil and Fausto:

> Any sovereign or broken yo-yo must feel like this after a short time of lying inert, rolling, falling: suddenly to have its own umbilical string reconnected, and know the other end is in hands it cannot escape. Hands it doesn't want to escape. Know that the simple clockwork of itself has no more need for symptoms of inutility, lonesomeness, directionlessness, because now it has a path marked out for it over which it has no control. That's what the feeling would be, if there were such things as animate yo-yos.(200-201)

Abandoned by Stencil on Malta—"a clenched fist around a yo-yo string"(418)—in Fausto's care, Profane still has no control of his own. Back on the street again, Valleta's Kingsway, he meets Brenda Wigglesworth, a college girl ending up her "Grand Tour"(426). He and his fellow tourist agree that beyond the tour is nowhere, "but some of us do go nowhere and can con ourselves into believing it to be somewhere: it is a kind of talent and objections to it are rare but even at that captious"(426–27). In a moment of sadness, the world-weary representative of mankind reflects on the consequence of constant motion: ". . . all his homes were temporary and even they, inanimate, still wandering as he: for motion is relative . . ."(427). Fausto promises to help Profane find work on the street or below it and, as if nothing else existed, Profane disappears from the novel running down the street hand-in-hand with Brenda as lights go out all over Valletta. Though neither Fausto nor Profane searches for information in the way Stencil does, neither one represents any alternative to the basic tour of life.

Pynchon provides a fully, if not systematically, developed structure in the tour. His own service in the navy provided him both with the experience of the form and with imaginative details. Having come of age in the 1950s, Pynchon was surely familiar with that generation's version of the open road, Jack Kerouac's among others. However, Pynchon complicates the conventional metaphor and form of the "road" with artful distractions, elaborate side trips, and the pleasures of self-conscious touristry. In Pynchon the tour is the basis of plot, but it is also theme; it is the structure of *The Crying of Lot 49* and *Gravity's Rainbow*. In *V.* the structure is diffuse, but more analytical than in later variations. Perhaps intentionally it displays conventional literary modes. In Fausto, for example, the tour is almost romantic; in Stencil, it is very low mimetic; and in Profane it is usually ironic. Of course Pynchon's use of the structure is itself ironic, but the distinction among "modes" serves a purpose by demonstrating, or revealing, how a tour-consciousness functions at every level from the scholarly to the profane, including the bureaucratic. It provides an artistic model that, once demonstrated, need not be replicated if it can be invoked. In subsequent novels, the tour is simply a fact of life, a communion.

The tour of Oedipa Maas, like *The Crying of Lot 49*, is more compact and efficient than its predecessor, Herbert Stencil's tour in *V.* The "modes" are no longer distinct, or even relevant, though they are replaced to some extent by mythic and Freudian referents. As her trip begins, the profane and romantic coincide. Returning from the suburban secular world of a Tupperware party to find she has been named executor of Pierce Inverarity's will, Oedipa recalls that she had "conned herself into the curious, Rapunzel-like role of a pensive girl somehow, magically, prisoner among the pines and salt fogs of Kinneret, looking for somebody to say hey, let down your hair" (10). Oedipa begins her search with a self-consciousness of inertia and potential energy. Inverarity had led her, for a time, away from Kinneret (an inert place) only for her to discover that he "had taken her away from nothing, there'd been no escape"(11). She had, as Profane suggested, conned herself for a while into believing nowhere to be somewhere, but the illusion could not last. She had asked herself, "If the tower is everywhere and the knight of deliverance no proof against its magic, what else?"(11). The answer is revealed in her pursuit of Inverarity's will. The illusion of movement is all that there is and in this, at least, she resembles her namesake, Oedipus, whose own tour never escaped its origins.

Oedipa's initial perception of her existence in an isolated system is not finally altered by her tour. Rather, Pynchon provides sufficient clues to suggest an unstated metaphor based on physics' various laws of motion. The law of conservation of momentum, for example, states that the total momentum of an isolated system remains constant. Further, Oedipa's own name suggests Newton's second law of motion in which *mass* is the term denoting a quantity of inertia. The law may be expressed as follows: the acceleration produced by a force acting on a body is directly proportional to the magnitude of its force and inversely proportional to the mass of the body. The greater the mass, the less the motion; or inversely, the greater the force, the greater the motion. Through his will, Inverarity is the force at work on Oedipa's mass. On several occasions Pynchon invokes the image of a pool table as the metaphor for a closed system, one that is frequently used by scientists to illustrate the predictability of motion within such a system. However, Pynchon also suggests the possibility of violating the laws of motion, a miracle, by the intrusion of one world onto another, like the "kiss of cosmic pool balls"(92). She will discover that there is no miracle at all. Rather, two worlds exist simultaneously if you are able to see them. Oedipa seems to encounter such a violation when she finds herself dancing at a deaf-mute convention: "There would have to be collisions. The only alternative was some unthinkable order of music, many rhythms, all keys at once, a choreography in which each couple meshed easy, predestined. Something they all heard with an extra sense atrophied in herself. She followed her partner's lead, limp in the young mute's clasp, waiting for the collisions to begin. But none came"(97). Later Emory Bortz will ask her if she thinks "a man's mind is a pool table?" (115). While Oedipa hopes for some violation of the conservation of momentum, such as she experienced briefly in the hands of her deaf dancing partner, she finds none. She is subject to the same laws as everyone else; even Stanley Koteks's promise that she will find "perpetual motion"(62) in Nefastis's machine is false. Oedipa is kept in motion by forces acting on her, as Stencil is kept in motion by V.'s force. Slowed by inertia, her own mass, she keeps moving by searching for information about the Tristero. Her attempt to identify the forces becomes a mode of existence, her own mass inextricably caught in death's gravitational pull—Inverarity's last will. Despite the efficacy of Pynchon's inertia model for Oedipa's adventure, the tour metaphor dominates *The Crying of Lot 49*.

A native of Southern California, Oedipa does not recognize anything unusual about San Narciso, the first stop on her tour, because she has yet to learn the difference between illusion and reality: "She left Kinneret, then, with no idea she was moving toward anything new"(12). Without benefit of a Baedeker or the clues that Inverarity's will eventually provides, she thinks to herself: "But if there was any vital difference between it and the rest of Southern California, it was invisible on first glance"(13). Her first glance is modified immediately, however, by the sense that what she can see actually conceals something else. By the end of the novel, she will know that there are coexistent worlds; her perception of California—all of America—will have changed in the interim. As Oedipa descends the highway into San Narciso, her sense of a concealed meaning beneath surface reality begins to take shape:

> Barbed wire again gave way to the familiar parade of more beige, prefab, cinderblock office machine distributors, sealant makers, bottled gas works, fastener factories, warehouses, and whatever. Sunday had sent them all into silence and paralysis, all but an occasional real estate office or truck stop. Oedipa resolved to pull in at the next motel she saw, however ugly, stillness and four walls having at some point

become preferable to this illusion of speed, freedom, wind in your hair, unreeling landscape—it wasn't. What the road really was, she fancied, was this hypodermic needle, inserted somewhere ahead into the vein of a freeway, a vein nourishing the mainliner L. A., keeping it happy, coherent, protected from pain, or whatever passes, with a city, for pain. But were Oedipa some single melted crystal of urban horse, L. A., really, would be no less turned on for her absence.(14)

With typical stylistic virtuosity, Pynchon's metaphor condenses and reifies the abstract interplay of illusion and reality. The movement of mind and body, each with its own vehicle, is a singular function of perception. Ugly details of the roadside coexist with fanciful illusions; the highway and the vein occupy the same space. Only a self-consciousness of the tour itself will make Oedipa's absence a presence, however tentative.

Oedipa senses that the surface of San Narciso cloaks some other reality, "as if . . . there were revelation in progress all around her" (28). Revelation proceeds at an accelerating rate as Inverarity's will begins to exert its influence on her. During her first night in San Narciso she discovers that Inverarity either owned or had an interest in almost every commercial enterprise in the area. In rapid succession she receives a letter with a curious misprint in the cancellation; sees the muted post horn of the Tristero for the first time in the ladies' washroom of The Scope bar; and begins the process of looking beneath the surface of Southern California:

So began, for Oedipa, the languid, sinister blooming of The Tristero. Or rather, her attendance at some unique performance, prolonged as if it were the last of the night, something a little extra for whoever'd stayed this late. As if the breakaway gowns, net bras, jeweled garters and G-strings of historical figuration that would fall away were layered dense as Oedipa's own streetclothes in that game with Metzger in front of the Baby Igor movie; as if a plunge toward dawn indefinite black hours long would indeed be necessary before The Tristero could be revealed in its terrible nakedness. Would its smile, then, be coy, and would it flirt away harmlessly backstage, say good night with a Bourbon Street bow and leave her in peace? Or would it instead, the dance ended, come back down the runway, its luminous stare locked to Oedipa's, smile gone malign and pitiless; bend to her alone among the desolate rows of seats and begin to speak words she never wanted to hear?(36)

She knows now that there is something beneath the surface. Its truth will come later, perhaps with the same unexpected sadness that awaited Narcissus in the disturbed surface of his own image.

She finds her next clue at Inverarity's fantasy-land housing development, Fangoso Lagoons, where everything is artificial, including a lake "at the bottom of which lay restored galleons, imported from the Bahamas; Atlantean fragments of columns and friezes from the Canaries; real human skeletons from Italy; giant clamshells from Indonesia—all for the entertainment of Scuba enthusiasts"(18). San Narciso is deliberately constructed of illusions; the detritus of the world is nothing but props for Inverarity's synthetic world. The similarity of Inverarity's use of human skeletons in his lake with the plot of a Jacobean revenge play produced by a local troupe leads Oedipa to the play and her first encounter with the word "Tristero." From this point on, other revelations "seemed to come crowding in exponentially, as if the more she collected the more would come to her . . ."(58). On her tour of Yoyodyne, she meets Stanley Koteks, sees the muted post horn again, and learns of Maxwell's demon. Other clues fall into place: a historical marker at Fangosa Lagoons; the text of the Jacobean revenge play; Mr. Thoth's memories of Wells Fargo; Genghis Cohen's discovery of stamp forgeries; Emory Bortz's footnote; and Nefastis's machine. Overwhelmed by her discovery of another world beneath the surface of California, Oedipa decides "to drift tonight, at random, and watch nothing happen, to be convinced it was purely nervous, a little something for her shrink to fix"(80). Instead, her motion predicted, she "collided with a gang of guided tourists" and "found herself being herded, along with other badged citizens"(81) toward a bar. Reminded "not to act like a bunch of tourists"(81), she is precisely a tourist, guided by clues emanating from Inverarity's apparently immortal will:

The city was hers, as, made up and sleeked so with the customary words and images (cosmopolitan, culture, cable cars) it had not been before: she had safe-passage tonight to its far blood's branchings, be they capillaries too small for more than peering into, or vessels mashed together in shameless municipal hickeys, out on the skin for all but tourists to see. Nothing of the night's could touch her; nothing did. The repetition of symbols was to be enough, without trauma as well perhaps to attenuate it or even jar it altogether loose from her memory. *She was meant to remember.* (86–87)

After her night of bus rides and walking, she realizes that "there had to exist the separate, silent, unsuspected world"(92), a world confirmed by her miraculous dance with the deaf-mute and by her encounter with an old sailor, the archetypal tourist. Following a Tristero courier, Oedipa finds herself back at Nefastis's apartment, where her tour of San Francisco had begun twenty-four hours earlier. With the physical tour completed, Oedipa exists in a world altered only by her perceptions of it, but completely unlike the one she had known before. After this experience there is nothing for her to do but follow the clues wherever they may lead. Alone in her room, she realizes that she is still in her tower, "for this, oh God, was the void. There was nobody who could help her. Nobody in the world" (128). She perceives the world differently than she did back in Kinneret with its Tupperware inertia; it has not changed—only she. Oedipa makes one last attempt at rationality in a phone call to the Inamorati Anonymous. After that "San Narciso at that moment lost . . . gave up its residue of uniqueness for her"(133) and became part of the American—and Freudian—continuity. Everywhere was the same: "If San Narciso and the estate were really no different from any other town, any other estate, then by that continuity she might have found The Tristero anywhere in her Republic, through any of a hundred lightly-concealed entranceways, a hundred alienations, if only she'd looked"(135). The distinction she perceives has little to do with place since everywhere is the same. Instead, it has to do with the difference between land and landscape. Oedipa thinks of the

America Inverarity's will revealed to her: "... as if they were in exile from somewhere else invisible yet congruent with the cheered land she lived in"(135). Oedipa sees clearly that there are both object and image, reality and illusion, but she does not yet know which is which: "Another mode of meaning behind the obvious, or none"(137). There is no choice but "waiting for a symmetry of choices to break down, to go skew"(136). After reviewing all the possibilities, Oedipa decides that if San Narciso is representative of America, "the only way she could continue, and manage to be at all relevant to it, was as an alien, unfurrowed, assumed full circle into some paranoia" (137). She can continue only as a tourist in her own country.

In *The Crying of Lot 49* Pynchon reduces the extravagances of Stencil's quest to essentials. Oedipa's search for clues to the identity of The Tristero has an economy and efficiency of plot that distinguishes it from the complexities of Pynchon's other novels. More importantly, Pynchon allows Oedipa Maas to reveal her consciousness of the tour far beyond what Stencil implies by his actions. Stencil in the role of tourist imitates Baedeker's stereotype; he is distinguishable among a crowd only by a suspected self-awareness of his touring for its own sake and by the commentaries of Fausto and Profane. Oedipa, on the other hand, begins as a Baedeker tourist but becomes a tourist of the mind as the focus of her observations shifts from image to object. Pynchon allows us to watch the transformation of her consciousness and, at the same time, experiments with perception. A place, whether San Francisco, Cairo, or London, is incidental to the way one sees it. While a tourist by definition goes to a place solely because it is that particular place, Pynchon suggests that the defining characteristic of tourism is the act of perception, regardless of where it is practiced. Thus freed from any dependency on a particular place, Pynchon's self-conscious tourists are able to recognize a difference between a place and its image, between land and landscape.

Tentative as it may be, Slothrop's search for the Schwarzgerät and the mysterious Imipolex G provides *Gravity's Rainbow* with the closest thing it has to a structure. Like *V.*, *Gravity's Rainbow* consists primarily of digressions from the search, but they are far more grandiose, complex, and dispersed than in *V.* Slothrop is introduced as an American lieutenant on loan to the appropriately named war intelligence unit ACHTUNG (Allied Clearing House, Technical Units, Northern Germany) where his job is investigating V-bomb incidents, "a Saint George after the fact, going out to poke about for droppings of the Beast . . ."(24). Already these bureaucratic searches for death contain the parameters of his particular grand tour: "Slothrop's Progress: London the secular city instructs him: turn any corner and he can find himself inside a parable"(25). Although his eventual goal is Rocket City, an alternate Celestial City, Slothrop's pilgrimage never goes beyond the tour; as Fausto predicted, everyone must turn the corner and find himself on the street of the twentieth century.

The secular city is reduced to a map on which Slothrop plots his sexual exploits with multicolored stars. It is also a map of the rocket-falls. Slothrop becomes important because of this correspondence, and his adventure is instigated by others who wish to observe his movements. Like Oedipa Maas, he is subject both to human control and to impersonal forces. Slothrop leaves London for the Casino Hermann Goering, a French resort recently reclaimed from the Germans. Appropriately attired for his new status as a misguided traveler, he appears in a flowered shirt decorated with hibiscus blossoms, an outrigger canoe, and "SOUVENIR OF HONOLULU," and he proudly proclaims, "This is the authentic item . . . not some cheap imitation"(184). A foreigner in London, Slothrop is a tourist at the Casino; his distinction between the authentic item and the cheap imitation is pure touristry, but one that will haunt him. Before his first day at the Casino is over, he has cause to reverse the assumption of his perceptions. After rescuing Katje Borgesius from an octopus under less than real circumstances, he has the first clue to his quest: "So it is here, grouped on the beach with strangers, that voices begin to take on a touch of metal, each word a hard-edged clap, and the light, though as bright as before, is less able to illuminate . . . it's a

Puritan reflex of seeking other orders behind the visible, also known as paranoia, filtering in"(188). When his identification papers are stolen and Slothrop is left in a citizenless state, he begins to think that he is "alone with the paraphernalia of an order whose presence among the ordinary debris of waking he has only lately begun to suspect"(202). Even objects are susceptible to different perceptions, like Baedeker sights: ". . . everything in this room is really being used for something different. Meaning things to Them it has never meant to us. Never. Two orders of being, looking identical . . . but, but . . ." (202).

After Slothrop confirms that there are at least two orders of being and that his perceptions are being manipulated, he flees the Casino and heads for Nice, where he assumes the identity of Ian Scuffling, an English war correspondent. From Nice he travels to Zürich, thus officially beginning his tour and quest. On the way, Slothrop confronts the fact that the War has left only a landscape—images created for purposes he cannot yet recognize; familiar objects turned into dream:

> A week later he's in Zürich, after a long passage by train. While the metal creatures in their solitude, days of snug and stable fog, pass the hours at mime, at playing molecules, imitating industrial synthesis as they are broken up, put together, coupled and recoupled. . . .
> The War has been reconfiguring time and space into its own image. The track runs in different networks now. What appears to be destruction is really the shaping of railroad spaces to other purposes, intentions he can only, riding through it for the first time, begin to feel the leading edges of. . . . (257)

Slothrop's objective—information about the Schwarzgerät—is as pure and innocent as any religious quest might be for a Puritan in Zürich, but Slothrop is less a pilgrim than a tourist. He might as well be a victim of Cook's, or an imitation victim like Maxwell Rowley-Bugge of V., as a victim of a plot in the way he puts the Baedeker-Land touch on Francisco Squalidozzi for a free meal. Squalidozzi's anarchist perspective gives Slothrop the first clear view of the land he has entered: ". . . this War—this incredible War—just for the moment has wiped out the proliferation of little states that's prevailed in Germany for a thousand years. Wiped it clean. *Opened it*" (265). It is not Germany (Baedeker's native land) that Slothrop will tour, but a state of mind. It is the Zone. On the way to Geneva, he realizes that there is nowhere to go because everywhere is the same: "Richard Halliburton, Lowell Thomas, Rover and Motor Boys, jaundiced stacks of *National Geographics* up in Hogan's room must've all lied to him . . ."(266). There is only the trip itself as Geli Tripping reminds him. Frontiers and subdivisions have all been suspended. It is an " 'interregnum.' You only have to flow along with it"(294).

At the Mittelwerke, Slothrop finds that tourism has already become big business: "Civilians and bureaucrats show up every day, high-level tourists, to stare and go wow"(295). Cameras are available for rent; souvenirs of various rocket parts are hawked; and there are special tours for those who want excitement. By slipping on a special Disney-design Space Helmet—for a few marks extra—the tourist can see a second order of being:

> Strangely, these are not the symmetries we were programmed to expect, not the fins, the streamlined corners, pylons, or simple solid geometries of the official vision at all—*that's* for the ribbon clerks back on the Tour, in the numbered Stollen. No, this Rocket-City, so whitely lit against the calm dimness of space, is set up deliberately To Avoid Symmetry, Allow Complexity, Introduce Terror (from the Preamble to the Articles of Immachination)—but tourists have to connect the look of it back to things they remember from their times and planet. . . .
> (297)

Still tracking down information, Slothrop leaves Nordhausen and the Brocken for Berlin aboard a hot-air balloon. Berlin proves to be a city of revelation, both about the quest he is on and, more importantly, about what the war has done to the two orders of being. Berlin is not "the city Slothrop used to see back in those newsreels and that National Geographic"(372). Suffering the tourist's ailment of having drunk the local water—from an ornamental pond—Slothrop ponders his progress while recuperating: "The Schwarzgerät is no Grail, Ace, that's not what the G in Imipolex G stands for. And you are no knightly hero. . . . But what you've done is put yourself on somebody else's voyage . . . you know that in some irreducible way it's an evil game. You play because you have nothing better to do, but that doesn't make it right"(364). Slothrop also begins to realize that even places may not be what they seem. The war has broken down more than buildings and sights. It makes it possible for the Zone's own tourist to ponder the object that persists after its image is gone. The Berlin to which a Baedeker no longer has reference offers few illusions:

> If there is such a thing as the City Sacramental, the city as outward and visible sign of inward and spiritual illness or health, then there may have been, even here, some continuity of sacrament, through the terrible surface of May. The emptiness of Berlin this morning is an inverse mapping of the white and geometric capital before the destruction— the fallow and long-strewn fields of rubble, the same weight of too much featureless concrete . . . except that here everything's been turned inside out. The straight-ruled boulevards built to be marched along are now winding pathways through the waste-piles, their shapes organic now, responding, like goat trails, to laws of least discomfort. The civilians are outside now, the uniforms inside. Smooth facets of buildings have given way to cobbly insides of concrete blasted apart, all the endless-pebbled rococo just behind the shuttering. Inside is outside. (372–73)

As Slothrop travels the Zone, quest dissolves into tour: "Slothrop and the S-Gerät and the Jamf/Imipolex mystery have grown to be strangers"(434). The search continues but it is a form, a reason for movement. He becomes more interested in the forces at work on him than in any finite object. After his Rocket-Man adventure in Potsdam, he returns to Berlin and "feels the whole city around him going back roofless, vulnerable, uncentered as he is, and only pasteboard images now of the Listening Enemy left between him and the wet sky"(434). Slothrop can now understand what Squalidozzi meant about the War's having opened the Zone and wiped it clean.

After the facades of reality are destroyed, nothing but illusion can remain.

Slothrop leaves Berlin with Margherita Erdmann and joins the traveling party abroad the *Anubis* as it makes its way down the Oder toward the Baltic and Swinemünde—rumored to be the place where he will find his information. The *Anubis* carries an international crowd of the war's refugees, people with nowhere to go and no place to stay. One of the passengers is Ensign Mortituri, who in May 1945 can still think of returning home to Hiroshima. But he speaks for the world as well as the Zone when he describes the course of the *Anubis* for Slothrop: "We'll all just keep moving, that's all. In the end it doesn't matter"(479). Slothrop still hopes that his trail of clues will lead to something, anything, even though he has no real expectations; at least he will keep up appearances for awhile:

> . . . he knows as well as he has to that it's the S-Gerät after all that's following him, it and the pale plastic ubiquity of Laszlo Jamf. That if he's been seeker and sought, well, he's also baited, and bait. The Imipolex question was planted for him by somebody, back at the Casino Hermann Goering, with hopes it would flower into a full *Imipolectique* with its own potency in the Zone—but They knew Slothrop would jump for it. Looks like there are sub-Slothrop needs They know about, and he doesn't: this is humiliating on the face of it, but now there's also the even more annoying question, *What do I need that badly?* (490)

Slothrop leaves the *Anubis* unceremoniously, to be hauled out of the Oder by Frau Gnahb and her son Otto, whose fishing smack carries a cargo of black market goods for the shadow world, including the film version of *Lucky Pierre Runs Amok,* which Pig Bodine had accumulated, or so he said in *V.* Slothrop accompanies the Gnahbs, der Springer (von Göll), and Närrisch from Swinemünde to Peenemünde, taking him ever closer to his phantom objective as he becomes increasingly less certain of what his objective really is. Although Peenemünde is "a holy Center"(508) of the Rocket, "Slothrop, as noted, at least as early as the *Anubis* era, has begun to thin, to scatter"(509). Unlike Stencil, who refuses to approach the truth that Malta might hold for him, or Oedipa, who waits for the symmetry of illusion and reality to break down, Slothrop does not know what he is approaching and he begins to break down instead of the symmetries: "Here he is, scaling the walls of an honest ceremonial plexus, set down on a good enough vision of what's shadowless noon and what isn't. But oh, Egg the flying Rocket hatched from, navel of the 50-meter radio sky, all proper ghosts of place—forgive him his numbness, his glozing neutrality. Forgive the fist that doesn't tighten in his chest, the heart that can't stiffen in any greeting . . ."(509–10). Like the travel-numbed tourist who mistakes Mont-Saint-Michel for just another old church, Slothrop has lost his ability to respond. Previous information, even "*A Cheapskate's Guide to the Zone*"(559), could not have adequately prepared him for this spectacle.

After an adventure with der Springer in which they ram and board the *Anubis,* Slothrop leaves for Cuxhaven having obtained the Springer's promise of help in getting him a "discharge"—ostensibly from the army, but also from the tour. Slothrop knows that he is losing his own identity to the Zone. His trip to Cuxhaven shows him the full extent of Baedeker Land: "The Nationalities are on the move. It is a great frontierless streaming out here. Volksdeutsch from across the Oder, moved out by the Poles . . . Poles fleeing the Lublin regime . . . Czechs and Slovaks, Croats and Serbs, Tosks and Ghegs, Macedonians, Magyars, Vlachs, Circassians, Spaniols, Bulgars stirred and streaming over the surface of the Imperial cauldron, colliding, shearing alongside for miles, sliding away, numb, indifferent to all momenta but the deepest, the instability too far below their itchy feet to give a shape to . . ."(549). It is pure movement that Slothrop sees and feels as entire populations trade spaces while retaining their separate illusions of nationality, order, and history.

Appropriately, Slothrop meets a Zone orphan named Ludwig along the way and helps him search for Ursula, a lost pet lemming that has apparently headed for the sea—pure movement again. Slothrop has time to reflect on the opportunity such freedom of movement offers for creating a new landscape as he follows the lemming. Since all the sights and preconceptions have been destroyed, there is a chance for rebuilding without perpetuating the dichotomy between object and image: "... for a little while all the fences are down, one road as good as another, the whole space of the Zone cleared, depolarized, and somewhere inside the waste of it a single set of coordinates from which to proceed ..."(556), just as the present two orders of being proceeded from Descartes's coordinates.

An accidental meeting with Major Marvy and Bloody Chiclitz puts Slothrop back on his quest temporarily, but his tendency is still toward Cuxhaven and discharge: "Like signals set out for lost travelers, shapes keep repeating for him, Zonal shapes he will allow to enter but won't interpret, not any more"(567). Like Oedipa, Slothrop finally takes for granted the signs of another order of being. He participates in a local festival as a hero-figure, a pig, only to lose his street clothes. Wandering in his pig costume, he happens upon Franz Pökler, to whom he tells the whole story of his quest and from whom he learns more about Laszlo Jamf. Like Stencil, Oedipa, or any traveler, Slothrop has to tell someone about the sights he has seen, the adventure he has had.

In Cuxhaven, Slothrop discovers that his trip has been monitored all along; he has been observed as he observes the Zone. With the help of the ubiquitous Pig Bodine, pig Slothrop escapes his followers and, more importantly, comes to realize that:

> ... the Zone can sustain many other plots besides those polarized upon himself ... that these are the els and busses of an enormous transit system here in the Raketenstadt, more tangled even than Boston's— and that by riding each branch the proper distance, knowing when to transfer, keeping some state of minimum grace though it might often look like he's headed the wrong way, this network of all plots may yet carry him to freedom.(603)

After his escape, Slothrop is left alone. He will get no discharge papers but he will need none where he is going. In the mountains outside Cuxhaven he thinks of the America he will never see again:

" . . . he can't let her go. She's whispered *love me* too often to him in his sleep, vamped insatiably his waking attention with come-hitherings, incredible promises. One day—he can see a day—he might be able finally to say *sorry*, sure and leave her . . . but not just yet. One more try, one more chance, one more deal, one more transfer to a hopeful line"(623). Despite all he has seen, he still clings to the illusion of return. He can never get off the bus voluntarily until he is home. It is a futile dream, like Ensign Morituri's dream of returning to Hiroshima.

One night he comes across a graffito on a public restroom wall: "ROCKETMAN WAS HERE"(624). But Slothrop did not write it. The historical Slothrop has been replaced by his own legend. He has become the Zone's Kilroy and its metaphorical tourist. In fact, he fulfills the prophecy of *V.*, in which Pynchon suggests a shift toward the rocket:

> Kilroy by 1940 was already bald, middle-aged. His true origins forgotten, he was able to ingratiate himself with a human world, keeping schlemihl-silence about what he'd been as a curly-haired youth. It was a masterful disguise: a metaphor. For Kilroy had sprung into life, in truth, as part of a band-pass filter, thus:

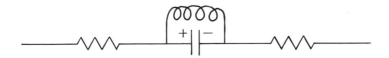

Unable to complete his search for information, unable to return to America, Slothrop fades into a metaphor. He scratches a new sign on the latrine wall:

"Only after he'd left it half a dozen more places did it dawn on him that *what he was really drawing was the A4 rocket,* seen from below" (624). Later in the day he makes the metaphor literal: "At last, lying one afternoon spread-eagled at his ease in the sun, at the edge of one of the ancient Plague towns he becomes a cross himself, a crossroads, a living intersection . . . "(625). His is also the shape of the Raketen-Stadt: " . . . the ceremonial City, fourfold as expected . . . built in mandalic form . . ."(725).

All that is left of Slothrop after this is a memory, frail and indistinct. There are glimpses of him still in the Zone, but no one can be certain who he is. Like Stencil and Oedipa, Slothrop does not complete his search. Instead of a Celestial City at the end of his progress, there is Rocket City, "a system of buildings that move, by right angles, along the grooves of the Raketen-Stadt's street-grid"(674). In this city, the land is landscape, the distinction between object and image blurred. It is a fantasy to be certain, but not that much different from the San Francisco Oedipa Maas discovers:

> Well, there is the heart of it: the monumental yellow structure, out there in the slum-suburban night, the never-sleeping percolation of life and enterprise through its shell, Outside and Inside interpiercing one another too fast, too finely labyrinthine, for either category to have much hegemony any more. The nonstop revue crosses its stage, crowding and thinning, surprising and jerking tears in an endless ratchet. . . . (681)

The film may slide across the spoked wheel in only one direction, but it goes on endlessly. While Oedipa can only wait for the symmetries to break down, Slothrop and his perceptions are united in the objective fantasy of a film world, the world where life can be recognized as real precisely because it is so representative. Just as Baedeker created Europe for prewar tourists by helping them perceive its form, film—as *Triumph of the Will* proved—helps break down the symmetries by presenting fantasy that appears to be objectively real. Film is the new Grand Tour; you do not even leave your seat if you are at the movies: " . . . there are also *spectators*, watching, as spectators will do, hundreds of thousands of them, sitting around this dingy yellow amphitheatre, seat after seat plunging down in rows and tiers endless miles, down to the great arena . . ."(679). In a sense, *Gravity's Rainbow* is a movie, or rather the imitation of a movie.

The remainder of Slothrop's trip is fragmentary: he tries to communicate with Squalidozzi on a half-wave antenna and listens "for news of unauthorized crucifixions"(681) such as his own; discusses American idioms with Säure; fantasizes an incident in the tranvestite toilet; reads that the atomic bomb has been dropped on Hiroshima; listens to a toilet that reminds him, alias the Kenosha Kid (Orson Welles's home town), that he is "trapped inside Their frame with your wastes piling up, ass hanging out all over Their Movieola viewer, waiting for Their editorial blade"(694); and has a man-to-man talk with his father about their respective modes of travel. His father calls his own dope trips "*vacations* . . . Cause you always do come back to old Realityland, don't you." But Slothrop imagines a trip "in a clean, honest, purified Electroworld"(699) that will never end. The last word on Slothrop as a person in *Gravity's Rainbow* comes when Bodine gives him a shirt that was soaked in John Dillinger's blood after the ambush outside the Biograph Theatre. It is a symbol for movieland—a reality that takes its cues from the screen—and an amulet for Slothrop's own last trip. When he was ambushed, Dillinger still had the vision of an unregenerate Clark Gable before him, the sense of actually being Blackie. As he was shot, Dillinger "found a few seconds' strange mercy in the movie images that hadn't quite yet faded from his eyeballs"(516). Movies can be invoked as proof against a less certain reality, a kind of grace for the moment when there is only a movie and no other reality to come back to.

Slothrop is gone. Only his fragments remain, memories that "have grown into consistent personae of their own"(742). There is rumor of Slothrop's joining an English rock group or returning home for the occupation of Mingeborough, but these no longer matter. Even the

Counterforce organized to search for Slothrop loses interest in him, ceases to search. The tour goes on with or without Slothrop, now one of the easily missed sights along the way, visible only on restroom walls: "Slothrop's Visitor by this time may be scrawled lines of carbon on a wall, voices down a chimney, some human being out on t^ie road, 'the object of life is to make sure you die a weird death' " (742). In Slothrop's case, there can be no doubt that his death, if that is what happened to him, is weird.

Slothrop's tour takes in most of Europe. As it progresses, he becomes increasingly general and diverse, while the places he visits tend to reflect an inner landscape. Early in his search, Slothrop offers the promise of becoming a representational character, a postwar Everyman, but this promise fades with his disintegration. If there is anything familiar about his tour, the convention lies only in his progress toward death, a pattern established by Adam. Pynchon offers still another variation on Stencil's search for his "own extermination" and Oedipa's "daily, tedious preparation for death." The specific interactions of Slothrop with his environment show only the more or less idiosyncratic experiences of any tourist in a technological landscape, but the trip itself has not changed. He is no redeemer.

His Tarot has "the cards of a tanker and feeb: they point only to a long and scuffling future, to mediocrity . . . to no clear happiness or redeeming cataclysm. All his hopeful cards are reversed, most unhappily of all the Hanged Man . . ."(738). It is the right card for a redeemer, but the wrong position. Slothrop imitates the Hanged Man when he lies down in the crossroads to become the living intersection " . . . where the judges have come to set up a gibbet for a common criminal who is to be hanged at noon"(625). Even a delegate from the Committee on Idiopathic Archetypes comes to investigate the incident.

Slothrop's fortune is told in the Celtic style—a cross. The Hanged Man is suspended from a gallows made of living wood; his legs are bent to form a cross. The cross in any Tarot generally means a union of positive and negative, vertical and horizontal, or the union of God with the earth. Slothrop in the intersection, the Hanged Man reversed, suggests preoccupation with the self, a false prophecy. He is no new Adam, but another repetition of the old one, the traveler. On the same day he becomes an intersection, Slothrop sees a rainbow, "a stout rainbow cock driven down out of pubic clouds into Earth, green wet valleyed Earth . . . "(626)—the Tarot's union of God and earth. The witch Geli Tripping provides a useful gloss on the union after she sees a surveyor in the Zone—"and she *feels the cross* the man has made on his own circle of visible earth . . . unconsciously a mandala . . ."(719). The cross is also the union of life and death, the world alive before man and the world dying after man. She waits for a sign from the goat-god Pan, he who haunts the nighttime traveler with panic fear: "Suddenly, Pan—leaping—its face too beautiful to bear, beautiful Serpent, its coils in rainbow lashings in the sky—into the sure bones of fright—"(720–21). Pan is like the presence "we are not supposed to be seeing"(720) beneath the surface. Slothrop's own mandala is a cross, the rocket seen from below. The rocket's parabolic path of flight describes a rainbow as well, another presence we are not supposed to be seeing, another union.

When Slothrop reads about the atom bomb that was dropped on Hiroshima, he sees a photograph "of a giant white cock, dangling in the sky straight downward out of a white pubic bush"(693). It is the rainbow of death, colorless. But there is more: "The white image has the same coherence, the hey-lookit-me smugness, as the Cross does. It is not only a sudden white genital onset in the sky—it is also, perhaps, a Tree . . ."(694). From his station of the cross at the roads' intersection, Slothrop sees a rainbow that is almost identical to that of the bomb, itself a Tree—the living wood of the cross. In a way, the atomic bomb and its symbolic potential for remote and mechanical death on a scale unimagined before 1945 is the ultimate reference for *Gravity's Rainbow*. The bomb is so definitive and absolute that it makes horror obsolete. The earlier destruction of the war—the bombing of Lübeck, the rocket attacks on London, or even the mass deaths of Auschwitz, Dachau, and Buchenwald—held a personal horror, a reality, for their witnesses, which was lost to the bomb's remoteness, its abstractness. The event of August irreversibly altered man's imagination and the Bomb, without even being named, dominates the postwar landscape. Consequently, Pynchon's inclusion of this detail of the Bomb and its Tree imagery has significance beyond Slothrop. It represents nothing less than man's final domination of the land and its permanent displacement by landscape. Pynchon's recognition of a Tree in the Bomb's unfolding shape is acknowledgement of a new Tree of Knowledge—a union of good and evil, man's mastery of energy for destruction and salvation. In leaving a simpler world behind after tasting the fruits of this new tree, man's journey into landscape carries with it an intensified consciousness of death.

All the images converge: the rainbow, the cross, the union of life and death, earth and sky, horizontal and vertical, and the serpent's coils. The iconography is complex and loosely associated, but all the symbols refer back to Adam's leaving the Garden on his endless journey. A tree marks the beginning and the end of that journey. Adam left Eden after tasting of the Tree of Knowledge; he and his descendants wander the world still searching out the Tree of Life. Slothrop had his origins in a Puritan past, an American Eden with trees that had to be cleared and transformed into a medium, which the Slothrops did. During his travels through the Zone, Slothrop becomes "intensely alert to trees, finally. When he comes in among trees he will spend time touching them, studying them, sitting very quietly near them and understanding that each tree is a creature, carrying on its individual life, aware of what's happening around it, not just some hunk of wood to be cut down"(552–53). In the Tarot, the two trees hold all its secret knowledge, the equilibrium between life and death. The Tree of Knowledge represents the polarity between two worlds, good and evil, paradise and earth; it offers knowledge of two orders of being. The Tree of Life represents balance and harmony; it is immortality to be sought—a union. Life is the journey between two trees—a quest, but for some only a tour.

THE LAND AND THE LANDSCAPE

The tour is a form of ritualized observation. Pynchon borrows a metaphor from physics that helps explain the tourist's double vision. On several occasions in *Gravity's Rainbow* he refers to the "Heisenberg situation. . . . It appears we can't have one property without the other, any more than a particle physicist can specify position without suffering an uncertainty as to the particle's velocity—"(348). The same principle is expressed by Dennis Flange in "Low-lands," when he says that the act of observing changes the data being observed. Each of Pynchon's protagonists shows some variation of the principle in operation. In fact, Pynchon takes quantum mechanics as a model for representing the world in his fiction. The "laws" of quantum mechanics are probabilistic rather than causal or deterministic, and they are based on the view that there are two simultaneous orders of being in micronature: particles and waves. In this theory, the bipartite unity of waves and particles limits what we can know about microphenomena to partial definitions. There is a symmetry between the particle and wave approaches to definition, both of which are equally valid. This dualism suggests a useful way of discussing reality, since it may be considered as either land or landscape, but either approach is independently incomplete. Even though a microparticle does in fact exist, it cannot be defined precisely because it simultaneously has properties of both particles and waves. Since criteria for finite measurement do not exist, uncertainty relations are all that can be known and they are expressions of the interdependence of continuities and discontinuities. The most that we can know about a microparticle, or reality, is a portion of the possible relationships among its characteristics such as time and energy or position and momentum. If we try to specify a particle's energy, for example, we can do so by decreasing the number of component waves having different energies. This process, however, allows the particle to disperse and spread throughout its configuration space. Certainty about one characteristic results in uncertainty about another and, therefore, about the actual particle.

Although an analysis of Pynchon's fiction, particularly *Gravity's Rainbow,* in terms of quantum mechanics might reward the effort, even this partial suggestion of a metaphorical structure indicates the extremely complex relationship between illusion and reality. They represent a unity, but neither is more fundamental than the other. The parallels go beyond the coexistence of two orders of being, however. As Stencil, Oedipa, and Slothrop demonstrate, the more certain they become about illusion, the less certain they are about reality. Slothrop even begins to disperse and spread throughout the Zone as his psychoanalytical observers learn more about the sexual energy he appears to derive from the Rocket. There is no doubt that Pynchon consciously uses the Heisenberg uncertainty principle as a metaphor in all his major works; whether he does so with an accuracy that would please a physicist is another matter. However clever the correspondences might be, they are secondary to experiencing the two orders of being. On this level, the Heisenberg principle has to do with defining one's own existence in terms of familiarity and strangeness—certainty and uncertainty—and the particular problem of observing one's own relationship with a dual reality.[3]

Although Pynchon does not refer explicitly to Georg Simmel, whose stranger theory is mentioned obliquely in *Gravity's Rainbow,* this German contemporary and friend of Weber, Husserl, and Rilke formulated a "culture-philosophy" that offers another perspective of the dualities that preoccupy Pynchon. According to Simmel, life is a process and constant flux, it can only be experienced. However, life produces objects, institutions, theories, and beliefs that have form and can be known. Once created, these forms exist as independent entities, can be experienced, and even shape experience for others. Reality is one such form, but it is only a form and has no higher claim than any other. In identifying the separation of form from life and noting its independent existence, Simmel suggests a way of perceiving land and landscape as forms that have the same content but allow different ways of experiencing it. The distinction being made may be a fine one, but it is another confirmation of the validity of Pynchon's equilibrium duality. Through the process of the tour, Pynchon shows not only that land and landscape coexist, but also that they are symmetrical approaches to the same experiences. One form may dominate the other, but it is no more or less arbitrary. Oedipa, Slothrop, and to a lesser degree Stencil discover that knowledge about their world is relative. What we normally mean by reality is so familiar that its forms have coincided with perception. As Simmel notes in his writings on landscape, it is only after we change our surroundings that a different feeling calls attention to the "causative" role of landscape in general. Unless we change scenery—travel, watch a movie, take drugs—we seldom recognize its influence on us.

The tour works well for Pynchon because its own form has evolved from travel as movement to travel as a mode of existence. At one time travel demanded a direct encounter with the land; there were no intermediaries, few expectations about what would be seen, no deliberate fabrications. When travelers such as Herodotus and Marco Polo began to give accounts of their movements, they had a profound impact on Western civilization in the images—landscapes—they created of strange places. During the eighteenth century travel began to evolve rapidly into tourism; by mid-century the Grand Tour had become an institution and as many as forty thousand English at a time were seeing the sights of Europe. It was a period when Johnson could say that "the use of traveling is to regulate imagination by reality" and when illustrators such as Thomas Rowlandson could satirize the Grand Tour knowingly. After World War Two the earth had become one continuous tourist attraction and travel a form of mass transit. No part of the globe was inaccessible to Cook's and its lesser counterparts, though some places held less interest than others. The development of tourism into a pastime for almost everyone depended on inexpensive transportation, the building of roads, and accessibility. The possibility of mass tourism, with its accompanying investment in railroads, automobiles, airplanes, and motel chains, demanded that tourists be attracted. If the land could not produce sufficient consumption, then landscape could; Johnson's dictum had been reversed. In 1955 (the year Benny Profane meets Brenda Wigglesworth on Malta) approximately one million Americans were abroad—most of them in Europe. Tourism had become a multibillion dollar international business with whole economies depending on the influx of tourist dollars. But these factors remain secondary to the essence of tourism: perception of forms, or "sight seeing," a term first used as late as 1847. Travel had been irreversibly changed by the two expectations of familiarity and strangeness.

The world Pynchon creates in his novels derives its validity from this paradoxical harmony of familiarity and strangeness, and its authenticity from the accumulation of details. His self-conscious identification of Baedeker Land implies a correspondence beyond the evidence of the novels. Pynchon deliberately builds his fictional world from the facts and artifacts of his readers' experience. In part, he fulfills the tour guide's responsibility for familiarity, but he also demonstrates the confluence of illusion and reality in form. The importance of facts to his fiction will be discussed subsequently, but the importance of form as a conceptual condition of both art and life requires attention now. Among countless examples perhaps the most obvious is the role Fritz Lang's 1929 movie *Die Frau im Mond* played in creating the A4 and the Rocket's form. Although "science fiction," it captured the imagination of a generation of young engineers, including von Braun, and was instrumental in the formulation of rocket clubs—like the Society for Space Navigation—throughout Germany in the prewar years. Lang's fanciful rocket not only looked like the A4, but in the crucial series of test firings before the V-2 became operational the first completely successful rocket had a picture of the woman on the moon painted on its side. Although Lang's rocket was based on a well-articulated theory, his illusion became reality. The famous Baedeker Raids on England are another example. After the British bombed the militarily unimportant city of Lübeck, the Germans ordered destroyed every sight in England that Baedeker had marked with an asterisk. Pynchon takes note of "the fire-raising at Lübeck and Hitler's order for 'terror attacks of a retaliatory nature' —meaning the V-weapons—"(151) in *Gravity's Rainbow* and uses it to suggest the way in which illusion and image can create their own reality:

> This is the kind of sunset you hardly see any more, a 19th-century wilderness sunset, a few of which got set down, approximated, on canvas, landscapes of the American West by artists nobody ever heard of, when the land was still free and the eye innocent, and the presence of the Creator much more direct. Here it thunders now over the Mediterranean, high and lonely, this anachronism in primal red, in yellow purer than can be found anywhere today, a purity begging to be polluted . . . of course Empire took its way westward, what other way was there but into those virgin sunsets to penetrate and to foul?
>
> But out at the horizon, out near the burnished edge of the world, who are these visitors standing . . . these robed figures—perhaps, at this distance, hundreds of miles tall—their faces, serene, unattached, like the Buddha's, bending over the sea, impassive, indeed, as the Angel that stood over Lübeck during the Palm Sunday raid, come that day neither to destroy nor to protect, but to bear witness to a game of seduction. It was the next-to-last step London took before her submission, before that liaison that would bring her at length to the eruption and scarring of the wasting pox noted on Roger Mexico's map, latent in this love she shares with the night-going rake Lord Death . . . because sending the RAF to make a terror raid against civilian Lübeck was the unmistakable long look that said *hurry up and fuck me,* that brought the rockets hard and screaming, the A4s, which were to've been fired anyway, a bit sooner instead. . . . (214–15)

It was not London or Baedeker sights that invited destruction, but their image. The creation of landscape is always a game of seduction and an image is nothing if it is not a self-fulfilling prophecy.

Pynchon's sole departure from fiction, or rather his only venture into journalism, occurred less than three months after the publication of his second novel. In many respects the article entitled "A Journey Into The Mind of Watts" is a continuation of his study of the land and landscape of Southern California in *The Crying of Lot 49*. Although Pynchon reveals no fundamental change in perspective, his use of the journalistic medium—*The New York Times Magazine*—with its particular audience expectations and its existence in a real world implies a great deal about the importance of form and perception in life as well as art. Watts rates no asterisks, but it exists as an image and it does invite raids; even at the last edge of America's western horizon, its sunset has long been polluted and penetrated. Significantly, the article is a "journey" into the "mind" or landscape of the place. Although it would be specious to attach great significance to Pynchon's choice of the term "journey" over "tour," his selection is conscious and consistent. "Journey" still connotes hardship, unformed perceptions of land, and it approximates the transformation of Stencil's, Oedipa's, and Slothrop's tours into their confrontations with two orders of being. Pynchon's journey into the mind clearly signals an effort to penetrate the surface and to deal with both orders. In short, this not quite expository piece is Pynchon's most direct and unmitigated treatment of land and landscape, if for no other reason than the freedom his departure from a narrative voice gives him to confront the reader directly.

The occasion for the article is the death of Leonard Deadwyler at the hand of a Los Angeles policeman, but the situation is a matter of perception: was he murdered or killed accidentally? The incident becomes the vehicle for exploring Watts and its image. The coroner's inquest found the policeman innocent of responsibility; the people of Watts found him guilty. The two opposite perceptions of the same incident and the same facts correspond precisely with the perceptions of two different places, both called "Watts." One is the land; it is strange and unfamiliar to the white police. The other is landscape; it is familiar and known territory to the same police. However, the residents of Watts can perceive the police only as tourists from an alien white Los Angeles, strangers whose continued presence must be accommodated and whose expectations must be satisfied. The result is the policeman's self-fulfilling perception of the image of the place: ". . . how very often the cop does approach you with his revolver ready, so that nothing he does with it can then really be accidental; of how, especially at night, everything can suddenly reduce to a matter of reflexes: your life trembling in the crook of a cop's finger because it is dark, and Watts, and the history of this place and these times makes it impossible for the cop to come on any different, or for you to hate him any less. Both of you are caught in something neither of you wants, and yet night after night, with casualties or without, these traditional scenes continue to be played out ..."(35). The something in which they are caught "is the co-existence of two very different cultures: one white and one black"(35). Pynchon takes the distinction beyond color: "While the white culture is concerned with various forms of systematized folly ... the black culture is stuck pretty much with basic realities ..."(35, 78). As far as Watts is concerned, the natives have only the land with few illusions about any separate existence it may have, and the tourists have only an image, never having gotten close enough to see anything else:

> The two cultures do not understand each other, though white values are displayed without let-up on black people's TV screens, and though the panoramic sense of black impoverishment is hard to miss from atop the Harbor Freeway, which so many whites must drive at least twice every working day. Somehow it occurs to very few of them to leave at the Imperial Highway exit for a change, go east instead of west only a few blocks, and take a look at Watts. A quick look. The simplest kind of beginning. But Watts is country which lies, psychologically, un-counted miles further than most whites seem at present willing to travel. (78)

If you ask any nonresident about Watts, two images come to mind: the riot and the Watts Towers. The first represents the strangeness of Watts: the land that is to be avoided, contained, and enclosed, by force if necessary. To outsiders, the Towers are a paradox, a familiar form with an alien manifestation; to residents, the Towers simply are. After the riots they were considered a target for demolition and renewal. The Towers represented the illusion of a place that could be accommodated: the landscape that could be remade—improved by social workers, agencies, triplicate forms, bureaucracies, "poverty warriors" who believed in a "form of semimiracle"(82) that was really only an imposition of the white culture onto the black. Pynchon has traveled in Watts and ironically reports that "everything seems so out in the open, all of it real, no plastic faces, no transistors, no hidden Muzak, or Disneyfied landscaping, or smiling little chicks to show you around. Not in Raceriotland"(78). Watts is a land of poverty. However, Raceriotland is a white image with little correspondence to people who live, love, and feel. The Watts Towers are important to the whites because they are a form, a touch of Disneyland; but to the people who live in Watts they are a symbol of what is not, of the waste and debris of their own land from which nothing really new can ever be made:

> It's part of their landscape, both the real and the emotional one: busted glass, busted crockery, nails, tin cans, all kinds of scrap and waste. Traditionally Watts. An Italian immigrant named Simon Rodia spent 30 years gathering some of it up and converting a little piece of the neighborhood along 107th Street into the famous Watts Towers, perhaps his own dream of how things should have been: a fantasy of fountains, boats, tall openwork spires, encrusted with a dazzling mosaic of Watts debris. Next to the Towers, along the old Pacific Electric tracks, kids are busy every day busting more bottles on the steel rails. But Simon Rodia is dead, and now the junk just accumulates. (78)

The reality of Watts exists in bitter contrast to Los Angeles, which, "more than any other city, belongs to the mass media. . . . It is basically a white Scene, and illusion is everywhere in it . . ."(78). Pynchon, a traveler beneath the surface, sees the land of Watts as a reality that exposes the landscape of the city that surrounds it: "Watts lies impacted in the heart of this white fantasy. It is, by contrast, a pocket of bitter reality. The only illusion Watts ever allowed itself was to believe for a long time in the white version of what a Negro was supposed to be. But with the Muslim and civil-rights movements that went too"(78). The white illusions are still projected into Watts without interruption by television, radio, and movies and imposed on it from a distance by the freeway tourists, but within Watts itself illusion is recognized for what it is. One black artist who intuitively understands that there is no reality without form by which it can be perceived, offers a fitting conclusion to Pynchon's journey: "There was this old, busted TV set; inside, where its picture tube should have been, was a human skull. The name of the piece was 'The Late, Late, Late Show' "(84).

Pynchon's journalism will not win him awards, but the article on Watts contributes to our understanding of his fiction. Without the complications of plot and characterization, he can show directly the coexistence of two orders of being. Although we must retain some skepticism as to how far a product of white illusions can travel into the mind of Watts, we can grant Pynchon credibility in the context of his fictional world. In trying to expose the difference between land and landscape from the perspective of the native, he clearly shows how one order intrudes on the other, how familiarity and strangeness are aspects of the same place. Natives can never be free of the tourist's synthetic reality and the realities of land are always present beneath the surface of landscape.

Pynchon's article on Watts also helps clarify the recurring theme of colonialism in his fiction. Although this particular aspect of his novels will be discussed in a subsequent chapter, it must also be considered here because colonialism consists of the forcible displacement of land by landscape, the conscious imposition of a synthetic reality onto an already existing reality. The Argentine anarchist Squalidozzi of *Gravity's Rainbow* offers the most succinct statement of this aspect of colonialism in words he wants to say, but cannot, to Slothrop:

> *We of all magical precipitates out of Europe's groaning, clouded alembic, we are the thinnest, the most dangerous, the handiest to secular uses. . . . We tried to exterminate our Indians, like you: we wanted the closed white version of reality we got—but even into the smokiest labyrinths, the furthest stacked density of midday balcony or courtyard and gate, the land has never let us forget. . . . (264)*

In its more blatant forms, colonialism is the most insidious aspect of Baedeker Land. However, it also occurs under the humanitarian guise of the social worker's attempt to remake the blacks of Watts into white imitations. More typically, it occurs in the form of a Baedeker guidebook designed to insulate the tourist from any real contact with the land or natives. The colonialist aspects of tourism are most evident in Pynchon's account of Cairo and Alexandria, in which various natives reveal their recognition of the illusions imposed on them. The café waiter Aïeul knows that he and his city exist as "picturesque but faceless Arabs; monuments, tombs, modern hotels. A false and bastard city; inert—for 'them'—as Aïeul himself"(52–53). Even the place itself can be changed by tourism: "The bierhalle north of the Ezbekiyeh Garden had been created by north European tourists in their own image. One memory of home among the dark-skinned and tropical. But so German as to be ultimately a parody of home"(76).

Pynchon provides ample enough evidence of colonialism's displacement of native reality to convince anyone of its perversity. In addition to incidents already mentioned, there are in *V.* the explorer Godolphin's invasion of Vheissu, the Gaucho's anarchist dream, the Bondel uprising, and the interesting detail of the anonymous soldier's personal colonialism in Africa; in *The Crying of Lot 49* there is Inverarity's corporate colonialism; in *Gravity's Rainbow* there are Frans Van der Groov's extermination of native dodoes, the Russians' campaign to give the natives of Central Asia a new alphabet and way of life, the Argentine anarchists' effort to create a new order based on von Göll's film, the displacements of the war that Slothrop repeatedly observes, the all-encompassing corporate imperialism of a meta-cartel, the rocket's own special hegemony, and Blicero's personal colonialism over Katje, Gottfried, and Enzian. There are numerous other examples, any one of which can represent the basic dislocation that colonialism brings with it regardless of the territory or the scale of the conquest. Although its horrors are most graphic in *V.*'s account of the Bondel uprising, colonialism's dependence on the duality of strangeness and familiarity in order to create a landscape is

most carefully drawn in the episode of *Gravity's Rainbow* that has
Tchitcherine in Kirghiz to impose the New Turkic Alphabet on the
natives: "He had come to give the tribesmen out here, this far out,
an alphabet: it was purely speech, gesture, touch among them, not
even an Arabic script to replace"(338).

Pynchon's account is based on the historical Latin alphabet revolution, the Turkological Congress held in Baku in 1926, and the Cyrillic
alphabet revolution of 1938. The Russians intended to undermine
Islam and to isolate the peoples of Central Asia from the Moslems
to the south by replacing Arabic with Latin and, later, the Cyrillic
alphabets. The intent of the Russians was to create an entirely new
reality, first by disrupting the entire economy and social structure of
the region, including the immigration of Russian settlers, and second
by imposing an alphabet that would require the natives to adopt a
new perceptual mode isolating them from their historical, ethnic, and
religious ties. Under the guise of drawing the peripheral nationalities
closer to the Russian center and a unified nation— "How could there
be Kazakh, Kirghiz—Eastern—reasons? Hadn't the nationalities been
happy? Hadn't fifty years of Russian rule brought progress? enrich-
ment?" (340)—Moscow forced a radical dislocation of the familiar by
the alien. There had been revolts and uprisings against the efforts of
1916 to change the land of Central Asia by replacing the natives.
Russian settlers panicked and began killing Sarts, Kazakhs, Kirghiz,
and Dungans like animals. Though they were not as efficient as von
Trotha had been in the Südwest, they persisted. The more subtle
though no less radical approach of changing the form—the alphabet
—and leaving the content ostensibly intact promised to be far more
effective. One of the natives, Džaqyp Qulan, was given a place in the
new power structure, but he—like all the other Nationals—remained
a native: "They throw amiable cigarettes, construct him paper existences, use him as an Educated Native Speaker. He's allowed his
function and that's as far as it goes . . ."(340).

Drawing upon the attendant facts of the alphabet revolutions,
Pynchon simultaneously shows how artifice replaces reality and ex-

poses the absurdity of the process for what it is. On one hand, the displacement works:

> Native printers get crash courses from experts airlifted in from Tiflis on how to set up that NTA. Printed posters go up in the cities, in Samarkand and Pishpek, Verney and Tashkent. On sidewalks and walls the very first printed slogans start to show up, the first Central Asian fuck you signs, the first kill-the-police-commissioner signs (and somebody does! this alphabet is really something!) and so the magic that the shamans, out in the wind, have always known, begins to operate now in a political way, and Džaqyp Qulan hears the ghost of his own lynched father with a scratchy pen in the night, practicing As and Bs.... (355–56)

At the same time, the bureaucracy of committees, congresses, and plenary sessions, which is the substance of the process, evokes some of Pynchon's most biting satire: committees steal letters from each other, play practical jokes, and even develop a "crisis over which kind of g to use in the word 'stenography' "(353)—all of which takes place against the reality that the establishment of the NTA is "an invitation to holy war"(354). Whole populations could be sacrificed to the image of a unified republic. When Tchitcherine witnesses a native singing duel, he "understands, abruptly, that soon someone will come out and begin to write some of these down in the New Turkic Alphabet he helped frame ... and this is how they will be lost" (357). The form will gradually give its shape to experience and the land will have been lost to landscape.

Whether it assumes the guise of tourism as reflected by the native narrators of Cairo and Alexandria, forceful domination such as that of the Südwest, or imposition of aesthetic forms such as the New Turkic Alphabet, colonialism is only one of Pynchon's several metaphors for the uncertainty relations of reality and illusion. Others work equally well and, at the same time, show both the diversity and completeness of infinite landscapes. Nor do these metaphors serve Pynchon exclusively in one domain. All the various landscapes give evidence of the world's closed system—its decadence and decay—at the same time suggesting that nature can be changed, like new molecules assembled from the debris of the given. It is not finally an optimistic view, but landscape does offer the illusion of hope. The dream, fantasy, or reverie is the most universal and accessible landscape imaginable. Available to all people at all times with or without artificial stimuli, it can be strange or familiar as necessary; it can be either an escape from reality or a preview of it. Dream is so much a part of Pynchon's fiction that it is usually unnoticeable. Of the dreams and fantasies that seek out strangeness and escape, those that simultaneously seek a confirmation of something real (and frequently painful) in illusion have a recognizable and recurring form. Although the pattern is established as early as "Low-lands," the siege party at Foppl's villa in *V.* offers a characteristic example as the assembled group collectively seeks its lost past in a recreation of the uprising of 1904. Kurt Mondaugen, "because of his peculiar habits of observation," is possibly the only one to escape the "common dream"(237) prescribed by Foppl. Though not entirely immune, Mondaugen provides commentary on the fantasy being nurtured around him. The party-goers recreate the dress and mannerisms of 1904, but they seek confirmation of the dream in killing the Bondel servants and torturing each other in every imaginable form of perversion. During a lapse of consciousness brought on by poor diet, Mondaugen has a surrealistic dream about colonialism. While the others enact dreams, he only dreams. His is a reflection of what he sees: "But his own musical commentary on dreams had not included the obvious and perhaps for him indispensable: that if dreams are only waking sensation first stored and later operated on, then the dreams of a voyeur can never be his own"(236). Mondaugen's voyeuristic dream is everything that the others desire. He awakens to find that his dream is being lived: "the discovery that his voyeurism had been determined purely by events seen, and not by any deliberate choice, or preëxisting set of personal psychic needs"(258). Shortly after this realization, he leaves Foppl's villa and its mass fantasy.

Mondaugen identifies the form of the dream that Pynchon gives full play in *Gravity's Rainbow.* The entire background of the novel is essentially the aftermath of Hitler's dream. It is reflected everywhere, but finds its most definite shape in Katje Borgesius, who, like Mondaugen, recognizes the form of the dream for what it is but still participates, " . . . plays at playing"(97). The dream that she, Gottfried, and Blicero enact is real in its pain though it is intended to protect them from reality; it is bizarre and yet familiar, as the narrator explains:

> How seriously is she playing? In a conquered country, one's own occupied country, it's better, she believes, to enter into some formal, rationalized version of what, outside, proceeds without form or decent limit day and night, the summary executions, the roustings, beatings, subterfuge, paranoia, shame . . . though it is never discussed among them openly, it would seem Katje, Gottfried, and Captain Blicero have agreed that this Northern and ancient form, one they all know and are comfortable with—the strayed children, the wood-wife in the edible house, the captivity, the fattening, the Oven—shall be their preserving routine, their shelter, against what outside none of them can bear—the War, the absolute rule of chance, their own pitiable contingency here, in its midst. . . . (96)

Katje performs a similar function under Edward Pointman's direction for General Pudding. The landscape of dream offers him something real, an escape from his memory of the dreamlike reality of his blunder during the First World War, which killed seventy percent of his troops. Although the sadomasochistic play is staged for him, Pudding complicitly enacts his own fantasy as protection against the dream he knows to be real:

> . . . no it's not guilt here, not so much as amazement—that he could have listened to so many years of ministers, scientists, doctors each with his specialized lies to tell, when she was here all the time, sure in her ownership of his failing body, his true body: undisguised by uniform, uncluttered by drugs to keep from him her communiqués of vertigo, nausea and pain. . . . Above all, pain. The clearest poetry, the endearment of greatest worth. . . . (234–35)

These and related incidents are evidence of the social equivalent of the Heisenberg uncertainty principle at work: the more we zero in on dream and fantasy, the less we know about reality, or what passes for reality. Dreams also function in the opposite direction, which is still another way of saying that reality and illusion are merely reciprocal functions. Other characters attempt to make their dreams more real and, usually, less painful. Perhaps the most obvious case is that of Esther Harvitz, who wishes to remake her Jewish nose: "Identical with an ideal of nasal beauty established by movies, advertisements, magazine illustrations. Cultural harmony, Schoenmaker called it" (91). Schoenmaker is, of course, the instrument of making dreams reality, a counterpart to Katje. Pynchon's account of the nose operation is bone-tinglingly realistic, one of the most effective passages in all his novels. Schoenmaker is a dream-maker but he has no illusions himself: "Trafficking in human vanity . . . propagating the fallacy that beauty is not in the soul, that it can be bought. Yes . . . it can be bought . . . I am selling it. I don't even look on myself as a necessary evil"(36-37). The narrator, however, makes clear that Schoenmaker's transformation of dream into reality parallels colonialism: "It was in short a deterioration of purpose; a decay"(89). Schoenmaker's mission of restoring reality had been transformed, subtly, into the creation of landscapes, the minimization of pain. There are others of this sort in *V.*: the Whole Sick Crew, whose ". . . pattern would have been familiar—bohemian, creative, arty—except that it was even further removed from reality . . ."(45-46) or Mélanie, who dreams of herself as a wind-up doll, ". . . not real but an object of pleasure"(379), as V. describes her. They are the human equivalents of Baedeker sights and Disneylands.

In *The Crying of Lot 49*, the reality-making, pain-reducing dream exists as the stage for Oedipa Maas's discovery of duality. The legacy of Inverarity's last will and testament is America, but not the America she thought it was. It is a fabricated fantasy land that has passed into reality without her, or anybody else's, noticing it or possibly even caring. The empire Inverarity built was the tangible product of his "need to possess, to alter the land, to bring new skylines, personal antagonisms, growth rates into being"(134). Consisting of investments in everything from real estate and defense contracts to Turkish baths and bone charcoal filtering processes, the patchwork estate has a meaning that is greater than any one of its many parts, but one that depended on Inverarity's private dream of how the world should be. When Oedipa first sees San Narciso, she recognizes it as "the place he'd begun his land speculating in ten years ago, and so put down the plinth course of capital on which everything afterward had been built, however rickety or grotesque, toward the sky"(12–13). He remade the land to fit his narcissistic dream. By the end of the novel Oedipa knows that San Narciso is "an incident among our climatic records of dreams and what dreams became among our accumulated daylight . . ."(133). San Narciso is finally indistinguishable from all the other tract towns of Southern California because America itself is indistinguishable from Disneyland. The only distinctions are among dreams. Fangoso Lagoons with its artificial entertainments for Scuba enthusiasts, the collection of imitation stamps that seemed to be "little colored windows into deep vistas of space and time"(28), Yoyodyne, the uncertain text of *The Courier's Tragedy*, Zapf's Used Books, Echo Courts, and all the other visible manifestations of Inverarity's "attempt to leave an organized something behind after his own annihilation"(58) turn out to be illusions masquerading as reality.

In addition to Inverarity's legacy, Pynchon includes other examples of reality remade by dream in three underground existences. The most important of these is of course the Tristero, which ostensibly exists in a shadow world but which, Oedipa discovers beneath the surface of California, is more a reality than an illusion. It is at least a parallel to the visible system and is proof that "there had to exist the separate, silent, unsuspected world"(92). As Oedipa presses at what she has always assumed to be real, she finds that it is facade; when she presses at the fantasy of the Tristero, it becomes more real. The Tristero has an ironic counterpart in the Peter Penguid Society, which is preoccupied with the duality of Marxism and fascism: "Un-

derneath, both are part of the same creeping horror"(33). The Pen-
guids are unable to make a clear distinction between them. Another
underground group is the Inamorati Anonymous, which is dedicated
to protecting its members from love and attendant illusions—"the
worst addiction of all"(83).

Dream in *Gravity's Rainbow* is perhaps all there is. The War, like
Inverarity's will, provides a background for the novel. It is pure
landscape:

> The War, the Empire, will expedite such barriers between our lives.
> The War needs to divide this way, and to subdivide, though its propa-
> ganda will always stress unity, alliance, pulling together. The War does
> not appear to want a folk-consciousness, not even of the sort the
> Germans have engineered, ein Volk ein Führer—it wants a machine of
> many separate parts, not oneness, but a complexity.... Yet who can
> presume to say *what* the War wants, so vast and aloof is it ... so
> *absentee.* Perhaps the War isn't even an awareness—not a life at all,
> really. There may only be some cruel, accidental resemblance to life.
> (130–31)

Perception is all that distinguishes life from the resemblance to life,
damnation from salvation. It is a matter of choice: "Is the baby
smiling, or is it just gas? Which do you want it to be?"(131). Against
this background, Pynchon provides numerous incidents of an individual's attempt to make the world conform to his perception, his
particular fantasy. None of them is more insistent than Edward
Pointsman's "own brown Realpolitik dreams"(50). Pointsman is the
incarnate symmetry of ones and zeros that Oedipa confronts toward
the end of her search:

> Like his master I. P. Pavlov before him, he imagines the cortex of the
> brain as a mosaic of tiny on/off elements. Some are always in bright
> excitation, others darkly inhibited. The contours, bright and dark, keep
> changing. But each point is allowed only the two states: waking or
> sleep. One or zero. "Summation," "transition," "irradiation," "concen-
> tration," "reciprocal induction"—all Pavlovian brain-mechanics—as-

sumes the presence of these bi-stable points. But to Mexico belongs the domain *between* zero and one—the middle Pointsman has excluded from his persuasion—the probabilities. (55)

For Pointsman, reality must be made to conform to his model, "the true mechanical explanation"(89). He hopes Slothrop will give proof to the validity of his dream, "a modest experiment" in which "the man will suffer—perhaps, in some clinical way, be destroyed—but how many others tonight are suffering in his name?"(144). Pointsman knows there is a duality. He fears it because he insists on being able to distinguish between illusion and reality. The possibility of an uncertainty relation is unthinkable heresy to Pointsman, a cause-and-effect man, but he knows that symmetries can go skew: "There is to this enterprise, Pointsman knows, a danger of seduction. Because of the symmetry. . . . He's been led before, you know, down the garden path by symmetry . . ."(144). But Pointsman will accept nothing less than the fulfillment of his dream and its promise of a Nobel Prize. Even though Slothrop escapes the Pavlovian's mechanical dream when he is confused with Major Marvy, there is no reason to believe that Pointsman will ever acknowledge anything but a deterministic reality, one he can shape in his own image.

Pointsman's mechanical view of the world and his sense of reality based on psychological fantasy establish essential criteria for other examples of landscape that recur in Pynchon's fiction. As suggested on several earlier occasions, science and technology provide Pynchon with many of his most important metaphors. But science and technology also have made possible a mass landscape on a scale that was unimaginable before the twentieth century. The effects of mass transportation on tourism, for example, are obvious, as are the results of electronic communications, cinematography, synthetics, V-2 rockets, atomic and hydrogen bombs, drugs, and numberless other technologies. These provide the means for literally transforming the land into something else: " . . . an announcement of Plasticity's central canon: that chemists were no longer to be at the mercy of Nature. They could decide now what properties they wanted a molecule to

have, and then go ahead and build it"(249). Although Disneyland
stands as one example of technology applied to dream, nowhere in
Pynchon is the relationship of technology to landscape more clearly
drawn than in Kekulé's dream of the benzene ring, which created "a
field of aromatic chemistry to ally itself with secular power, and find
new methods of synthesis . . ."(412).

Nothing in all of Pynchon's fiction rivals his accomplishment in
showing how technology and its secular allies have reshaped the
world. From Inverarity's personal dream in *The Crying of Lot 49* to
the impersonal meta-cartel of *Gravity's Rainbow,* there is a shift of
emphasis, a growing anxiety, that commands our attention; there
appears to be a global conspiracy that will accept nothing less than
its own image of reality. With technology at its command, the meta-
cartel appears to have unrestrained control over nations as well as
individuals. The importance of technology is perhaps best summarized by Walter Rathenau, "prophet and architect of the cartelized
state"(164), who is summoned from among the dead during a seance
for the "corporate Nazi crowd"(164). A Jew, Rathenau had been
sacrificed to racial purity on June 24, 1922, even though he was the
German Foreign Minister. He speaks with authority, though the
Nazis will "warp, they will edit, into a blessing"(165) whatever the
ghost has to say. He describes the only world possible after technology's transformation:

> Problems you may be having, even those of global implication, seem
> to many of us here only trivial side-trips. You are off on a winding and
> difficult road, which you conceive to be wide and straight, an Auto-
> bahn you can travel at your ease. Is it any use for me to tell you that
> all you believe real is illusion? I don't know whether you'll listen, or
> ignore it. You only want to know about your path, your Autobahn."
> (165)

Though they are only a small part of the meta-cartel, the Nazis
represent the process of turning dream into reality; only Rathenau
tries to tell them that this synthetic reality is still illusion. A few
minutes later, he adds: "If you want the truth—I know I presume—

you must look into the technology of these matters. Even into the hearts of certain molecules . . ."(167). It is only from a perspective such as death that illusion can be recognized for what it is; another ghost collaborates Rathenau's perspective: " . . . the illumination out here is surprisingly mild, mild as heavenly robes, . . . glimpses into *another order of being* . . ."(239). Slothrop and his earlier counterparts get a glimpse of the two orders of being, but not a clear view. Theirs is rather like "some alkaline aftertaste of lament, an irreducible *strangeness*, a self-sufficiency nothing could get inside . . ."(240).

The evidence of technology's landscape hardly needs documentation since it is omnipresent in Pynchon's novels, but two tangible results of technology—dope and film—recur with such frequency as to require special attention. Both are extended metaphors for alternate landscapes and both have an element of irreducible strangeness. They are alternate forms of the tour and, accordingly, media for the meta-cartel's controlling images of reality. In a world gone synthetic, with illusion accepted as reality everywhere, drugs offer no "real" escape. But by removing their users one step from the usual landscape, they do offer the possibility of an alternate perception of the world. In *The Crying of Lot 49*, for example, LSD, mescaline, psilocybin, and related drugs are part of the psychotherapist Hilarius's experiment, which he describes as "the bridge, die Brücke. . . . The bridge inward"(7). Drugs bridge a logical gap between inside and outside. They permit fantasy to be projected into the world and then perceived as real. Where one person sees a few flecks of shimmering light, another may see a resplendent rainbow with the help of LSD— a bridge between imagination and experience. Psychologists' case studies repeatedly verify the fact that hallucinations can displace reality and that fantasy invokes real experiences. The effects of LSD on Oedipa's husband have already been noted; according to Mucho, "You take it because it's good. Because you hear and see things, even smell them, taste like you never could. Because the world is so abundant. No end to it, baby"(107). LSD causes his dreams to change.

In *Gravity's Rainbow,* drugs have become a mode of existence and, perhaps, a part of the control system of the meta-cartel that sprang from Kekulé's dream. In the seance, Rathenau identified a succession of technologies derived from Kekulé's molecular discovery, each of which had its corporate counterpart in the meta-cartel that included, among others, IG Farben, Shell Oil, Grössli, Sandoz, Psychochemie AG, and General Electric. The drug Oneirine is one of the latest in the line of discoveries. Although drugs function as a complex metaphor with multiple applications, they are always a means for avoiding present circumstances, for seeming to escape reality. Slothrop's disintegration at the end of *Gravity's Rainbow,* even the fragmentary structure of the novel itself, may suggest a drug-facilitated perspective. This possibility of individualized illusion is a problem for the meta-cartel that produced Oneirine and that seeks nothing less than total, uniform control. The legendary IG salesman Wimpe explains the problem to Tchitcherine: "We seem up against a dilemma built into Nature, much like the Heisenberg situation. There is nearly complete parallelism between analgesia and addiction. The more pain it takes away, the more we desire it"(348). The cartel needs total, predictable control for its synthetic reality to displace any other reality that might happen to exist. It is a matter of perception fundamentally, but the cartel has gone beyond the basics: " . . . we need fewer of these unknowns, not more. We know how to produce real pain. Wars, obviously . . . machines in the factories, industrial accidents, automobiles built to be unsafe, poisons in food, water, and even air—these are quantities tied directly to the economy. We know them, and we can control them. But 'addiction'? What do we know of that? Fog and phantoms"(348–49). An exchange between Wimpe and Tchitcherine clarifies the magnitude of the landscape involved and the cartel's underlying assumption:

"Well—you won't find many addicts among us. The medical profession is full of them, but we salesmen believe in real pain, real deliver-

ance—we are knights in the service of that Ideal. It must all be real, for the purposes of our market. Otherwise my employer—and our little chemical cartel is the model for the very structure of nations— becomes lost in illusion and dream, and one day vanishes into chaos. Your own employer as well."
"My 'employer' is the Soviet State."
"Yes?" Wimpe did say "*is* the model," not "will be." (349)

In comparison with this "little" cartel, Inverarity, the Tristero, and V. look like mere amateurs.

However, the fears of the cartel to which Wimpe admits are realized in several characters, including Pig Bodine. In a song entitled "The Doper's Dream," he expresses the basic duality of worlds between "Doperland" with its own peculiar landscape of seeming freedom and "this cold, cold world . . . m' prison's whurever I be . . ." (369). Dope permits dreams in a world that has exhausted most dreams by transforming them into a synthetic reality; beyond Disneyland there is Doperland. One of the natives of Doperland, Säure (acid) Bummer, tells Slothrop of the confusion that resulted in Berlin when the Germans diverted potassium permanganate (used to identify cocaine) to the Rocket: "Well, without that Purpurstoff you can't deal cocaine honestly. Forget honesty, there just wasn't any *reality*", or "without the permanganate there was no way to tell anything for sure"(375). Representing no cartel but his own, Säure is an addicted ironic counterpart to the IG salesman Wimpe.

Bodine proves that Oneirine can intrude into reality and change present circumstances. The drug—which he had slipped into the coffee urn aboard his destroyer—intervenes between the *John E. Badass* and a torpedo: "The property of time-modulation peculiar to Oneirine was one of the first to be discovered by investigators. . . . So, out in the mellow sea-return tonight, the two fatal courses do intersect in space, but not in time"(389). Greta Erdmann also discovers Oneirine "and the face of her afflicted home planet was rearranged in the instant"(464). Yet Oneirine is still only another landscape, regardless of its modulations or rearrangements: "Greta was meant to find Oneirine. Each plot carries its signature. Some are God's, some masquerade as God's. This is a very advanced kind of forgery. But still there's the same meanness and mortality to it as a falsely made check"(464). The party crowd aboard the *Anubis* offers ample evidence of this fact. Near the end of the novel—after Slothrop's personal disintegration and amid the general disintegration of Doperland—we learn of a unique Oneirine characteristic: hallucinations recur.

Whereas other sorts of hallucinations tend to flow by, related in deep ways that aren't accessible to the casual dopefiend, these Oneirine hauntings show a definite narrative continuity, as clearly as, say, the average *Reader's Digest* article. Often they are so ordinary, so conventional . . . that they are only recognized as hauntings through some radical though plausible violation of possibility: the presence of the dead, journeys by the same route and means where one person will set out later but arrive earlier, a printed diagram which no amount of light will make readable. . . . (703)

Like other landscapes, Oneirine hallucinations eventually become familiar—a shift in the uncertainty relation. Perception that is drug-induced, however, usually includes a paranoid response to the realization that reality is as ephemeral as dream: "Like other sorts of paranoia, it is nothing less than the onset, the leading edge, of the discovery that *everything is connected*, everything in the Creation, a secondary illumination—not yet blindingly One, but at least connected, and perhaps a route In for those like Tchitcherine who are held at the edge . . ."(703). Drugs not only make hallucinations appear to be real, but they have the potential for showing their users that illusion and reality are related. The route, or bridge, inward gives the observer the power to create whatever reality, however interconnected, he wants and the drug permits.

The other perception-inducing products of technology that Pynchon uses extensively as an alternate landscape are film and similar visual media. As early as *V.* he noted its potential in Fergus Mixolydian, who implanted electrodes in his skin and attached them to

his television: "When Fergus dropped below a certain level of awareness, the skin resistance increased over a preset value to operate the
switch. Fergus thus became an extension of the TV set"(45). His
landscape was ready-made and always available. Pynchon makes a
more sophisticated and complex use of film and television in *The
Crying of Lot 49*, as already noted on several occasions, both in the
novel's own plot structure and as a metaphorical device; the analogy
of Oedipa's being a film projector, for example, is sustained by the
world she projects. In *Gravity's Rainbow*, film becomes a self-
sufficient landscape of its own and the novel even functions as a
movie with frozen time frames, a cast of Hollywood extras, images
of reality, and a continuity of form rather than experience; most of
the important characteristics of film's synthetic reality and its capacity for altering perception have been discussed in other contexts. The
capacity of film to create a sense of reality from fantasy is the source
of its power; its magic lies in its potential for transforming reality to
coincide with the form it projects. Von Göll can believe that his fake
film of a black German military group, produced for the Allied propaganda machine, actually is incarnated in the Schwarzkommando—
"summoned, in the way demons may be gathered in, called up to the
light of day and earth . . ."(275–76). Discovering that the Schwarzkommando are "leading real, paracinematic lives," von Göll sees his
mission as "to sow in the Zone seeds of reality"(388). By the end of
the novel, he has produced a movie that goes on indefinitely, twenty-
four hours a day, and is designed to take back these seeds of reality:
"Part of a reverse world whose agents run around with guns which
are like vacuum cleaners operating in the direction of life . . ."
(745). As might be expected, von Göll uses a special film invented by
Laszlo Jamf, "which somehow was able, even under ordinary daylight, to render the human skin transparent to a depth of half a
millimeter, revealing the face just beneath the surface"(387). Film
demonstrates, in a way everyone recognizes, that life and illusion are
both a matter of form. Von Göll's movie *Alpdrücken*, for example,
presents the image of copulation that Franz Pökler recreates in his

bedroom; the results are Bianca on one side of the film and Ilse on the other; both are the experience of form. Pökler will think of his daughter as *"A film. How else? Isn't that what they made of my child, a film?"*(398). But when he is at work on the Rocket, watching movies of its flight, he also knows that form intrudes on the other side of reality: " . . . proof that these techniques had been extended past images on film, to human lives"(407). Slothrop repeatedly encounters the problem of film's providing a form that is both illusory and real. In Berlin, for example, he mistakes the Reichstag building for King Kong and bodies of the dead dug from beneath the rubble for loaves of bread; film has given him an image of reality that is more than a momentary lapse: "But it was more than an optical mistake. They are rising, they are transubstantiated . . ."(368). Early in the novel, Pointman's PISCES colleagues use drugs to gather information from Slothrop about American Negroes that they can then incorporate in von Göll's Schwarzkommando films. Slothrop's hallucination is cinemagraphic, opening with an exchange with the Kenosha Kid, who is presumably Orson Welles; he is puzzled by an imagined movie because there are more people than there are supposed to be:

Q. Then what about all the others? Boston. London. The ones who live in cities. Are those people real, or what?
A. Some are real, and some aren't.
Q. Well are the real ones necessary? or unnecessary?
A. It depends what you have in mind.
Q. Shit, I don't have anything in mind.
A. *We* do.
   For a moment, ten thousand stiffs humped under the snow in the Ardennes take on the sunny Disneyfied look of numbered babies under white wool blankets, waiting to be sent to blessed parents in places like Newton Upper Falls. It only lasts a moment. (70)

Although Slothrop is not even aware of it, this scene answers one of the major questions of the novel: Is Slothrop real? Both Slothrop and the reader learn that he is a film character, an image that can be manipulated like a part of any other landscape. Slothrop's personal sense of reality is irrelevant to everyone but him. By the end of the novel he is a "Sentimental Surrealist" and "They called him the 'Kenosha Kid,' though this may be apocryphal"(696). He and the others have been living the "fake film-lives of strangers"(684), playing parts in a movie under someone else's direction. One of the Argentinians who wait for von Göll to bring their anarchist dream to life knows that the world is one giant sound stage for a movie:

> The sets for the movie-to-be help some. The buildings are real, not a false front in sight. The boliche is stocked with real liquor, the pulpería with real food. The sheep, cattle, horses, and corrals are real. The huts are weatherproof and are being slept in. When von Göll leaves—if he ever comes—nothing will be struck. Any of the extras who want to stay are welcome. Many of them only want to rest up awhile for more DP trains, more fantasies of what home was like before the destruction, and some dream of getting somewhere. They'll move on. (613)

When Slothrop confronts von Göll with the possibility that life is not really paracinematic, the director lets him know that it is only a matter of time: "Not yet. Maybe not quite yet. You'd better enjoy it while you can. Someday, when the film is fast enough, the equipment pocket-size and burdenless and selling at people's prices, the lights and booms no longer necessary, *then* . . . then . . ."(527). Because all is not yet landscape, or at least not yet a homogeneous landscape, Slothrop is still able to detect a duality of illusion and reality; strangeness and familiarity have not yet been completely synthesized. The plans have been formulated and the technology is being improved daily.

In one of the last fragmentary sections of the novel, called "Some Characteristics of Imipolex G," the narrator suggests the way in which Kekulé's molecular discovery, the synthetic revolution, corporations, drugs, film, and Slothrop's quest are related in the meta-cartel's technological capability for creating landscape. Imipolex G is a climactic symbol because it is a synthetic skin, a permanent replacement for all the other surfaces:

It is entangled with the bones and ducts, its own shape determined by how the Erection of the Plastic shall proceed: where fast and where slow, where painful and where slithery-cool . . . whether areas shall exchange characteristics of hardness and brilliance, whether some areas should be allowed to flow over the surface so that the passage will be a caress, where to orchestrate sudden discontinuities—blows, wrenchings—in among these more caressive moments. (699)

The new surface can be made to respond to predetermined images by a coordinate system of wires, by a beam-scanning system, or by "the projection, *onto* the Surface, of an electronic 'image,' analogous to a motion picture"(700). Thus, Imipolex G can be controlled at the Surface . . .

(or even below the outer layer of Imipolex, down at the interface with What lies just beneath: with What has been inserted or What has actually *grown itself a skin of Imipolex G*, depending which heresy you embrace. We need not dwell here on the Primary Problem, namely that everything below the plastic film does after all lie in the Region of Uncertainty, except to emphasize to beginning students who may be prone to Schwärmerei, that terms referring to the Subimipolexity such as "Core" and "Center of Internal Energy" possess, outside the theoretical, no more reality than do terms such as "Supersonic Region" or "Center of Gravity" in other areas of Science). . . . (700)

And Subimipolexity is no more—or less—real than the "perception-conscious (Pcpt.-Cs.) systems" Freud theorizes in the fourth section of *Beyond the Pleasure Principle*. The ubiquity of Imipolex and its related landscapes has made illusion familiar—a substitute for reality —which is, of course, the only important lesson of Slothrop's search for the substance that appears to have exercised such great control over him. In conformity with the Heisenberg principle, the consequence is that what lies beneath the surface has become strange. If Slothrop's quest seems bizarre, it is only because the object of his search lies in the Region of Uncertainty. The one certainty of his tour is that images are all he can see on the surface, and they can be changed with the flick of a switch.

In his novels and stories Pynchon does not propose or intimate anything fundamentally new about the very old problem of the relationship of illusion to reality, though he does offer some new approaches. Even those readers least impressed with Pynchon's handling of complex philosophical problems and most depressed by his stylistic facility will recognize in his fiction a continuity with older formulations of the problem, both literary and philosophic, popular and psychoanalytic. That his novels can hold everything from Whitehead and Heisenberg to comic books and Disneyland in a single form is less a sign of interosculation than confirmation of Whitehead's conclusion that everything *is* related and that modes of perception *do* intersect. The analysis of this problem in terms of land and landscape is consistent with Pynchon's fiction in establishing a model that can accommodate Mickey Mouse and the unyielding philosopher. In a variety of ways, such as those detailed above, Pynchon systematically, though fancifully, explores the nature of the relationship between reality and illusion. The Pointsmans of the world, with their fixed categories of Inside and Outside, real and false, have their counterparts in the von Gölls, who slide back and forth between categories without detecting any interruption. In between are the Oedipa Maases and Tyrone Slothrops, who occupy the realm of probabilities and uncertainty relations. By experiencing the forms of both the Pointsmans and the von Gölls, they at least recognize that reality is relative and a matter of perception, even if they can do nothing about their own situations.

The landscapes of Disney, dope, film, and tourism depend on a conscious recognition of form, and therefore artificiality, for their effect in shaping experience. However, a sense of familiarity is also essential. Repetition, prior knowledge, and experience itself can make even the strangest landscapes familiar. Familiarity in turn makes a landscape appear real, allows it to function as land. Although Pynchon's novels offer some of the strangest landscape of contemporary fiction, they do nonetheless have a familiarity about them. The

Heisenberg principle of observation that operates within the novels functions at the reader's level as well, reinforcing the sense of duality that the characters experience. Through his use of facts and details carried over from the reader's own experience, Pynchon creates a sense of place and event that self-consciously calls attention to the coexistence of reality and fiction. The emergence of a genre of fictional history, particularly during the last decade, may in time diminish the singular importance of Pynchon's contribution, but not the efficacy of his representation of the relationship between illusion and reality, the way life and art overlap.

One of Pynchon's most effective means of creating a sense of familiarity is that of accumulating details. The 1899 Florence episode in *V.* is typical. Woven in among the dialogue and plot are descriptive details that have the accuracy of a Baedeker (even the same words) and can, therefore, evoke the illusion of authenticity in the fiction. The story has an immediate familiarity for readers who have been to Florence. Mantissa and Cesare sit in front of a wine shop on the Ponte Vecchio, whose shops, reports Baedeker, have belonged to goldsmiths since the fourteenth century; Mantissa is described as if he were the creation of a goldsmith. They drink Broglio, the variety of Chianti Baedeker recommended in Florence at the time; they drink from a "fiasco," which Baedeker describes as a straw-covered flask holding three ordinary bottles. They watch tourists returning to their hotels on the Lungarno, where, Baedeker notes, the best ones are located. Mantissa's map of the Uffizi is accurate and even the location (western wall of the Sala di Lorenzo Monaco) and dimensions of Botticelli's *Birth of Venus* (175 by 279 centimeters) are precise. The narrator notes that there are 126 steps from the Gallery to the Piazza della Signoria, which in fact there are. Streets in the novel intersect where they are supposed to intersect, buildings are in their right locations, and historical references to monuments, artists, and plazas are accurate. All of Pynchon's descriptions of places are built on such scattered but concrete details, which substantiate the entire description even though most of it may be invented. New York, Paris, London, Cairo, Alexandria, Los Angeles, San Francisco, Berlin, Nordhausen, Baku, Zürich, St. Louis, Boston, Valletta, and other cities are described in precise enough detail to convince those who have been there of Pynchon's accuracy and to make them almost familiar to strangers. Details that are fictional seldom seem incongruous or improbable, even if they are strange.

Other details are similarly introduced into the novels for the same documentary reasons. The description of Esther's "nose-job," the popular legend of alligators in New York City sewers, von Trotha's atrocities in the Südwest, Thurn and Taxis, the interlocking corporations, rocket technology, drugs, films, comic books, television programs, bureaucratic procedures, laws and theories of physics, chemistry, psychology, political science, anthropology, sociology, biology, and mathematics, several discrete philosophies, sexual perversions, pinball, music, poetry, and other novels are only a few of the categories of details that enter Pynchon's work not simply as decoration but as functional elements of fiction. The curious who seek to verify any of these details often find that they are facts and that Pynchon has been scrupulous in representing them. However, these researches are far less rewarding than the realization that the facts drawn from the world outside Pynchon's fiction are indistinguishable from those invented by the author.

Likewise, Pynchon makes extensive use of historical events and actual people in his fiction. Despite the context, these events and people tend to gain an aura of reality from their imaginative treatment. The intrigues in Cairo during the Fashoda incident, the colonial and military policies in the Südwest, the bombing of London, the alphabet revolutions of Central Asia, the postwar distribution of goods, people, and geography, the security at the Potsdam conference, and the prewar corporate negotiations are represented accurately but embellished with enough of Pynchon's own details to make them convincing as experiences remembered as well as history. A number of historical figures become characters, such as Mickey

Rooney, Jack Kennedy, Malcolm X, and Walter Rathenau. Countless others have prominent roles but do not interact with the other characters; among the more important are Henry Adams, Rilke, Eliot, Wittgenstein, Kekulé, Mann, Weber, Wagner, Rossini, von Braun, Pavlov, Freud, Borges, Leibnitz, Descartes, Einstein, Maxwell, and Disney. When Pynchon's fictional characters such as Bodine, Weissmann, Mondaugen, Hogan Slothrop, and Bloody Chiclitz reappear in successive stories and novels, they too take on an existence apart from the particular story they are in. The result is always the same whether the characters are real or imagined: they are familiar to the reader and they are evidence of coexisting worlds.

In *Gravity's Rainbow* Pynchon's ability to recreate the sense of a place and time has increased although he is less interested in the physical than the mental landscape. His rendering of the bureaucratic idiocies of the White Visitation, for example, has an ambiance of truth to it that allows the fictional institution to represent any number of real counterparts: the acronyms, the struggles for funding, interoffice intrigue, incompetence at the top, doctrines of belief, rules, procedures and protocols, trivial seriousness, irrelevancy of purpose, committees, delays, and reversals are as common to universities, government agencies, and institutions as to the special wartime intelligence unit. However, Pynchon is perhaps at his best in describing the dislocation and strangeness, the nervous fear and unrelenting horror of the war, which are masked by a surface of calm and casual jocosity. The rocket attacks on London, with as many as sixty strikes in a week, had such an unsettling effect that fantasy and illusion became more real than "the plaster smell, the gas leaking, the leaning long splinters and sagging mesh"(24) that followed. The V-2 rocket, which gave no warning of its coming, was ever-present nonetheless, about to fall: the rocket, both imagined and real, poised in the sky just beyond sight. Pynchon recreates this landscape of anxiety indirectly and slowly through the accumulation of details. In an unusually elaborate embellishment of the London scene, he draws a memorable picture of the delicate balance between madness and sanity. The occasion is Slothrop's visit with Mrs. Quoad, who stuffs him full of disgusting wartime candies: wine jellies, Marmalade Surprises, rhubarb creams, cherry-quinine *petit fours,* and a jar full of patriotic candies, including a chocolate hand grenade, "a .455 Webley cartridge of green and pink striped taffy, a six-ton earthquake bomb of some silver-flecked blue gelatin, and a licorice bazooka" (118). Slothrop tries the hand grenade: "Under its tamarind glaze, the Mills bomb turns out to be luscious pepsin-flavored nougat, chockfull of tangy candied cubeb berries, and a chewy camphor-gum center. It is unspeakably awful. Slothrop's head begins to reel with camphor fumes, his eyes are running, his tongue's a hopeless holocaust. Cubeb? He used to *smoke* that stuff"(118). The episode is perhaps the funniest of all Pynchon's novels, but it is also one of his finest recreations of life. While the piece of candy itself comments on the discrepancy between appearance and reality, the incident is characteristic of the nervous humor that helped Londoners survive their anxiety. Anyone who sampled one of those candies can still recall the taste thirty years later; Slothrop's exaggerated agony is a shared experience. Using such fine points of intersection with his reader's memory and experience, Pynchon is able to build an extremely complex and comprehensive sense of the place and times from minutia. It is the details, the unimportant details like the taste of bittersweet candies, that are remembered most vividly and that give memory its sense of reality.

Details are discovered, selected, altered, combined, and with them a landscape is created. Perception, finally, is all that distinguishes illusion from reality, and illusion is always partial. Whether observed or represented, reality necessarily involves illusion because it has no form of its own and cannot make itself visible without an image being imposed. If one purpose of criticism is to invent such images, Pynchon has prevented definitive perceptions by forcing critics into uncertainty relations with his observable world and thus into distracting complexity. Criticism serves no useful purpose in burdening art with implications beyond its own pretensions. Pynchon's art is neither simple nor unpretentious, but it does nonetheless lay claim to the basic act of coping with an environment that has grown beyond any one person's ability to apprehend it as an entity. Pynchon lures his readers into exotic regions, dazzles them with chimeras of possibilities, but he never strays from fundamental conditions and ordinary themes, however elaborately they may be embellished. When criticism is least able to describe or is most complex, it is Pynchon who can speak for the critic by showing how the earth's own substance is literally transformed into dream—into Baedeker Land.

Land and landscape are the poles of Pynchon's fictional world, related in the life of man's illusions. In one of the least ambiguous passages of *Gravity's Rainbow,* Pynchon unmasks the illusions he so generously provides his characters. Appropriately, the spokesman is Walter Rathenau, philosopher of the world built from Kekulé's molecule, summoned from among the dead to speak the "truth" about the land and the "terrible structure behind the appearances of diversity and enterprise"(165). It is a truth that "will be repressed or in ages of particular elegance be disguised as something else"(164). He speaks to those who have inherited his world: "Imagine coal, down in the earth, dead black, no light, the very substance of death. Death ancient, prehistoric, species *we will never see again.* Growing older, blacker, deeper, in layers of perpetual night. Above ground, the steel rolls out fiery, bright. But to make steel, the coal tars, darker and heavier, must be taken from the original coal. Earth's excrement, purged out for the ennoblement of shining steel. Passed over" (166). That is the illusion of change, the serpent's promise of new from the old. Rathenau, however, knows that there is more: "But this is all the impersonation of life. The real movement is not from death to any rebirth. It is from death to death-transfigured. The best you can do is to polymerize a few dead molecules. But polymerizing is not resurrection"(166). Landscape is a function of life, a dream that the land can be changed. But even as it is changed, there is no real change: "The persistence, then, of structures favoring death. Death converted into more death. Perfecting its reign, just as the buried coal grows denser, and overlaid with more strata—epoch on top of epoch, city on top of ruined city. This is the sign of Death the impersonator" (167).

3 Death Transfigured

Earth, is not this what you want: *invisibly*
to arise in us? Is it not your dream
to become one day invisible?—Earth! invisible!
What do you charge us with if not transformation?
Earth, my love, I will. Oh believe me, I need
no more of your springtimes to win me; *one,*
ah just one is already too much for my blood.
Unutterably I am resolved to be yours, from afar.
You were always right, and your holiest occurrence
is our intimate companion, Death.

From R. M. Rilke's Ninth
of *The Duino Elegies*

EARTH'S MINDBODY

If the final measure of life is death, then death must be implicit
everywhere in life. It is a pervasive artistic theme that haunts all
others. The two approaches to Pynchon's fiction already examined
claim their separate metaphors, but it becomes obvious that they are
only other ways of talking about the probabilities and uncertainties
of death. Although entropy is a measure of probability, it implies the
process of transformation. There can be no more direct expression of
human entropy then the sailor Mehemet's simple "the only change
is toward death. . . . Early and late we are in decay"(433). While it
is the role of art and human invention to embellish and disguise
simple facts, complex formulations can always be reduced to Mehemet's cheerful observation. Kekulé's serpent may offer a more elegant

image, but it too brings the same message: Rebirth is an illusion; the only transformation is, as Walter Rathenau expressed so well, "from death to death-transfigured." Despite its other connotations, the tour conceals the same inherent truth: reality and illusion are continuous, functions of the same uncertainty relation. Both the isolated system and the tour take their shapes from the earth's change toward death, from the nature of things. Death in new appearances and death exalted are the ends of transfiguration, not rebirth. Synthesis and control give the illusion of rebirth, making something new from the debris of the given—like the Great Synthesist Wallace Carothers' discovery of nylon—but this is deliberate resurrection, an impersonation of nature. Rathenau's coal-tar image of death is simultaneously metaphorical and literal. More importantly, it suggests the duality of life and death contained within the same structure—not quite a unity, but an interrelationship that tries to say life and death are aspects of the same form. Man needs death to live and lives only to die. There is no cycle, only continuity.[1]

Gravity's Rainbow's Lyle Bland—an American shadow of Rathenau —helps explain the knowledge, which follows departure from the surface world, of life and death's duality. In life, both Rathenau and Bland had been prophets of illusion and deception—Rathenau through the cartelized state, Bland through his own Institute and Foundation. With the help of Masonry magic, not unlike a Maxwell's demon, Bland leaves his body for journeys into the interface between life and death: "He knows where he is when he's there, but when he comes back, he imagines that he has been journeying underneath history: that history is Earth's mind, and that there are layers, set very deep, layers of history analogous to layers of coal and oil in Earth's body"(589). Significantly, Bland's experience is a journey and he receives instruction in the "techniques of voyage"(589). Though he early learns that distinctions between good and evil are meaningless, he cannot yet help making a distinction between mind and body. The Cartesian problem persists until the last, but even that dissolves:

Because it's hard to get over the wonder of finding that Earth is a living critter, after all these years of thinking about a big dumb rock to find a body and psyche, he feels like a child again, he knows that in theory he must not attach himself, but still he is in love with his sense of wonder, with having found it again, even this late, even knowing he must soon let it go. . . . To find that Gravity, taken so for granted, is really something eerie, Messianic, extrasensory in Earth's mindbody . . . having hugged to its holy center the wastes of dead species, gathered, packed, transmuted, realigned, and rewoven molecules to be taken up again by the coal-tar Kabbalists of the other side, the ones Bland on his voyages has noted, taken boiled off, teased apart, explicated to every last permutation of useful magic, centuries past exhaustion still finding new molecular pieces, combining and recombining them into new synthetics—"Forget them, they are no better than the Qlippoth, the shells of the dead, you must not waste your time with them. . . ." (590)

The living, shells of the dead, give up their uniqueness for those who see the continuity embraced in Earth's mindbody. They may be forgotten. Others on this side of life are left with delusions and other comforts.

If Walter Rathenau, as an apparently disinterested party, speaks the truth about life's being a movement toward death transfigured, then the characters of Pynchon's novels and stories should reveal various degrees of the transfiguration, all of which confirm death. Amid the variety of human activities that validate Rathenau's conclusion, love is one aspect to which Pynchon repeatedly turns for evidence—even in spite of a certain sympathy for human compassion. Within the traditions of western civilization Pynchon has a complete love-death structure to draw upon, including Freud's compendium, which begins with the conclusion that the goal of all life is death. Although Freud is augmented with such diverse perspectives as those of Rilke, Wagner, Weber, Schrödinger, Nietzsche and Frazer, Pynchon's concerns with the synthesis of life and death, the consequences of reducing human life to a process of control, and the particular way in which love becomes a ministry of death are ultimately his own. Rathenau, Bland, and other visitors have an easy familiarity with continuity. Qlippoth still scuffling with life display their uncertainties most vividly in the vicissitudes of love, while bureaucracies efficiently turn death into profit. Lyle Bland's mind-body analogy is a paradigm for the way in which both life and death are transfigured, made continuous.

QLIPPOTH IN LOVE

Drawing heavily on the death and wasteland images of Conrad and Eliot, an ironic appreciation of sacraments, and the intellectual's disaffection for the banalities of business, government, and social life, Pynchon published four stories before *V.* that established his preoccupation with life as tedious preparation for death. These and his three subsequent stories reveal the themes of transfiguration developed so masterfully in the novels. "Mortality and Mercy in Vienna" is noteworthy for using the Eucharist as a deadly redemptive process for saving a society from its own decadence. In a perverse act of love, Cleanth Siegel acts on his one bit of information about Ojibwa Indians to unleash a primitive holy ghost. The story also introduces the pig as an ancient symbol of death transfigured. "Low-lands" introduces Pig Bodine, the notion of the garbage dump as a layered deposit of organic death, and the act of love's transfiguring death in Dennis Flange's acceptance of Nerissa. "Entropy," of course, makes the closed system explicit. It is also the most successful of the seven stories. In both plots of "Entropy" the possibility of love is treated as an important sign of life. This is only a slight modification of the notion of redemption in the earlier stories, where the idea of rebirth through sacrifice is an act of love. In "Entropy" Meatball Mulligan's friend Saul has recently separated from his wife over an argument about communication theory and concludes that the problem is one of relational disorganization: "Tell a girl: 'I love you.' No trouble with two-thirds of that, it's a closed circuit. Just you and she. But that nasty four-letter word in the middle, *that's* the one you have to look out for"(285). Love is an act of unification and community; it is a relational process, or circuit, between "I" and "you." Death, on the other hand, is a process of individuation and separation; an awareness of personal death isolates the individual from all others. In the instance of an individual's sacrificing his life for the redemption of the community, love and death are unified. If the possibility of individuality paradoxically decreases as entropy increases, then love can be viewed as a process of transferring energy, both sexual and social, from areas of high to areas of low concentration. As a force of equilibrium, love is another name for entropy and dying may thus be viewed as an act of self-love. In Pynchon's fictional world—as in life —paradox and ambiguity reign. Man cannot bring himself to affirm life by affirming death because, Freud would say, his death instinct is repressed. Consequently, man flees death in his normal pursuit of life and transforms death into an enemy of life.

Saul's discussion of love amid the increasing chaos of Mulligan's party points out one way that life unconsciously affirms death. The party is a community act in which people come together—one of the least complex manifestations of eros. However, the party is simultaneously a demonstration of the social equivalent of entropy and a transformation toward death, as the party disintegrates and disorder increases. The relational interaction between "I" and "you"—love and all such union-seeking relations—must always intervene between a complete union even while it relates. Consequently, Mulligan's efforts to restore order among his individual guests, an act of compassion if not love, will be subject to ambiguity, redundance, irrelevance, leakage, and, of course, noise.

The party's affirmation of life and union has its counterpart in Callisto's hothouse apartment above Mulligan's. Callisto fears a literal entropic heat death and maintains his own controlled, but isolated, environment. Though he is able to maintain a higher temperature inside than outside, his intellectual environment rapidly approaches equilibrium. Callisto affirms death under the illusion that he affirms life. Although they take opposite forms, the party and the hothouse are related; they have a point of intersection in love as well as entropy. Callisto tries to preserve a dying bird by holding it in the warmth of his arms, resisting entropy with love. Acquainted with the theories of Clausius, Gibbs, and Boltzmann as well as Adams, Callisto makes a connection between love and the forces of death, "realizing like his predecessor that the Virgin and the dynamo stand as much for love as for power; that the two are indeed identical . . . "(280). Love does not save the bird. When Callisto is immobilized by his failure, his girl friend, in another act of love, smashes the window of his apartment to violate the closed system and to permit an equilibrium of temperatures inside and outside, thus affirming life and death in the same act as "their separate lives should resolve into a tonic of darkness . . . "(292). Love unmasks the illusions of both social union and personal isolation—the instincts of life and death—by demonstrating that they are continuous, that they are functions of each other. Entropy may increase toward death but it is also the process of life.

V.'s thematic and structural complexities tend to obscure the underlying simplicity of its single great melody or, more accurately, fugue. The history of V. and the actual V. are parallel themes that form the novel's mindbody, to use Lyle Bland's terminology, and that are imitated in most of the novel's development of secondary characters and actions. While V. can be approached from several perspectives, the Adamsian metaphor of Virgin-dynamo and the implication of an entropic history dominate; in this respect, at least, the novel is a logical extension of the preceding stories. Some surgery is required however, if we are to apprehend the structure of death and to learn how the mind and body of V. are made continuous. V.'s mind, or history, can be reconstructed through Stencil's and others' recollections; it is a ritual transition from comparative innocence to an unnamable but destructive force. Similarly, V.'s body progresses from life to inanimateness. In Sidney Stencil's metaphor, V.'s history is the hothouse and her body is the street, but they are the same regardless of what metaphors are used. These parallel themes are developed contrapuntally and when viewed as a single composition they constitute one of Pynchon's most remarkable images of death transfigured. V. anticipates the processes that control *Gravity's Rainbow*: her own continuance depends increasingly on being able to synthesize an artificial existence from the wastes she makes of life around her, to make something new from the debris of the given, to turn a profit by taking energy from the rest of the world. Reduced to a human scale, V. is a microcosm of the later meta-cartels; consequently, we are able to witness her own collapse, unlike that of her successors, when she exhausts her artificial resources.

V.'s dual themes resound in the experiences of other characters, and V. imparts a centrifugal energy to the novel even as she disintegrates. Profane, Stencil, Rachel Owlglass, the Winsomes, Godolphin, and the others are too thinly drawn to exist without V.'s superstructure. Reciprocally, they also help define the meaning of V. Her history, for example, not only makes Herbert Stencil plausible, but it is our knowledge of V. that informs his petty existence. The fact that his search simultaneously allows him to maintain a "sense of animateness" and leads inevitably to "his own extermination" makes sense only in the context of V. Similarly, our knowledge of V.'s history places Esther Harvitz's cosmetic and abortion operations, the decadence of the Whole Sick Crew, or Father Fairing's sewer parish into a much larger frame of reference, the "eternal drama of love and death"(83). Mafia Winsome, who believes "the world can only be rescued from certain decay through Heroic Love"(113), parodies V. in her using up men—"nothing really but a frequency"(113)—and yet Mafia substantiates V.'s disembodied presence. Of the secondary characters Benny Profane is most able to exist on his own and yet he too reveals the influence of V.'s body in his drift toward the inanimate. One of the street's permanent citizens, Profane has multiple symbolic experiences—as a yo-yo, an angel of death, the "god of a darkened world"(17), a human kilroy, or a "schlemihl Redeemer" (427)—which all point inevitably to V.; he "was looking for something too to make the fact of his own disassembly plausible as that of any machine"(30). Profane reduces V.'s symbolic abstractions to the mundane as, for example, in his conversations with the appropriately named robot, SHROUD:

> "What do you mean, we'll be like you and SHOCK someday? You mean dead?"
> Am I dead? If I am then that's what I mean.
> "If you aren't then what are you?"
> Nearly what you are. None of you have very far to go.(267)

Triviality, however, cannot hide the iron edges of truth when SHROUD reminds Profane of "thousands of Jewish corpses, stacked up like those poor car-bodies"(275). It is at his level that V. has her greatest impact: "Schlemihl: It's already started"(275).

Although V.'s transfiguration of death requires the more familiar surroundings of a Profane, Esther, or Winsome to be felt, it is the intellectual center of the novel and the foundation of Pynchon's canon. The historical V. is the record of a transformation that precedes ostensibly along religious lines. V. is created from Victoria Wren by the accretion of experience not unlike the transfiguration of organic death into coal. Her earliest chronological appearance is as a girl of eighteen in Cairo with her father. During this episode we learn that she left the novitiate because she had been unable to stand the competition for the Son of God. Although she did not leave the Catholic church, its mass became "the stage or dramatic field already prepared, serviceable to a seedtime fancy" for her creation and manipulation of a dream world in which God "fought skirmishes with an aboriginal Satan out at the antipodes of the firmament ... "(61). Throughout her career the church and its iconography provide the props for enacting her dreams as she takes religion into her own hands in a cult of power and control. More importantly, the church's poles of good and evil, eternal life and eternal death, are the extremes she will reconcile. V. does not seek her role in the image of an antichrist, but in a merger or fusing of life and death. Despite V.'s initial femininity the progress of transformation is toward the unity of the Trinity and, most likely, the Holy Ghost—a force. While usually regarded as masculine, the spirit in its earliest forms was feminine (including the Hebrew *shekinah* and the Roman Venus's dove) and its gender is still a matter of controversy. This facet of V.'s metamorphosis accounts for both a fusion of masculine and feminine principles and her essentially asexual final role.

When V. next appears in Florence a few months later, she is "self-proclaimed a citizen of the world"(151) and she has taken the important step of secularizing her religious fancy, "crystallized into a nunlike temperament pushed to its most dangerous extreme. . . . it was as if she felt Christ were her husband and that the marriage's physical consummation must be achieved through imperfect, mortal versions of himself—of which there had been, to date, four"(152). A very earthly Virgin indeed, V.'s first role is that of the Shulamite. It is a logical first step because the Bride is the aspect of the Virgin that overcomes death through love; "love is strong as death" according to the "Song of Solomon," which engenders the Bride's legend. The Christian belief in eternal life through death is the foundation of V.'s own cult, but it is corrupted by her secular ends. As the narrator suggests, her adaptation of the Virgin becomes increasingly willful: " . . . her entire commitment to Roman Catholicism as needful and plausible stemmed from and depended on an article of the primitive faith which glimmered shiny and supreme in that reservoir like a crucial valve-handle: the notion of the wraith or spiritual double, happening on rare occasions by multiplication but more often by fission, and the natural corollary which says the son is doppelgänger to the father. Having once accepted duality Victoria had found it only a single step to Trinity"(183). The Bride is doppelgänger to the Mother, as is past to present, life to death, the historical V. to the physical V.

Florence, where Signor Mantissa tries to steal Botticelli's *The Birth of Venus,* is the scene of two important events in the history of V. Faith and the church alone are inadequate; she must incorporate an article of control and Machiavelli seems to be ideal: "skill or any virtú was a desirable and lovely thing purely for its own sake; and it became more effective the further divorced it was from moral intention"(182–83). The birth of V. and her marriage of the two orders are celebrated in a ritual of violence that becomes characteristic. Victoria had justified her deflowering in Cairo with the violent emotions of the Fashoda crisis. In Florence the revolt of the Figli di Machiavelli is a ceremony of blood, which Victoria watches without emotion "as if she saw herself embodying a feminine principle, acting as complement to all this bursting, explosive male energy. Inviolate and calm, she watched the spasms of wounded bodies, the fair of violent death, framed and staged, it seemed, for her alone in that tiny square" (192–93). Sidney Stencil will later recall having "dragged her away from an unarmed policeman, whose face she was flaying with pointed fingernails"(458–59). It is a consummation.

V. rather than Victoria first appears in Paris in 1913: " . . . Victoria was being gradually replaced by V.; something entirely different, for which the young century had as yet no name"(386). In her relationship with Mélanie she approximates the role of Mother and "one solution to a most ancient paradox of love: simultaneous sovereignty yet a fusing-together. Dominance and submissiveness didn't apply; the pattern of three was symbiotic and mutual"(385). V., Mélanie, and their mirror image form the Trinity Victoria had imagined in Florence. Life and death are fused in her love-play: "It was a variation on the Porpentine theme, the Tristan-and-Iseult theme, indeed, according to some, the single melody, banal and exasperating, of all Romanticism since the Middle Ages: 'the act of love and the act of death are one.' Dead at last, they would be one with the inanimate universe and with each other. Love-play until then thus becomes an impersonation of the inanimate, a transvestism not between sexes but between quick and dead; human and fetish"(385). Mélanie is V.'s fetish offspring, the fruit of her union with the world, who comes not as a savior but a witness: " . . . so the Kingdom of Death is served by fetish-constructions like V.'s, which represent a kind of infiltration"(386). In keeping with V.'s dramatic form, Mélanie is crucified during her dance of the "Sacrifice of the Virgin," and V. as an essentially human personage vanishes "from Paris and as far as anyone on the Butte could say, from the face of the earth"(390). The sacrifice probably occurs in August, which coincidentally is the month of the Feast of the Virgin's Assumption and signals V.'s transition to a role as the Queen. The Virgin is the only other mortal besides Christ whose body ascends uncorrupted and inert, if not inanimate; V.'s own concern with preserving her body reinforces the religious parallel. As Queen, V. begins her reign over decadence and completes the evolution of a feminine counterpart of the masculine Trinity. The transfiguration of death proceeds both by V.'s bodily transubstantiation and by her emergence as the century's new goddess.

When Stencil encounters her on Malta in 1919 after the horrors of a world war, he reflects on the new politics and violence of the street, a communion of opposition to established order, which like death "cuts through and gathers in all ranks of society"(443). He thinks last of the church—the Virgin's continuing presence—awaiting the Third Kingdom: "Violent overthrow is a Christian phenomenon"(444). Stencil's rumination completes the picture of V.'s transformation:

> The matter of a Paraclete's coming, the comforter, the dove; the tongues of flame, the gift of tongues: Pentecost. Third Person of the Trinity. None of it was implausible to Stencil. The Father had come and gone. In political terms, the Father was the Prince; the single leader, the dynamic figure whose virtù used to be a determinant of history. This had degenerated to the Son, genius of the liberal love-feast which had produced 1848 and lately the overthrow of the Czars. What next? What Apocalypse?
>
> Especially on Malta, a matriarchal island. Would the Paraclete be also a mother? Comforter, true. But what gift of communication could ever come from a woman....(444)

Even Stencil's conversation with Veronica Manganese is haunted by V.'s presence. He concludes that the past and present, hothouse and street, have been resolved in her by some magic: "No doubt I have passed and repassed you, or your work, in every city Whitehall has called me to." To which she responds with rare peace: "How pleasant to watch Nothing"(459). She, not Stencil or the narrator, capitalizes the *N*; it is a boast.

V. subsequently appears as a comforter in several places. She apparently accompanied D'Annunzio into Fiume after leaving Malta, perhaps even bestowing the gift of communication. In 1922 she is present for another siege at Foppl's villa in the Südwest, where she orchestrates an elaborate decadence against boredom that calls for the recreation of an earlier uprising and the public enactment of private dreams, including old Godolphin's dream of annihilation; this too is one means of bestowing the gift of tongues. In a particularly detailed episode, she induces in Kurt Mondaugen a surrealistic dream about "the destroyer and the destroyed, and the act which united them"(245); it details the way in which colonial soldiers found their own life-sustaining force in the death of helpless victims. At the dream's end there is a vision of the future in which killing could come only "with a logic that chilled the comfortable perversity of the heart, that substituted capability for character, deliberate scheme for political epiphany . . . the engineering design for a world he knew with numb leeriness nothing could now keep from becoming reality . . ." (254). It is, obviously, the design for V.'s world and the plan for *Gravity's Rainbow*.

Her final appearance is described by Fausto Maijstral in his confession. It is a report both enriched and complicated by Fausto's own religious experiences to the point where the two lives cannot be separated. V. and Fausto are ironic counterparts in their respective relationships with the church as unordained priests, their salvations, their abilities to balance life and death, even their competition for Elena Xemxi. More importantly, their apposition in the novel climaxes V.'s personal transformation and her transfiguration of death as the historical and physical V. become one.

In essence Fausto recapitulates V.'s transformations, though on different terms. He had planned to become a priest and take the church as his bride. The war, however, confronts him with an unresolvable equilibrium of life and death, control and chance, while Elena confronts him with love. Fausto progresses through four stages of innocence, doubt, nonhumanity, and a new consciousness (perhaps loosely related to Jung's four stages of the anima, which V. manifests). In the crucial second and third stages he approximates V. in his conclusions: "Decadence, decadence. What is it? Only a clear movement toward death or, preferably, non-humanity. As Fausto II and III, like their island, became more inanimate, they moved closer to the time when like any dead leaf or fragment of metal they'd be finally subject to the laws of physics. All the time pretending it was a great struggle between the laws of man and the laws of God" (301). He recognizes entropy as the law of physics that takes the inevitable human form in which the illusion of life merely cloaks death's transfiguration. In his self-conscious writings he even describes the illusion in terms of mothers who "perpetuate a fictional mystery about motherhood": " . . . the same forces which dictate the bomb's trajectory . . . have focussed somewhere inside the pelvic frontiers without their consent, to generate one more mighty accident. It frightens them to death. It would frighten anyone"(301). Fausto's view of the life-death struggle, which V. resolves with her personal transformation, becomes a conflict of accident and control; the same fusion of life and death occurs regardless of how or why entropy increases.

As Fausto begins to identify Malta as his Paraclete, V. walks its streets as the Bad Priest in a transvestism not of sexes but of animate and inanimate. Described as a sinister figure with the mouth of Christ, she infiltrates the animate, searching for souls, preaching that only Christ is strong enough to coexist with the sickness of giving birth—what Fausto calls a mighty accident. She infects Elena with a sense of disease and even though Paola is born Elena wonders to her death whether it would have been better to accept the Bad Priest's offer of an abortion. The children, of course, are her particular interest—she advises the girls to become nuns and avoid the "pleasure of intercourse, pain of childbirth"; the boys are told to be like a crystal, "beautiful and soulless"(319). She seeks the undifferentiated sexlessness of the inanimate in denying girls motherhood and urging boys toward the anima. However, the children's "view of death was nonhuman"(311) and they are unpersuaded. Rather, they see the Bad Priest, like enemy planes, only as another of the multiple evils—"vectors of evil—pointing inward. Good, i.e., at bay. The Virgin assailed. . . . The woman passive. Malta in siege"(317). The metaphor, of course, is Fausto's and reveals more about him than about the children. Yet the children do see things as they are without the complicated rationalizations of a Fausto or a V. It is this commonsense—"non-human"—perception that permits them to make a game of watching her and leads eventually to V.'s destruction.

V.'s disguise—the illusion that is so important to Fausto—is merely a curiosity to the Maltese children. Near the end of her career V. has nearly completed the process of "bodily incorporating little bits of inert matter"(459), which began forty-five years earlier with an ivory comb depicting five crucified soldiers. Relating both to the comb of the matriarchal love-death goddess and the poison comb of the Snow-white (Lisa) legend, V.'s comb is a fitting symbol of an attempt to make her body and life conform to the deliberate transfiguration of her identity. From the time of her fetishism with Mélanie and her political and social decadences of Malta, Fiume, and the Südwest until her final religious decadence, V.'s own body has been a monument of her drive to establish life only as a measure of decay, to become an incarnate law of physics. Her illusion, however, depends on its being perceived through the adult fictions of continuity, cause and effect, or a humanized history endowed with reason. The children of Malta see only an evil priest made harmless by a fallen beam. It is merely a game when they remove her clothing and find that "she comes apart"(321), but it is nothing less than the Virgin assailed. The children take away their treasures while Fausto watches the dismantling of illusion. For V., whose bare scalp reveals a two-color crucifixion, her death is an unholy Eucharist and the ultimate consummation of her life; all the symbols, roles, and transfigurations culminate in an accident. For Fausto, who violates his covenant with God by administering the last sacrament, her death—preceded by Elena's a few hours before—is the beginning of nonhumanity. The author of the confession admits to committing murder by a sin of omission. He inherits V.'s "physically and spiritually broken world"(286). In his slow return to humanity, he recognizes that if he must live in a universe of things he must also suffer illusions because they, at least, permit survival. His comfort is Malta, the rock, inert but alive with his metaphors.

By taking Catholicism as the dramatic form of her life's unfolding and by exhausting the church's multiple personifications in her own image, V. seeks the subversion of one of society's strongest beliefs: the triumph of life over death and order over chaos. Within the novel only Sidney Stencil and Fausto Maijstral signal any significant recognition of her design or the form itself. The perversion of holy transformations and the mockery of an inanimate transubstantiation are powerful forms nonetheless, and they take their fragmentary toll of countless characters. As the goddess of a new consciousness, V. invokes the laws of physics as proof against the laws of God and the laws of man. There is little doubt that the process she claims as her own survives her death as an unseen presence in the novel, whether or not it is finally her work or the reflection of circumstances. If there is any doubt that her body is the visible sign of her mind—as it has been recorded—it is only Fausto's detecting in inhuman cries a hatred for her sins. But V.'s life was never merely sinful. Her enactment of disintegration encompassed the church, and her body's earthly change was an ultimate transmigration since even God could not restore life to soulless things. After V. only her form remains. Regardless of any uncertainty raised by Fausto's conviction, the history of V. is perhaps Pynchon's most elaborately developed process, one that infiltrates at least our reading of all his subsequent works.

The telescopic complexities of V. are succeeded by the efficient simplicity of *The Crying of Lot 49*. Although there are echoes and reverberations throughout the novel, the idea of death transfigured is contained in Oedipa Maas's efforts to unravel Pierce Inverarity's will, his "attempt to leave an organized something behind after his own annihilation"(58). It would be a mistake to view Pynchon's second novel as simplistic or to suggest that he is dealing with trite ideas. Rather, he has focused the novel more directly on the duality of life and death without feeling obligated to display his erudition and without attempting to incorporate every available myth of Western civilization. Though less complex, Pynchon's thematic treatment of death transfigured is more sophisticated than in earlier works. Whereas *V.* is largely a device for exhibiting the author's cleverness and, therefore, designed for the reader's tracking down clues, *The Crying of Lot 49* shows Oedipa Maas's personal confrontation with the facts of her isolation and inevitable death. She is what makes the novel interesting. Because Oedipa's own discoveries must carry proof of the novel's accomplishment, she is more a recognizable character possessed of human frailties than the representatives of theory, myth, and religion that people *V.*

Pynchon's presentation of death transfigured in *The Crying of Lot 49*, however, is ostensibly based on Oedipa's namesake and Freud's psychoanalytic use of the myth. Though it does not depend on reference to Oedipal literature for its revelations, the novel's development assumes that the reader will make several identifications and correlations. Oedipa bears an obvious relation to the tragic hero of literature, who is confronted with and consumed by the mystery of life. Oedipus is an instrument of death, from the prophecy at his birth that he would murder his father until his own death at Colonus. Oedipa most nearly resembles him in her searches for the key to the sphinx-riddle of Inverarity's will, but her name is given additional significance by the Freudian concept of becoming the father of one's own self in a narcissistic flight from death. As a female, Oedipa certainly refers to Freud's notion of the primal, pre-Oedipal mother, which he discovered to be the substructure for his entire concept of the Oedipus complex. By feminizing Oedipus, Pynchon may also be suggesting the hermaphroditic unity of opposites, which Freud saw as the goal of the human body, as it struggles to overcome the dualities of life and death; this unity is also a theme of Rilke's, developed in *Gravity's Rainbow*. The Freudian construct helps explain Inverarity's empire (headquartered in San Narciso) as a narcissistic attempt to escape death, and his interest in Oedipa as a means of reestablishing contact with the feminine other. In both the mythic and psychoanalytic references to Oedipus, however, Pynchon evokes the fundamental idea of individuation, or isolation, as the manifestation of death and of the basic duality; the appearance of death is transformed by the death instinct's development into the principles of negation and aggression. Thus the path of Oedipa's search takes her, at once, toward increased isolation and the discovery of duality. The fact of her isolation is obvious and inevitable; the possibility of a Tristero, however, places her in an ambivalent relationship with life and death.

Oedipa's quest begins in a tower, "its height and architecture, are like her ego only incidental: . . . what really keeps her where she is is magic, anonymous and malignant, visited on her from outside and for no reason at all"(11). Though the magic might be variously named id, probabilities, uncertainties, or accident, it forces her to seek order and control as a defense against disintegration and the void outside. She is summoned from her tower by the will of a dead lover whose intentions are at best uncertain. She encounters her first Oedipal situation at the Echo Courts Motel, where Metzger tells her his mother "was really out to kasher" him and then adds, "You know what mothers like that turn their male children into"(16). She also is provided with a theme song by a rock group called the Paranoids, who sing about a "*lonely girl in your lonely flat, well, that's where it's at*"(25). Amid evidences of the "American cult of the dead"(42) Oedipa discovers in *The Courier's Tragedy* a theatrical rehearsal to the drama that unfolds on the stage of Southern California; it had been fashioned for an audience "preapocalyptic, death-wishful"(44). The play also includes another Oedipal affair and another literal Eucharist, but its importance is in revealing the presence of the Tristero, the

Adversary. The play's director, who claims that he gave "life" to words, is a model for Oedipa; he has projected a world in the same way she is to bring Inverarity's death "into pulsing stelliferous Meaning"(58). Although the director dies, Oedipa continues her effort to give her clues meaning and life, to exert some control over the void. In the process she encounters the Inamorati Anonymous, "a society of isolates"(85) that was born out of a vision that love and death are the same thing and, therefore, dedicated itself to denying love.

She finds clues to the Tristero's existence everywhere and sees in them a pattern of the instinctual death-wish, but not yet the secret or truth that the Tristero might hold for her:

> She faced that possibility as she might the toy street from a high balcony, roller-coaster ride, feeding-time among the beasts in a zoo— any death-wish that can be consummated by some minimum gesture. She touched the edge of its voluptuous field, knowing it would be lovely beyond dreams simply to submit to it; that not gravity's pull, laws of ballistics, feral ravening, promised more delight. She tested it, shivering: I am meant to remember. Each clue that comes is *supposed* to have its own clarity, its fine chances for permanence.(87)

She thinks the clues may be compensation for having lost the "cry that might abolish the night"(87), a cry that will open Pynchon's third novel. She continues her search amid more clues; the "legend DEATH ... DON'T EVER ANTAGONIZE THE HORN"(90) becomes the name for what she finds: an advertisement for the "Alameda County Death Cult"(90); "a child roaming the night who missed the death before birth as certain outcasts do the dear lulling blankness of the community; a Negro woman with an intricately-marbled scar along the baby-fat of one cheek who kept going through rituals of miscarriage each for a different reason, deliberately as others might the ritual of birth, dedicated not to continuity but to some kind of interregnum . . ."(91). She finds, in short, that, simultaneously with the world of pulsing suburban life, Tupperware parties, and psychologists, "there had to exist the separate, silent, unsuspected world"(92).

Oedipa's recognition that life is death transfigured occurs during her encounter with an aged sailor, whom she treats "as if he were her own child"(93) in her vague role as primal mother: "It was as if she had just discovered the irreversible process"(95), which is both the process of entropy and the great paradox of life, "where death dwelled in the cell though the cell be looked in on at its most quick" (96). Oedipa, like Fausto, recognizes that all beliefs about life are lies at best, but also necessary illusions. She tries to check her impressions with the psychoanalyst Hilarius, "a good enough Freudian"(99), who has his own fears about being visited by "angels of death"(102). In the midst of his own paranoia, he advises her to cherish her fantasy: "What else do any of you have? Hold it tightly by its little tentacle, don't let the Freudians coax it away or the pharmacists poison it out of you. Whatever it is, hold it dear, for when you lose it you go over by that much to the others. You begin to cease to be"(103). He urges her to maintain the illusion of the Tristero's being a fantasy, as if the truth—whatever it may be—were too great to face directly.

Oedipa continues along her path of increasing isolation, being stripped of her men, love, community, and sense of order one by one: her psychoanalyst gone mad; her husband, as she says, gropes away, "hopelessly away, from what has passed, I was hoping forever, for love; my one extra-marital fella has eloped with a depraved 15-year-old; my best guide back to the Trystero has taken a Brody. Where am I?"(114). She finds that she is not only isolated but in the presence of "some opposite Principle, something blind, soulless; a brute automatism that led to eternal death"(116). Like a corporate V., the Tristero, regardless of any actual existence, came to "symbolize the Other"(117) for the radical Puritan sect called the Scurvhamites. But even as these extremists postulated the Other, they looked upon it "with a certain sick and fascinated horror" until "one by one the glamorous prospect of annihilation coaxed them over . . ."(116). In the Tristero's legend WASTE—We Await Silent Tristero's Empire—

Oedipa detects a motto for her own existence: "For this, oh God, was the void. There was nobody who could help her. Nobody in the world. They were all on something, mad, possible enemies, dead" (128). When Oedipa thinks she is pregnant, it is with "disembodied voices from whose malignance there was no appeal, the soft dusk of mirrors out of which something was about to walk, and empty rooms that waited for her"(131). No redeemer will be born of her; there will be no rebirth, no resurrection.

Inverarity's will, a message from the dead, has stripped away layers of history and accumulated waste to show Oedipa the dualities of life and death and the coexistence of competing fantasies. Inverarity may have tried only to show her the void through her discovery of the Tristero or he may have tried to survive death by extending his will through her. Regardless of his intent, the effect on Oedipa is similar to the effect of the Bad Priest's disassembly on Fausto. Inverarity, whose inanimate empire had been his life, holds within his death's grasp both life and death. Oedipa sees them as a symmetry of possibilities, "either an accommodation reached, in some kind of dignity, with the Angel of Death, or only death and the daily, tedious preparations for it"(136–37). She occupies the position in between, where such distinctions have no meaning; there can only be a continuity even if it cannot be confirmed. The last image of the novel is an auctioneer, spreading "his arms in a gesture that seemed to belong to the priesthood of some remote culture; perhaps to a descending angel"(138). He begins the ritual of celebrating the secular Eucharist of Inverarity's corporate body, distributing pieces of the estate to the highest bidder. It is the now familiar ceremony of death transfigured.

In V. Pynchon created a complex symbolic form to represent the idea of personal and historical entropy. In The Crying of Lot 49 he added flesh and plausible human character to the form. In Gravity's Rainbow he retains the formality of character, but abstractions again become the harmonic center. The novel begins with a quotation of Wernher von Braun: "Nature does not know extinction; all it knows is transformation. Everything science has taught me, and continues to teach me, strengthens my belief in the continuity of our spiritual existence after death"(1). The novel ends with one of von Braun's rocket progeny at the last delta-t above the movie house that holds us all; it shines like a "bright angel of death"(760). In between these images of death are such countless variations on the single theme of continuity that a mere catalogue would fill several pages. The closest approximation to a thematic statement occurs in the "net of information that no one can escape"(165), which Walter Rathenau casts over the world's living in his message from the other side of death. In a way *Gravity's Rainbow* is a net of information about death, designed to entangle readers in the certain complexities of its weave.

The course of Tyrone Slothrop's progress toward death has already been described in sufficient detail. It is worth repeating the observation, however, that his search provides the structural framework for the novel. This fact invests his relationship with the Rocket with a special significance. He is characterized by his detractors as being "in love, in sexual love, with his, and his race's, death"(738), or as being a "rocket-creature, a vampire whose sex life actually *fed* on the terror of that Rocket Blitz"(629). The Rockets fall on London like giant phalluses of death, and Slothrop's own aroused penis is a wraith of each Rocket's fall. The war and its varieties of death are related to love in a number of ways, but the Rocket is "programmed in a ritual of love . . . at Brennschluss it is done—the Rocket's purely feminine counterpart, the zero point at the center of its target, has submitted" (223). The Rocket provides the only genuine unity for the novel's multiple plots; it subsumes Slothrop's quest and integrates other characters and other preoccupations into the pattern established in earlier of Pynchon's works: love, death, and life are the same.[2] The matrix of the Rocket, its home in the German Mittlewerke, has the shape of double S's—the lightning stroke, the Schutzstaffel emblem, and the double integral sign: "But in the dynamic space of the living Rocket, the double integral has a different meaning. To integrate here is to operate on a rate of change so that time falls away: change is stilled. . . . 'Meters per second' will integrate to 'meters.' The moving vehicle is frozen, in space, to become architecture, and timeless. It was never launched. It will never fall"(301). The double-S shape is "the shape of lovers curled asleep"(302) and it is also the "ancient rune that stands for the yew tree, or Death"(302).

In his complex Rocket symbol Pynchon integrates life and death with as many attendant forms as possible, from mathematics to vegetation myths. He goes to great lengths to ensure that the Rocket is perceived as the integrating form that is as complete and conclusive as the isolated system. The Rocket's shape—a parabola—is also the shape of God's rainbow promise and gravity's rainbow law. The Rocket's imagery defines a system of death transfigured. Katje Borgesius explains the parabola to Slothrop. Before they became lovers, they had already been joined by the Rocket's trajectory: "You were in London . . . while they were coming down. I was in 's Gravenhage . . . while they were going up. Between you and me is not only a rocket trajectory, but also a life. You will come to understand that between the two points, in the five minutes, *it* lives an entire life" (209). It is the shape to which everything else has reference:

> But it is a curve each of them feels, unmistakably. It is the parabola. They must have guessed, once or twice—guessed and refused to believe—that everything, always, collectively, had been moving toward that purified shape latent in the sky, that shape of no surprise, no second chances, no return. Yet they do move forever under it, reserved for its own black-and-white bad news certainly as if it were the Rainbow, and they its children. . . . (209)

Another devotee of the Rocket, Miklos Thanatz, adds one more important bit of lore to the myth Slothrop is assembling about the Rocket. He sees it "as a baby Jesus" possessing a "Max Weber charisma . . . some joyful—and *deeply* irrational—force the State bureaucracy could never routinize, against which it could not prevail . . ." (464). Thanatz's image is one of redemption and resurrection, like God's rainbow promise, but the Rocket has replaced Pynchon's earlier enigmatic redeemers and, therefore, promises no rebirth, only death transfigured; it can be changed as Victoria Wren changed Catholicism's dramatic field.

A perfect symbol of the continuity between life and death, the Rocket offers both the illusion of control and the illusion of its own independent life, all the while promising death. It supersedes Fausto's clumsy metaphors and Inverarity's corporate life. Slothrop begins to understand the real power of such uncertainty when he descends into the Mittlewerke's underground chambers: "Ghosts used to be either likenesses of the dead or wraiths of the living. But here in the Zone categories have been blurred badly. The status of the name you miss, love, and search for now has grown ambiguous and remote, but this is even more than the bureaucracy of mass absence—some still live, some have died, but many, many have forgotten which they are" (303). The ambiguity is everywhere, not just in the earth's recesses. The war, of which the Rocket is the most powerful emblem, has affected even the children, whose "non-human" perception is the same as the guileless recording angels of *V.* In one episode, children gathered for a matinee performance of *Hansel and Gretel* are startled by a rocket blast and begin to cry. The performers stop, as they have many times before, to sing a song which ends "And those voices you hear, Boy and Girl of the Year,/ Are of children who are learning to die . . ."(175). One of the children returns to her "fatherless" home to see his ghost, only the father's shell, for he has been the victim of "death-by-government—a process by which living souls unwillingly become the demons known to the main sequence of Western magic as the Qlippoth, Shells of the Dead. . . . It is also what the present dispensation often does to decent men and women entirely on this side of the grave"(176). Growing-up is learning how to die, how to fabricate flattering illusions.

The Rocket is everywhere in *Gravity's Rainbow* and symbolically hangs above the novel like the rocket above the Orpheus Theatre at the book's conclusion. It enters the consciousness of every character, and its meaning, like the permuted names of God, may vary but it remains unchanged. Like Pynchon's other major symbol, the Great

Serpent, the Rocket promises certain death and a continuity with life: "So, yes yes this is a scholasticism here, Rocket state-cosmology . . . the Rocket does lead that way—among others—past these visible serpent coils that lash up above the surface of Earth in rainbow light, in steel tetany . . ."(726). The cosmology has interpretations as varied as the people who use it:

> But the Rocket has to be many things, it must answer to a number of different shapes in the dreams of those who touch it—in combat, in tunnel, on paper—it must survive heresies shining, unconfoundable . . . and heretics there will be: Gnostics who have been taken in a rush of wind and fire to chambers of the Rocket-throne . . . Kabbalists who study the Rocket as Torah, letter by letter—rivets, burner cup and brass rose, its text is theirs to permute and combine into new revelations, always unfolding . . . Manichaeans who see two Rockets, good and evil, who speak together in the sacred idiolalia of the Primal Twins (some say their names are Enzian and Blicero) of a good Rocket to take us to the stars, an evil Rocket for the World's suicide, the two perpetually in struggle.(727)

Regardless of the schools of thought, the Rocket, finally, is the instrument of death: ". . . these heretics will be sought and the dominion of silence will enlarge as each one goes down . . . they will *all* be sought out. . . . each Rocket will know its intended and hunt him, . . . shining and pointed in the sky at his back, his guardian executiner rushing in, *rushing closer* . . ."(727). Though the image is radically different, its fundamental design differs little from Victoria Wren's doppelgänger vision or Inverarity's organized "something."

This aspect of the Rocket is best represented by the alleged Manichaean duality of Blicero and Enzian, each with his own Rocket. In their separate ways, both seek an affirmation of the unity. Amid their duality is Slothrop's quest for his Rocket-bound identity and Tchitcherine's similar quest to destroy his black doppelgänger. The Rocket holds all four within its power, as well as others such as Katje, Gottfried, Thanatz, Pointsman, and Pökler, but the relationship of Blicero and Enzian has special significance. Infatuated with Rilke's

Duino Elegies, Blicero found Enzian in the Südwest when he was there as Weissmann. The young boy, "using the Herero name of God," had wanted sex: "... to the boy Ndjambi Karunga is what happens when they couple, that's all: God is creator and destroyer, sun and darkness, all sets of opposites brought together, including black and white, male and female ..."(100). It will take the Rocket to show Blicero how life and death can be physically brought together, but he already knows Rilke's principle. With "some precognition," he "gave his African boy the name 'Enzian,' after Rilke's mountainside gentian of Nordic colors ..."(101), the young wraith of Blicero's Gottfried. There is another precognition, however. Imparting technological knowledge and his beliefs, Blicero has made Enzian his complementary opposite, black to his white, unified in their devotion to the Rocket. It should perhaps be expected, then, that "Enzian" is also the name of a surface-to-air, radio-controlled missile developed by the Germans late in the war—complete with the cruciform wings and fins of the Zone Herero's Rocket mandala. Gottfried is the doppelgänger of Enzian, but Enzian is the doppelgänger of Blicero. Blicero had been a "pierced Jesus"(324) for Enzian and had demanded that "he enter the service of the Rocket"(324). Enzian in turn had repeatedly escaped death as a child in a "Herod myth"(323). Gottfried, "God's peace," completes the trinity of "an entire system *won,* away from the feminine darkness, held against the entropies of lovable but scatterbrained Mother Nature"(324). It is the modern myth in which "the Kingdom of Lord Blicero"(486) is the personalized kingdom of death. Blicero took his own name from a town near the Rocketworks, finding "the name Bleicheröde close enough to 'Blicker,' the nickname the early Germans gave to Death"(322).

From the time he left for the Südwest with a copy of *The Duino Elegies* in his kit until the last days of the war, Blicero's career sought the consummation of life and death under his personal, godlike control. He devoted the last days of his life to building the Rocket that will permit him, like Rilke's angels, to be at home in the continuous regions of life and death. Before the launch, "he is now always the same, awake or asleep—he never leaves the single dream, there are no more differences between the worlds: they have become one for him"(721). He explains to Gottfried, his youthful lover, his plans for realizing Rilke's transformation; there is no specific reference, but the following lines from "The Ninth Elegy" are familiar as the source of Enzian's name and indicative of Blicero's purpose in seeking the literal form for the poet's physical language:

> For the wanderer brings down from the mountainside
> not a handful of earth to the valley, all indescribable,
> but the word he has gained there, pure, the yellow
> and blue gentian. Are we perhaps here only to say: house,
> bridge, brook, gate, jug, olive tree, window,—
> at best: pillar, tower . . . but to *say* them, understand me,
> *so* to say them as the things within themselves never
> thought to be. Is not the hidden craft
> of this secretive earth when she urges two lovers on,
> that in their feelings each and every thing should be transported?
> Threshold: what is it for two
> lovers that they wear down a little
> the older threshold of their own door. They too, after
> the many before them, and before all those to come . . ., lightly.[3]

Blicero launches the blue and yellow Gottfried to the sky in Rocket 00000. He is specially prepared: "Deathlace is the boy's bridal costume . . . the 00000 is the womb into which Gottfried returns" (750). Most importantly, "in one of his ears, a tiny speaker has been surgically implanted. . . . and the words of Weissmann are to be . . . sent out to the Rocket. But there's no return channel from Gottfried to the ground. The exact moment of his death will never be known" (751).

Before the sacrifice, Blicero prepares Gottfried to enter the "Other Kingdom"(722) with what may be his credo: "America *was* the edge of the World," Blicero says, ". . . the site for its Kingdom of Death. . . . But Europe refused it"(722). America had offered the last 'lusion of uniting life and death in the same act that unites destroyer ind destroyed, but "now we are in the last phase. American Death has come to occupy Europe"(722). Like the dream soldier of *V.*, who predicts that an engineering design will replace individual acts of consummation, Blicero knows that death has dominion and that his act is romantic fancy. He refers not to the Allies but to the structure of death when he says that technologically perfected death has come to occupy Europe: "The savages of other continents, corrupted but still resisting in the name of life, have gone on despite everything . . . while Death and Europe are separate as ever, their love still unconsummated. Death only rules here. It has never, in love, become *one with* . . ."(722–23). In an ultimate symbolic act, Blicero plans nothing less than the consummation. Addressing Gottfried in his symbolic role as sacrificial victim and son, Blicero explains that their particular form of love—"lovers whose genitals *are* consecrated to shit, to endings . . . as many in acts of death as in acts of life . . ."(722)—will end for them at least the generation of death:

> "Can you feel in your body how strongly I have infected you with my dying? I was meant to: when a certain time has come, I think that we are all meant to. Fathers are carriers of the virus of Death, and sons are the infected . . . and, so that the infection may be more certain, Death in its ingenuity has contrived to make the father and son beautiful to each other as Life has made male and female . . . oh Gottfried of course yes you are beautiful to me but I'm dying. . . ."(723)

The narrator says that this scene should be read as a Tarot card, what is to come. Although there is no card for it in the deck, Weissmann's own card of what will come is The World, a card symbolizing the final attainment of man, the state of cosmic consciousness toward which all other cards point.[4]

This is Blicero's dream. It is perhaps important only as a dream, his desire. With the last edge of the world lost, the Kingdom of Death is everywhere. Blicero knows that his Rocket will fall back to earth and death, but for a moment—at Brennschluss—Gottfried and at least his words will be at a new edge where life and death are undifferentiated at last. Blicero presumably dies, but that no longer matters after his transfiguration. Enzian conjectures: ". . . he may have changed by now past our recognition. We could have driven under him in the sky today and never seen. Whatever happened at the end, he has transcended. Even if he's only dead"(660–61). Thanatz knows Blicero survives his last stand in the Lüneburg Heath: "He is the Zone's worst specter. He is malignant, he pervades the lengthening summer nights. Like a cankered root he is changing, growing toward winter, growing whiter, toward the idleness and the famine"(666). He has become Death the impersonator.

Blicero is mirrored by Enzian, who moves through the Zone assembling pieces of failed machinery to create Rocket 00001, which will apparently carry him northward to the final zero, an emulation. The reciprocal imagery is completed by the fact that Blicero's own act had been a consummation of Enzian's knowledge of death from the colonialists. Thus Blicero had begun his ceremonial speech to Gottfried before the launch: "And sometimes I dream of discovering the edge of the World. Finding that there *is* an end. My mountain gentian always knew. But it has cost me so much"(722). Enzian knew about an end from the time of von Trotha's atrocities, when he learned that there was "no return. Sixty per cent of the Herero people had been exterminated. . . . Captivity, sudden death, one-way departures were the ordinary things of every day"(323). Like Fausto, Enzian learned that there was no rebirth or resurrection, ". . . no difference between the behavior of a god and the operations of pure chance" (323).

Enzian is the leader of the Zone-Hereros, an uneasy alliance of those who, like Enzian, believe in the system of the Rocket and the Empty Ones, who "calculate no cycles, no returns, they are in love with the glamour of a whole people's suicide . . ."(318). There is a difference in form although both tend toward death: "It was a simple choice for the Hereros, between two kinds of death: tribal death, or Christian death. Tribal death made sense. Christian death made none at all"(318). They both opt for tribal death. The Empty Ones "can guarantee a day when the last Zone-Herero will die, a final zero to a collective history fully lived"(318). As if they will become one of the vanished species that Rathenau mentions, they intend to complete the extermination begun in 1904 and their method is a "nonrepeatable act" that "embraces all the Deviations in one single act" (319), including masturbation, abortion, sterilization, homosexuality, sadism, masochism, onanism, necrophilia, bestiality, pedophilia, lesbianism, coprophilia, urolagnia, and fetishism; it is a list of names all of which mean racial suicide. The Empty Ones' dream of the Final Zero is a total denial of life. It is the colonial policy stripped of all illusion: no transcendence, transformation, or transfiguration.

Enzian's dream is more complex. Based on the Herero traditions, missionary Christianity, and the experience of von Trotha translated into a technological world, "it began when Weissmann brought him to Europe: a discovery that love, among these men, once past the simple feel and orgasming of it, had to do with masculine technologies, with contracts, with winning and losing . . . by understanding the Rocket, he would come to understand truly his manhood . . ." (324). Imbued with Rilke's poetry, Enzian detects a chance correlation between the Herero mandala and the Rocket that seems to point toward destiny: "There may be no gods, but there is a pattern: names by themselves may have no magic, but the *act* of naming, the physical utterance, obeys the pattern"(322). Blicero's Rocket 00000 is fired to the north and built in Nordhausen; "North is death's region" (322) for the Hereros. This and Blicero's own name indicate "to Enzian yet another step to be taken toward the Rocket, toward a destiny he still cannot see past this sinister cryptography of naming, a sparse pattern but one that harshly will not be denied . . ."(322). The Rocket appears to be a force, "some immachination, whether of journey or of destiny, which is able to gather violent political opposites together in the Erdschweinhöhle as it gathers fuel and oxidizer in its thrust chamber: metered, helmsmanlike, for the sake of its scheduled parabola"(318). The Rocket promises a unity of opposites, life and death, in a mystical replication of the Herero village; the symbol is the launch switch of the Rocket and the village plan:

One of Enzian's followers explains the symbolism to Tyrone Slothrop, who has his own version of the Rocketfin Cross:

> Andreas sets it on the ground, turns it till the K points northwest.
> "Klar," touching each letter, "Entlüftung, these are the female letters.
> North letters. In our villages the women lived in huts on the northern
> half of the circle, the men on the south. The village itself was a
> mandala. Klar is fertilization and birth, Entlüftung is the breath, the
> soul. Zündung and Vorstufe are the male signs, the activities, fire and
> preparation or building. And in the center, here, Hauptstufe. It is the
> pen where we kept the sacred cattle. The souls of the ancestors. All the
> same here. Birth, soul, fire, building. Male and female, together.
> "The four fins of the Rocket made a cross, another mandala.... Each
> opposite pair of vanes worked together, and moved in opposite senses.
> Opposites together. You can see how we might feel it speak to us, even
> if we don't set one up on its fins and worship it. But it was waiting
> for us when we came north to Germany so long ago ... even confused
> and uprooted as we were then, we *knew* that our destiny was tied up
> with its own. That we had been passed over by von Trotha's army so
> that we would find the Aggregat."(563)

Enzian finds his Rocket's symbolism in the "gathered purity of opposites, the village built like a mandala" (321). Nearly universal in
form, though not necessarily in interpretation, the mandala also appears in Blicero's Rocket imagery: "The symbol used is a rude mandala, a red circle with a thick black cross inside, recognizable as the
ancient sun-wheel from which tradition says the swastika was
broken by the early Christians, to disguise their outlaw symbol"
(100). Enzian sees his people's role as that of "the scholar-magicians
of the Zone, with somewhere in it a Text, to be picked to pieces,
annotated, explicated, and masturbated till it's all squeezed limp of
its last drop ... well we assumed—natürlich!—that this holy Text

had to be the Rocket . . ."(520). Throughout *Gravity's Rainbow* the Rocket is a text whose complex imagery is explicated by everyone, with varying degrees of sophistication. That the Rocket is often a book of doom foretelling death is obvious in its physical capacity for destruction; but the Rocket contains the gathered purity of opposites, ascent as well as descent, and its powers far exceed those of steel and amatol. Viewed as a whole, the Rocket-text speaks of a life-death continuity. The text itself is mystical; words and the objects they stand for, the symbolism, are interchangeable in a way that transcends rational explanation yet holds the promise of an ultimate truth. The text's interpreters must of necessity be priests and magicians, for only their cryptography of naming can hold such contradictions intact.

Enzian cannot escape Christian corruption, and though his experience in the Südwest taught him that there is no resurrection, he cannot avoid the Christian symbols or the savages' resistance in the name of life. The Rocket is a journey or destiny that promises not rebirth or resurrection, but a return to the unity of death transfigured: "What Enzian wants to create will have no history. It will never need a design change. Time, as time is known to the other nations, will wither away inside this new one. The Erdschweinhöhle will not be bound, like the Rocket, to time. The people will find the Center again, the Center without time, the journey without hysteresis, where every departure is a return to the same place, the only place . . ."(318– 19). The similarity of the consequences of his journey with the ends of the Empty Ones permits a rapprochement: "The Eternal Center can easily be seen as the Final Zero"(319). However, he still wonders about all the connections, the chance correlation: ". . . if the Zone-Hereros are meant to live in the bosom of the Angel who tried to destroy us in Südwest . . . then: have we been passed over, or have we been chosen for something even more terrible?"(328).[5]

When the Zone-Hereros find Thanatz and he tells them about the Schwarzgerät, "how it was used, where the ooooo was fired from, and which way it was pointed"(673), Enzian prepares for the firing of 00001. Until Thanatz, he had been unable to complete the symbolism of his own flight northward; his response to the information about the passenger of 00000 is not recorded, but it is certain that he will personally choose to consummate the coupling of opposites begun in the Südwest years before. At the end of his preparations, Enzian reflects on the cooperation among the Empty Ones and his own people, "talking for the first time since the dividing along lines of racial life and racial death began . . . reconciled for now in the only Event that could have brought them together . . ."(673). The Hereros themselves represent the same unity that the Rocket's flight will seek, even if it is a temporary alliance. On the trip north, Enzian begins having long talks with Christian, one of his followers, in an effort to tell him everything he knows or has dreamed. He talks of the Rocket they are transporting: "It comes as the Revealer. Showing that no society can protect, never could. . . . They have lied to us. They can't keep us from dying, so They lie to us about death. A cooperative structure of lies. . . . Before the Rocket we went on believing, because we wanted to. But the Rocket can penetrate, from the sky, at any given point. Nowhere is safe. We can't believe Them any more. Not if we are still sane, and love the truth"(728). It is a simple message, but since "the history of the old Hereros is one of lost messages"(322) Enzian wishes to take no chances. The Rocket reveals the world of probabilities and uncertainties that missionaries had cloaked with images of resurrection and the will of God, that colonialists had masked with their policies of death, and that Blicero had sought to dominate—all of which are methods of control unveiled by the Rocket's "life of its own" and its accidental similarity to the Herero mandala. Enzian's Rocket will be a denial of the structures of control and, consequently, a threat to routinized death.

Enzian's sudden discovery of control is a revelation that gives his Rocket its political as well as symbolic function and helps explain the "They" pronoun reference in his advice to Christian. Riding through the bombed ruins of a refinery (named after Laszlo Jamf) he realizes that it is not ruined, but "modified, precisely, *deliberately* by bombing that was never hostile, but part of a plan both sides—'*sides?*'—had always agreed on ..."(520). Part of the "exact industrial process of conversion"(520), the modified refinery shows Enzian the truth about death revealed by Walter Rathenau and contained in Kekulé's serpent:

It means this War was never political at all, the politics was all theatre, all just to keep the people distracted ... secretly, it was being dictated instead by the needs of technology ... by a conspiracy between human beings and techniques, by something that needed the energy-burst of war, crying, "Money be damned, the very life of [insert name of Nation] is at stake," but meaning, most likely, *dawn is nearly here, I need my night's blood, my funding, funding, ahh more, more.* ... The real crises were crises of allocation and priority, not among firms—it was only staged to look that way—but among the different Technologies, Plastics, Electronics, Aircraft, and their needs which are understood only by the ruling elite.... (521)

Enzian, however, sees that technology is not all that is involved: "Go ahead, capitalize the T on technology, deify it if it'll make you feel less responsible—but it puts you in with the neutered, brother, in with the eunuchs keeping the harem òf our stolen Earth for the numb and joyless hardons of human sultans, human elite with no right at all to be where they are—"(521). Enzian uses words almost identical to Rathenau's announcement that the "industrial process," which at first passed over the coal-tars of "Earth's excrement," is actually a "sign of revealing," "of unfolding" in its "impersonation of life" and deliberate resurrection(166). Enzian independently begins to zero in on the same underlying truth: "Up here, on the surface, coal-tars, hydrogenation, synthesis were always phony, dummy functions to hide the real, *the planetary mission* yes perhaps centuries in the unrolling ..."(521). The polymerization of molecules is not resurrection and the impersonations produced by the meta-cartels of technology are not life, but the illusion of control. Enzian imagines clustered pygmies who "breed in the tanks at the interface between fuel and water-bottom" on the other side of "the whole bacteria-hydrocarbon-waste cycle"(523). His reference to pygmies is ironic since it evokes an image of Wagner's Nibelungs, an image that also applies to the Schwarzkommando, who, in their struggle to assemble their Rocket from debris and waste, unavoidably promise ruination to the very structure that stole life from them in the Südwest and uses them in Europe. Tempted by an even greater mission than assembling Rocket 00001, Enzian thinks that "somewhere, among the wastes of the World, is the key that will bring us back, restore us to our Earth and to our freedom"(525). The restoration may be in Rilkean transformation, the continuity of life and death, which lies outside the corporate structure of lies, but it also lies in the force of gravity that awaits Rocket 00001.

Though not in the service of the Rocket, Enzian's half-brother shares something of the same mission, the same sense that all movement is toward death transfigured. Tchitcherine has "German dreams of the Tenth-Elegy angel coming" (341) and his search for Enzian is the only constant in his life. His fate is inextricably tied to Enzian's. In 1904 their father's ship had sailed into Lüderitzbucht in the Südwest. After two days of hauling coal on board, he could take no more of his own thoughts: ". . . the slowly carbonizing faces of men he thought he knew, men turning to coal, ancient coal that glistened . . . a conspiracy of carbon, though he never phrased it as 'carbon,' it was power he walked away from, the feeling of too much meaningless power, flowing wrong . . . he could smell Death in it"(351). He found life in a Herero girl and produced a son he never saw. This same blackness preoccupies Tchitcherine. He wants to destroy the black ghost that haunts his career and has come, increasingly, to define his identity. The Russians find his mission useful though they do not know why, but Tchitcherine knows that his usefulness is "a death sentence"(611).

Under the shadow of his half-brother, Tchitcherine is given assignments that always put him at the edge of dying for the Marxist dialectic. He tries to understand why he is supposed to die, why he is passed over, not realizing that he shares Enzian's preterite origins and a destiny that calls for a return to the earth. (While Enzian is directly related to the earth through the Erdschweinhöhle totem and being passed over by von Trotha, Tchitcherine is related to what Rathenau call "preterite dung" [166] through the molecular synthesis of coal-tars and the production of the drug Oneirine.) He is held always at the edge of revelations until he finally sees that a new state is being formed from the debris of the German dream "... and the Rocket is its soul"(566). Tchitcherine will never cross the border of the new state but he can recognize it in the shape of Oneirine, one of the state's by-products. Wimpe the drug salesman had explained it all to him before:

"The basic problem," he proposes, "has always been getting other people to die for you. What's worth enough for a man to give up his life? That's where religion had the edge, for centuries. Religion was always about death. It was used not as an opiate so much as a technique—it got people to die for one particular set of beliefs about death. Perverse, natürlich, but who are you to judge? It was a good pitch while it worked. But ever since it became impossible to die for death, we have had a secular version—yours. Die to help History grow to its predestined shape. Die knowing your act will bring a good end a bit closer. Revolutionary suicide, fine. But look: if History's changes are inevitable, why not not die? Vaslav? If it's going to happen anyway, what does it matter?"(701)

Oneirine shows Tchitcherine that religion, Marxism, and history are techniques—precisely the same technologies that Enzian saw in a more recognizable form. The result of many years of Oneirine use is a haunting, which in Tchitcherine's case is a confirmation of his fear that the Marxist Theory of History has been a lie; he foresees that he will be sent back to Central Asia, which "in *his* dialectic, his own life's unfolding, ... is, operationally, to die"(706). If there is no resurrection and if history is a lie, the only alternative is death transfigured, the very process that makes Oneirine from earth's excrement. Tchitcherine is presumably saved from revolutionary suicide and his dialectical victimization by the same sort of magic that Enzian finds in the promise of his Rocket's return to the center, to the earth.

His salvation comes from Geli Tripping, a witch and "the only one in the Zone who loves him completely"(719). Tchitcherine has been pursuing the Rocket on his government's behalf without any belief in it other than the hope it will lead him to Enzian. In the absence of his own beliefs, Geli brings him back to the earth's center, whose very processes of transformation her magic reveals:

> This is the World just before men. Too violently pitched alive in constant flow ever to be seen by men directly. They are meant only to look at it dead, in still strata, transputrefied to oil or coal. Alive, it was a threat: it was Titans, was an overpeaking of life so clangorous and mad, such a green corona about Earth's body that some spoiler *had* to be brought in before it blew the Creation apart. So we, the crippled keepers, were sent out to multiply, to have dominion. God's spoilers. Us. Counter-revolutionaries. *It is our mission to promote death.* The way we kill, the way we die, being unique among the Creatures. It was something we had to work on, historically and personally. To build from scratch up to its present status as reaction, nearly as strong as life, holding down the green uprising. But only nearly as strong.
>
> Only nearly, because of the defection rate. A few keep going over to the Titans every day, in their striving subcreation (how can flesh tumble and flow so, and never be any less beautiful?), into the rests of the folk-song Death (empty stone rooms), out, and through, and down under the net, down down to the uprising. (720)

She recites a charm in the name of the angels of the Kabbala, including Metatron, the recording angel, which preserves Tchitcherine until she finds him beside a stream. He finally meets Enzian in the middle of a bridge over the stream; they talk for a moment and pass without recognizing each other or caring. Tchitcherine no longer needs to die for history, Them, or his mission. Geli has shown him Earth's mind-body.

Geli has a counterpart in Katje Borgesius, a more secular witch who tries, too late, to save Slothrop. She is not an opposite or even a parallel to Geli, but she is a double agent on both sides of the war and both sides of the life-death question. A veteran of Blicero's Kinderofen love-games, of sending Jewish families to their death, of calling in RAF bomber strikes, she knows "that inside herself, en-closed in the *soignée* surface of dear fabric and dead cells, she is corruption and ashes . . ."(94). She is also one who knows the meta-solution. After recalling that life is all a game, she is the player who will say "*fuck it* and quit the game, quit it cold . . ."(107). There is something, too, of her Dutch ancestor, Frans Van der Groov, in her. He spent his life helping to complete the extermination of Dodoes on Mauritius, birds that he saw as the embodiment of an argument against a Godly creation: "Was Mauritius some first poison trickle through the sheltering dikes of Earth? Christians must stem it here, or perish in a second Flood, loosed this time not by God but by the Enemy"(110). Overcome by the slaughter, Frans wonders if a con-version of the Dodoes might not be possible—a redemption—but there is none. The Dodoes only die and the colonialist structure of death goes on. From Frans Katje inherits her knowledge of man's mission to promote death.

Unwilling to remain indebted to the British for helping her leave Blicero's game, she agrees to help Pointsman with his Slothrop project. Amid the conspiracy he detects around him, Slothrop thinks that Katje may be "as much a victim as he is—an unlucky, an unac-countably *futureless* look . . ."(208). Along with her other tasks in preparing Slothrop for his unwitting mission, she tells him about the life and death of the Rocket, something she knows and was not programmed to say: "Katje has understood the great airless arc as a clear allusion to certain secret lusts that drive the planet and herself, and Those who use her—over its peak and down, plunging, burning, toward a terminal orgasm . . ."(223). After Slothrop leaves, Katje returns to the White Visitation—a name that takes on special signifi-cance for her—to perform still another service for Those who use her, in a terminal orgasm of sorts. To retain funding for his project, Pointsman has Katje enact a fantasy of Brigadier Pudding's guilt for having lost seventy percent of his troops during the previous war. The general is summoned by the voice of Metatron through a series of rooms like the antechambers of the Throne in Isaac's vision at the moment of sacrifice. She waits in the last chamber: "Domina Nocturna ... shining mother and last love ..."(232), whom Pudding must entertain with stories of death, "myth, and personal terror ..." (234). It is a scene inspired by Sacher-Masoch, an enactment of love-in-death that takes the form of coprophilia. But to Katje it is only another game, a reversal of roles. Weissmann had said "her masochism ... is reassurance for her. That she can still be hurt, that she is human and can cry at pain"(662). She finds no life in the games. After discovering a film in which she plays herself, she leaves Pointsman's game, as she had Blicero's, opting for the meta-solution. She finds the only possible alternative: "Dialectically, sooner or later, some counterforce would have had to arise ..."(536).

Katje the controlled actress has her counterpart in Margherita Erdmann the movie actress and another presence of death, like her name —"Earth, Soil, Folk ... a code"(395). She also plays a role as the mistress of the night, but it is not a game for her. Obsessed with the horrible fantasy of being Jewish in the days before the Polish invasion, she sacrifices Jewish children in a black mud pool, proclaiming "I wander all the Diaspora looking for strayed children. I am Israel. I am the Shekhinah, queen, daughter, bride, and mother of God. And I will take you back, you fragment of smashed vessel, even if I must pull you by your nasty little circumcised penis—"(478). She plays another role for Pökler and the Germans who watch her pornographic movies. To Slothrop's impotent Tannhäuser she plays Lisaura—not an Elizabeth, but someone else, perhaps another singer like Lissauer, whose "Hymn of Hate" casts her in a more appropriate role. All the men who loved her from their side of the film had "gone to war or death, and she is left nothing but God's indifferent sunlight in all its bleaching and terror"(364). The refrain of the popular Great War poem—that God punish England—may give her lines for her role with Slothrop, who poses as an English correspondent. She also plays Katje for Blicero just before he launches Rocket 00000 and wears a costume made of the same Imipolex G that is Gottfried's shroud. She may even play the role of an unrepentant Gretchen who kills her own daughter, or she may simply reenact Blicero's sacrifice, for she had seen her daughter Bianca in Gottfried. In all her roles, Margherita takes her own life and continuing existence from the death she inflicts on others or from the presence of death. She can have no life outside of the structure of death: " 'Greta Erdmann' is only one, these dames whose job it is always to cringe from the Terror ..."(689).

Her husband, however, has become the "leading theoretician" of sadism and masochism in the Zone:

> "Why will the Structure allow every other kind of sexual behavior but *that* one? Because submission and dominance are resources it needs for its very survival. They cannot be wasted in private sex. In *any* kind of sex. It needs our submission so that it may remain in power. It needs our lusts after dominance so that it can co-opt us into its own power game. There is no joy in it, only power. I tell you, if S and M could be established universally, at the family level, the State would wither away."(737)

He has learned his ideology from Blicero; he watched the launching of Gottfried and saw Bianca in him too. But he could not see past the form of Blicero's ceremony, lacking the conviction of the mysteries. Like Margherita, Thanatz is "just a loser at-the-game, of love ..." (671). With Margherita, he shares "a world below the surface of Earth or mud—it crawls like mud, but cries like Earth, with layer-pressed generations of gravities and losses thereto—losses, failures, last moments followed by voids stringing back, a series of hermetic caves caught in the suffocated layers, those forever lost ... from someone, who'll ever know who? a flash of Bianca in a thin cotton shift ... the lashes now whose lifting you pray for ... will she see you?"(672). Theirs is a love of death, but it remains unconsummated; life is incidental.

Pynchon creates a structure of death transfigured in *Gravity's Rainbow* so complex and abstract that more than the 760 pages of his novel would be required to unravel, explicate, and analyze it, and the result would be only another version of "Europe's Original Sin—the latest name for that is Modern Analysis"(722). The word "death" and its cognates appear hundreds of times in *Gravity's Rainbow;* as one of the word-counters of the novel, Milton Gloaming, says, the situation is "the same as it's always been at these affairs . . . 'death' " (32) is the term most frequently used. The notion of death transfigured articulated by Walter Rathenau is a statement of fact or observation rather than belief, one repeatedly confirmed by others. From his perspective among the dead, he has seen that the Earth's own process is a one-way continuity of life becoming death, one form giving way to the other even as the Earth itself runs down—but not at all the horrible specter that the living seem to think it, as Lyle Bland and Geli Tripping reveal in their visions. Various characters, particularly Blicero and Enzian, act on their respective beliefs about death's transfiguration, but Pynchon does not imply a philosophy. Rather, he creates the evidence of Earth's process at work in the lives of people. Most of the characters show signs of the conflict between their coming to terms, personally and individually, with the process, and their sense that their lives and deaths are being manipulated by an elite that has violated the process and takes life to feed its own needs for energy, power, and consumption. The source of anxiety, even desperation, for Pynchon's characters lies in the fact that they are human: "the one species cursed with the knowledge it will die . . ."(230). Death is a fact that humans must acknowledge, with which they must come to terms. It is this fact that corrupts life, infects it. Webly Silvernail, a Pointsman subaltern with a mystic's vision, explains the corruption to the animals in the psychologist's laboratory, animals that, like most people, are subjected to "rationalized forms of death"(230) for the benefit of the few:

> "I would set you free, if I knew how. But it isn't free out here. All the animals, the plants, the minerals, even other kinds of men, are being broken and reassembled every day, to preserve an elite few, who are the loudest to theorize on freedom, but the least free of all. I can't even give you hope that it will be different someday—that They'll come out, and forget death, and lose Their technology's elaborate terror, and stop

using every other form of life without mercy to keep what haunts men down to a tolerable level—and be like you instead, simply here, simply alive. . . ."(230)

Pynchon's structure of death is continuous throughout his stories and novels, which is not to accuse him of mere repetitions and rephrasings. Rather, the structure has grown more complex and sophisticated as Pynchon's art matures. Similarities occur among characters like Siegel, Flange, Stencil, Profane, Oedipa, and Slothrop or others like V., Inverarity, and Blicero. They are not, however, the same pasteboard embodiments of theory tiresomely recycled through new situations. Pynchon's art is too accomplished to permit such resignation. The artist's creation of the images of death—a knowledge—depends on his personal accommodation of experience. Freud described the artist's role as making the unconscious conscious, liberating the instincts. Rilke called it a wise blindness, letting one's self go. Pynchon's vision has enlarged and his art has changed. The structure of death in his fiction has evolved from a representation of probabilities to a reflection of his own uncertainties. As historians increasingly abandon history for other comforts, it may well be that Pynchon's images will someday be our best representation of an age, but for now they are mysteries to be probed. For some they may be vehicles for return, a way of seeing past the entanglements of our own impending deaths, the uses we make of our fellow humans, our world.

CARING

The structure of death tends to pervert love to its own form—homosexuality, fetishism, narcissism. The narrator of *Gravity's Rainbow* explains that it was not always this way: "In the trenches of the First World War, English men came to love one another decently, without shame or make-believe, under the easy likelihoods of their sudden deaths. . . . But the life-cry of that love has long since hissed away into no more than this idle and bitchy faggotry. In this latest War, death was no enemy, but a collaborator. Homosexuality in high places is just a carnal afterthought now, and the real and only fucking is done on paper . . ."(616). Through love, life seeks an accommodation of death. It may be an ennobling transformation as found in Rilke's poetry or an act of desperation as in Thanatz's sadomasochism. Both possibilities, however, are intellectualized—perhaps routinized—systems of thought and both can serve as retreats from humanity into process. Bureaucracies are the real mistresses of the night: "a million bureaucrats are diligently plotting death and some of them even know it, many about now are already into the second or third pint or highball glass, which produces a certain desperate aura here"(17). However, when systems are disturbed by war, drugs, or sudden revelation, a humanity—something personal—may emerge to gnaw at the paper barriers, to claim a brief life of its own while no one is watching. Though overshadowed by the machination of systems, a human tenderness persists throughout Pynchon's stories and novels: irrational love amid death, a caring.

Its occurrences are relatively scarce and often fragmentary. In Pynchon's stories, Nerissa, Aubade, and the children of Mingeborough show evidence of caring. Pynchon himself openly cares in his essay on Watts. In the novels there are others: Porpentine, whose humanity betrays a weakness in him; Fausto, who recognizes "the need to care"(304); possiblly Fina Mendoza, who seems to care about Profane but who incites a gang rape (appropriately, her guardian is Sister Maria Annunziato); Rachel Owlglass, whom, despite her mother's instinctive need for dependents, others can recognize as "a good woman, member of a vanishing race"(40); Benny Profane, who cares about Paola in spite of himself; Oedipa Maas, who can mother an old sailor and care about Driblette; Geli Tripping, who saves Tchitcherine with her love; Slothrop, who cares about Tantivy Mucker-Maffick and, on occasion, Katje; Ludwig, who loves his lemming despite knowing what will happen to her, "thinking that love can stop it from happening"(556); and even Pig Bodine, who in *Gravity's Rainbow* is finally overcome by a "transvestism of caring"(742) for the first time in his life. There are others who care quietly, secretly, afraid that admission might deprive them of feeling.

In *V.*, Paola Maijstral and McClintic Sphere not only affirm caring, but come close to finding an alternative to the system that would deprive them of their humanity. They have both known colonialism and the forces unleashed by V. Although McClintic is the one who gives words to their feelings, Paola is the principal actor despite her silence. Her origins on Malta gave her a unique beginning. She is Maltese, "pure and a motley of races at once"(290), which may account for the way in which she continually shifts roles and yet remains somehow the same, "one girl: a single given heart, a whole mind at peace"(294), as her father prays for her. Fausto says she had "only one father, the war; one mother, Malta her women"(304). He also takes note of her birth during the siege, good assailed by bad; in a sense, a war continues all about her, preserving the validity of childhood metaphors. In Fausto's view the most important fact of her upbringing was that he and his wife left her to the care of other children and the very old, forces that may have neutralized each other and permitted her to create her own discrete world. He describes her and the other children as recording angels and "poets in a vacuum, adept at metaphor"(318). In short, the conditions were perfect for Paola's escaping the education to death promoted by the Church, the State, and others and permitting the childhood experience to pass for her model of reality. But there is another ironic side of Paola that her father may not recognize.

Fausto thought that the name his wife gave to Paola—"for happy" (300)—was ironic because her soul would become "torn and unhappy" (300). Perhaps he does not realize the real irony of her name: she is to be blown by the winds of passion. Appropriately, "Maijstral" is the name for a seasonal Maltese wind, and her given name is a play on a wind-blown masculine counterpart, Paolo Malatesta, whose history with Francesca da Rimini is still one more variation on the Tristan-and-Iseult theme. While the association is loose, there is ample evidence that Pynchon intends Paola to represent a humanized reconciliation of dualities. Paolo and Francesca were celebrated by Gabriele D'Annunzio in a drama dedicated to and enacted by Eleonora Duse, with whom V. identifies during the siege at Foppl's villa. The implications are reinforced by the apparent fact that Paola inherits both the innocence of Victoria and the knowledge of V. In a direct reference to the Victoria Wren of Alexandria, Paola is called "the most buoyant balloon-girl in the stretch of sewer we occupied that season"(310); she plays a war game as an Italian dirigible that always outwits its RAF enemy. More importantly, Paola becomes the custodian of Victoria and V.'s ivory comb, which was removed during the disassembly of the Bad Priest.

Circumstances have combined to permit Paola instinctive knowledge of death with its corruption, life with its impersonation. Although it may be a defect, her ability to avoid the extremes of involvement and to see the continuity of life and death, good and evil, place her in a special category. She can be a prostitute and a good wife without a contradiction. As a barmaid, she is named Beatrice—like all the other barmaids—but if Paola's namesake Paolo was condemned to the second, carnal circle of Dante's Inferno, then the revelatory Beatrice, and guide through Paradise, represents her other side. She stimulates Roony Winsome to lust and Bodine to attempted rape; she frightens Stencil; and she inspires Profane to become her guardian. She holds dualities in dynamic tension, inflaming and inspiring, but above all else she is an enigma.

It is Paola's relationship with the black jazz musician McClintic Sphere that speaks. She leaves the decadence of the Whole Sick Crew for Harlem, a "rooming (and in a sense cat) house"(262), the name of Ruby, and a new identity as a prostitute. McClintic is a man also haunted by dualities—by racial lines, by people who do not understand his music or who choose to misunderstand it, by the matter of having or losing Paola. Foreshadowing Oedipa Maas and Roger Mexico, he has found a metaphor for the duality in an electrical circuit called a flip-flop, which could be either one of two ways when turned on: "And that . . . can be yes or no, or one or zero. And that is what you might call one of the basic units, or specialized 'cells' in a big 'electronic brain' "(273). McClintic rephrases the metaphor in social terms for Paola: "Ruby, what happened after the war? That war, the world flipped. But come '45, and they flopped. Here in Harlem they flopped. Everything got cool—no love, no hate, no worries, no excitement. Every once in awhile, though, somebody flips back. Back to where he can love. . . ." After a moment he adds, "But you take a whole bunch of people flip at the same time and you've got a war. Now war is not loving, is it?"(273). McClintic understands the duality very clearly. What he does not yet know is that the only alternative to a world that is either flip or flop is personal and between the circuit's system: Paola, for example.

The closest Paola ever comes to an utterance that reveals her function is when she tells McClintic that "a whore isn't human" and that a "whore lives in one place and stays there. Like some little virgin girl in a fairy tale. She doesn't do any traveling, unless she works the streets"(271). A whore is not human but neither is a fairy-tale virgin. The alternatives are "either the street or all cooped up"(271), which are still the hothouse and the street that Sidney Stencil believed had been reconciled in V. As V.'s heiress, Paola will learn to reconcile the whore and virgin in herself, but she does not make the reconciliation into a system. It is merely a personal means of survival. Later she tells him who she is and about Malta and her father. She tells him she will have to return to Malta, "a cradle of life"(358) as she calls it. Hers may be a symbolic return to childhood origins, but it is at least a necessary stage in her own development. Before leaving, however, Paola must herself learn one more bit of magic.

By nothing more than her presence, which confronts McClintic with the "matter of having her or losing her"(280), she brings him to the point of seeing "that the only way clear of the cool/crazy flipflop was obviously slow, frustrating and hard work. Love with your mouth shut, help without breaking your ass or publicizing it:

keep cool, but care"(342–43). He sees that there is no system that can do it: "Not even I love you is magic enough"(343), he tells Paola. She remains an enigma, however, and her silence only implies that she has learned something from McClintic. When she returns to Malta, she also returns to her husband. Their reconciliation is brief and formal. Assuming still one more role, she promises to wait for him in Norfolk, a faithful Penelope spinning a yarn for his return. When he says "I love you"(417) she gives him her ivory comb as stronger magic than the redundant words—a promise. They part without touching or kissing, cool but caring.

Oedipa Maas is the next of Pynchon's major characters to occupy the zone between one and zero, between the symmetries of routinized life and death. Though she does appear to care for other people, Oedipa is alone. All her men have been removed from her by the systems. Absence is proof of her ability to care. In keeping with her female Oedipal role, all the normal forms of love she encounters are either fraudulent, perverted, or both. When she concludes her conversation with the anonymous inamorato in The Greek Way, Oedipa is overcome by the despair of her own ironically parallel isolation— ". . . when nobody around has any sexual relevance to you" (86). She is primal in her mother-love for her childlike husband, Baby Igor, the old sailor she cradles as a child, even Driblette. But it is the void that concentrates Oedipa's love, her caring for a humanity that has grown past knowing itself. At the novel's beginning she recalls the tears she shed—"she could carry the sadness of the moment with her that way forever"(10)—after seeing a painting of frail girls trying to fill the earth's void with a tapestry. Grace Bortz later interprets her harassed style as something caused only by kids. At the novel's end when she confronts the void as her own with nobody to help her, she imagines she is pregnant. Though she has no correspondent, Oedipa cares in the same way Paola does in her eternal and lonely waiting or Roger Mexico will in Jessica's absence. In retrospect, she prefigures the earth's repressed mindbody Geli Tripping describes—a mass that hugs dead species to some still vital center—while she waits, as at

Driblette's grave, for some "winged shape, needing to settle at once in the warm host, or dissipate forever into the dark"(121).

It is not until *Gravity's Rainbow* that Pynchon explores fully other personal situations of caring. One of these involves the failed love of the Pöklers—Franz, Leni, and Ilse. Franz is lured by the singular beauty of the Rocket: "These were the kinds of revenants that found Franz, not persons but forms of energy, abstractions . . ."(161). Too late the absence of Leni and the uncertainty of his own daughter will show him his loss—a void he attempts to fill after the war. Leni, however, has always cared. When confronted with the possibility that love is another form of capitalist control—"Pornographies: pornographies of love, erotic love, Christian love, boy-and-his-dog, pornographies of sunsets, pornographies of killing, and pornographies of deduction . . . they're approaches, more comfortable and less so, to that Absolute Comfort"(155)—she responds, "I know there's coming together"(155). Franz turns away from Leni's offers of love, leaving her isolated with her dreams of tenderness, her masturbation, and her caring for Ilse. She had tried to explain her feelings to Franz, her love that had grown to embrace the promise of revolution, but he had "this way of removing all the excitement from things with a few words. Not even well-chosen words: he's that way by instinct" (159). Her own intuitive sense of what love could accomplish were it not for the pornographies of power is one of the clearest expressions in *Gravity's Rainbow*: " 'It all goes along together. Parallel, not series. Metaphor. Signs and symptoms. Mapping on to different coordinate systems, I don't know . . .' She didn't know, all she was trying to do was reach"(159).

Leni's sense of the way love can fuse love and death into a meaningful continuity is precisely the same as Paola and Sphere's, or Oedipa Maas's, or Roger Mexico's. More importantly, Leni is the natural, instinctive counterpart to the intellectualized and systematized fusion that V., Inverarity, and Blicero seek so desperately. Leni and Blicero, for example, share exactly the same dream: "Leni saw a dream of flight. One of many possible. Real flight and dreams of flight go together. Both are part of the same movement. Not A before B, but all together . . ."(159). The only thing that distinguishes Leni and her caring from Blicero and his love is the absence of control. Leni does not wish to control the fusion, but simply to merge. In one of the most impressive metaphors of *Gravity's Rainbow* she defines with aesthetic precision the phenomenon that is consuming Franz: "It moves slowly, so slowly and so far away . . . but it will burst out. It is the grim phoenix which creates its own holocaust . . . *deliberate resurrection.* Staged. Under control. No grace, no interventions by God"(415). Their forms are identical, but caring and the pornography of love are exactly the opposite of each other. Like the living and the dead, however, they are often confused. Leni loses Franz to the grim phoenix but her caring sustains her during her passage through the novel.

Leni's caring in part structures the novel and by its clarity defines the difference between caring and the illusions of love. Leni has a male counterpart in the statistician Roger Mexico, who loses his chance for union with Jessica Swanlake to the grim phoenix as well. As already noted, Mexico belongs to "the domain *between* zero and one," which denies him the illusory comforts of absolutes and certainties. Jessica's humanity is temporary, made possible by the war, while Roger's caring is constant and the disruptions of the war give him respite from his loneliness. It is a time in between past and future: "If they have not quite seceded from war's state, at least they've found the beginnings of gentle withdrawal . . . [from] abstraction, required pain, bitter death"(41). Roger looks upon the war from the viewpoint of a statistician whose only belief is in probabilities, looking with an "angel's-eye view"(54) at the distribution of death he knows goes on whether there is a war or not. He holds an attraction for Jessica during the war because death, delivered by the rockets, is random and uncertain and he is the minister of probabilities. Under these circumstances, she is willing to use him though she knows her future is with the familiar, safe bureaucrat Jeremy.

Roger and Jessica temporarily "merged into a joint creature un-aware of itself"(38) that exists with a life of its own. Roger, of course, is a man divided by his knowledge of death and his desire to escape it. Love, he thinks, may be a way of holding off the dark probabilities: "Jessica was all that made it human or tolerable"(125). With her, he can even imagine a reprieve: "he was seeing the honest half of his life that Jessica was now, how fanatically his mother the War must disapprove of her beauty, her cheeky indifference to death-institutions he'd not so long ago believed in . . ."(126). Their alliance is magical: "They confuse everyone. They look so innocent. People immediately want to protect them: censoring themselves away from talk of death, business, duplicity when Roger and Jessica are there" (121). For Roger, it is nothing less than a miracle:

> His life had been tied to the past. He'd seen himself a point on a moving wavefront, propagating through sterile history—a known past, a projectable future. But Jessica was the breaking of the wave. Suddenly there was a beach, the unpredictable . . . new life. Past and future stopped at the beach: that was how he'd set it out. But he wanted to believe it too, the same way he loved her, past all words— believe that no matter how bad the time, nothing was fixed, everything could be changed and she could always deny the dark sea at his back, love it away. And (selfishly) that from a somber youth, squarely founded on Death—along for Death's ride—he might, with her, find his way to life and to joy. He'd never told her, he avoided telling himself, but that was the measure of his faith. . . . (126)

Roger confuses Jessica. When she is with him she is in the presence of a love she cannot understand. He seems to hate everything that is normal for her: "he hates England so, hates 'the System,' gripes endlessly, says he'll emigrate when the War's over . . ."(126). Jessica thinks it will be "safer with Jeremy"(126) after the war, when things are back to normal. Jessica is only a receiver of Roger's love. Though she warms him, makes him think of life, she is passive. It is he alone that is in the void between his cold statistician's knowledge of death and the routinized death of the System. Roger thinks that Jeremy *is* the System and all its assertions:

> —that we are meant for work and government, for austerity: and these shall take priority over love, dreams, the spirit, the senses and the other second-class trivia that are found among the idle and mindless hours of the day. . . . Damn them, they are wrong. They are insane. Jeremy will take her like the Angel itself, in his joyless weasel-worded come-along, and Roger will be forgotten, an amusing maniac, but with no place in the rationalized power-ritual that will be the coming peace. She will take her husband's orders, she will become a domestic bureaucrat, a junior partner, and remember Roger, if at all, as a mistake thank God she didn't make. . . . (177)

He begins to see what will happen when the war is over; " 'The War' was the condition she needed for being with Roger. 'Peace' allows her to leave him"(628). It will go on in people like Jeremy, who will standardize and perpetuate the war and it will go on in Jessica— "You're catching the War," Mexico thinks. "It's infecting you and I don't know how to keep it away"(177).

Peace comes and Jessica, believing in Jeremy, his illusions, and his comforts, returns. Roger's usefulness is over, his resources too meager to hold her when death is no longer random: "The paranoia, the danger, the tuneless whistling of busy Death next door, are all put to sleep, back in the War, back with her Roger Mexico Years. The day the rockets stopped falling, it began to end for Roger and Jessica. As it grew clear, day after safe day, that no more would fall ever again, the new world crept into and over her like spring . . ."(628). Roger knows that "there's *something* still on, don't call it a 'war' if it makes you nervous, . . . but Their enterprise goes on"(628). In this enterprise, the rockets will continue to go up, without the killing (at least temporarily), and Jeremy and his Jessica will be pushing the button. Jessica belongs to the new world, Roger to his private vision of a war that goes on. In her absence, Roger's ability to care will isolate him: "He is losing more than single Jessica: he's losing a full range of life, of being for the first time at ease in the Creation"(629). Without a person for him to care about, Roger will care for a ghost—Slothrop —and dedicate himself to searching for the only person he knows who may have come to terms with gravity and the war that continues, "a culture of death"(176).

Pynchon insists that the capacity to care is a fragile and rare emotion amid so many easy feelings mass produced and manipulated by the system that passes for life. The isolation of Mexico may be the most poignant moment in all Pynchon's fiction. It is a loneliness that hurts because it touches nerves of memory, childhood dreams of what life was supposed to be like. By comparison, other moments of passion appear fabricated, taken from movie-screen images. By means of his rarity, Roger Mexico may be a secular Rathenau pointing out that if there is no resurrection—only death transfigured— then individual acts of caring may be the best we can hope for. Though it is a potential for everyone, it is also seldom realized, a fantasy to be cherished. At Christmas Roger and Jessica visit a church and Roger thinks about resurrection. In a vision that parallels Rathenau's and Leni Pökler's, he sees huge piles of children's toothpaste tubes being melted, transformed, into the goods of war in a deliberate rather than divine or natural resurrection. It is the same continuity of life and death, the movement toward death transfigured, that echoes Rathenau throughout the novel. Regardless of the ceremony of the church, he knows that any redeemer will not survive, that the "true king only dies a mock death"(131), and that the real king is death with the rocket as his Christmas star: ". . . what kind of a world is it . . . for a baby to come in tippin' those Toledos at 7 pounds 8 ounces thinkin' he's gonna redeem it, why, he oughta have his head examined . . ."(135). In spite of his statistician's faith in probabilities, Roger can think to himself, "you wish you'd picked him up, held him a bit. Just held him, very close to your heart, his cheek by the hollow of your shoulder, full of sleep. As if it were you who could, somehow, save him"(135–36). But there is no resurrection, "no counterfeit baby, no announcement of the Kingdom, not even a try at warming or lighting this terrible night, only, damn us, our scruffy obligatory little cry, our maximum reach outward . . ."(136). What little possibility there is for humanity, for caring, is invested in the likes of Leni Pökler and Roger Mexico and in "the path you must create by yourself, alone in the dark. Whether you want it or not, whatever seas you have crossed, the way home . . ."(136).

4 In Which Various Things Come Together

The theory claims the role of a great scientific theory.
Its synthetic power allows us to apprehend many dis-
parate facts. In its development, it rediscovers some
banal facts as landmarks; others, unexpected (for
example, the uncertainty principles), justify it as a
method of presentation.

Abraham Moles in
Information Theory and Esthetic Perception

PARANOIA

If criticism offers any theory of Pynchon's fiction, its synthetic power
may be only a socially acceptable form of paranoia, in which the critic
voluntarily becomes the center of an elaborate plot hatched by some
remote author. An exhausting array of facts seduces admirer and
skeptic alike into the comfortable fantasy of their own ordered labyrinths, coaxing them with numbing certainty and indifferent guile.
By remaining personally and aesthetically remote Pynchon feeds a
contemporary mania for the very idea of paranoia. In a world that has
seen this particular psychosis become a principle of international
politics in such forms as the cold war, of international economics in
giant oil, chemical, and communications cartels, or of religions in the
hundred or so holy wars that have occurred in the past three decades,
the question of who is paranoid and who is not is vital and relevant,
and perhaps always has been. Pynchon forces his readers—and most

acutely, his critics—to resolve this question before reaching any conclusion and thus forces them to demystify or naturalize his texts.
Assuming that the preceding chapters have established the plausibil-
ity of structure, the reader is put in precisely the same situation as
Oedipa Maas: either there is a coherent structure to Pynchon's fiction
or the reader imagines it; or Pynchon has deliberately launched a plot
aimed at the reader to make him or her sense a structure; or the reader
fantasizes such a plot. A meta-solution is possible, but it requires
ignoring the evidence of the novels.

The critical concern about structure is real since it is, finally, the
center of Pynchon's fiction—the minotaur of his particular labyrinth.
Although originally one of the Hippocratic categories of mental illness referring to deterioration, paranoia was given its modern conno-
tation primarily by Emil Kraepelin at the end of the last century. It
now generally refers to a form of psychosis based on a logical structure of relationships that interprets reality in terms of evidence of
persecution. The paranoid believes that someone or some group is out
to get him and sustains this belief with evidence that to his mind is
irrefutable. Two characteristics of paranoia are particularly noteworthy: it is a psychosis of interpretation and it depends on a careful
ordering of unconnected evidence to prove the existence of persecution. Paranoia is a highly rigorous, integrative, self-preserving mode
of behavior amid assumed or real cultural chaos. It is often mistaken
for normalcy and not infrequently is a formula for political and
economic success precisely because its methods are those most highly
regarded by the sane portion of humanity. When put in terms of
control or power, paranoia's imaginary premises of persecution are
indistinguishable from facts and certainly have to be considered
within the realm of reality. Pynchon was prophetic, but not the least
bit ironic, in beginning the fourth section of *Gravity's Rainbow,* "The
Counterforce," with a quotation from Richard M. Nixon: "What?"
(617). Thus paranoia retains its usefulness as a clinical classification,
but its application goes far beyond any psychological condition.
Paranoia, in one sense, is no more of a disorder than guilt and the

term, at least, is used with an easy familiarity that raises hardly anyone's eyebrows.

Paranoia serves Pynchon well as a model, or extended metaphor, for a number of reasons, not the least of which is its decontaminated, socially acceptable use as description of real, imagined, and unconfirmed conspiracies. Its logical structure—the process of relating evidence—implies a structure for his own fiction, not unlike a great scientific theory. Although the clinical paranoid would organize uncertainties out of existence, Pynchon bases his use of the paranoia metaphor precisely on uncertainties, because both ambiguity and the more specific implications of uncertainty relations nourish paranoia and make any psychosis difficult to establish clinically. The question of whether a conspiracy is real or not remains an open one, a matter of interpretation. Paranoia also offers the advantage of allowing him to work with a dialectic of good and evil, the persecuted victim and the enemy conspiracy, without obligation to substantiate, defend, or even explain. Again, it is a matter of interpretation, of designing a logical structure that will accommodate all the evidence. It is for this reason that paranoia may be the closest we can come to naming any theory that explains Pynchon's fictional world. From this perspective it is not difficult to see why so many themes, ideas, characters, evidences . . . are related. In the paranoid interpretation of Pynchon's stories and novels, the isolated system, the manipulation of reality and illusion, and the movement toward death transfigured are all logically related. They are evidence of some cosmic-scale, elitist conspiracy determined to use most of humanity and all of the earth's resources for its own ends, to derive its life from the death of everyone else. It is at this point that the reader, like Tchitcherine after taking Oneirine, is overwhelmed by the possibility that there really is a connection: "Like other sorts of paranoia, it is nothing less than the onset, the leading edge, of the discovery that *everything is connected,* everything in the Creation . . . "(703).

A conspiracy or plot is a defining characteristic of all Pynchon's novels. Although the uncovering of each conspiracy supplies the momentum for all the novels, and although the conspiracies each show all the characteristics of paranoia, the device is not simply repeated. In fact, the most paranoid among us might suspect that there is only one conspiracy and that the more we read the more evidence we uncover that points to some grand design we cannot quite see. After all, Kurt Mondaugen and young Weissmann were together with V. in the Südwest; Mondaugen went to work for the same Bloody Chiclitz who hired Benny Profane, who was a business partner of Pierce Inverarity, and who had been involved in the postwar scramble for the German technology—which Weissmann/ Blicero and Mondaugen had developed; and, of course, a seemingly unaging Pig Bodine appears in a variety of places. How much coincidence can be tolerated before being organized into a system varies with the paranoid, but there is certainly evidence of something. Beyond these superficial relations, however, lies a connection that reflects Pynchon's serious concerns and his maturity as an artist. Any reader must be impressed with the fact that Pynchon not only returns to the idea of conspiracy for each novel, but he also increases the complexity of its function and of his own vision. It would be tempting merely to ascribe his preoccupation with paranoia to the disorder and suspicion of the decades since World War One, and the development of his vision to cynicism and experience. Surely these factors are involved, but more significant is the possibility that Pynchon views paranoia as a social and aesthetic form rather than as metaphor or psychosis—a form for relating the individual to community, to some external truth (or system of belief), for counteracting what appears as an increasingly entropic world. Delusion, illusion, fantasy, or hallucination is no longer a defining characteristic of paranoia as a form. Given the reality that is considered sane, paranoia may be regarded as a form of life amid so much waste, so much death.

The quests of Stencil, Oedipa, and Slothrop have already been considered in sufficient detail to demonstrate, on reflection, that these searches for evidence of conspiracy may all be classified as paranoid. Earlier discussions, however, did not make explicit the way in which paranoia is a socializing form aimed at preserving life, nor did they suggest the degree to which Pynchon's use of the form has changed from *V.* to *Gravity's Rainbow.* That Stencil, Oedipa, and Slothrop can simultaneously be engaged in a traditional quest, a Dashiell Hammett-like pursuit of clues, a stylized recapitulation of life, a movement through time, a tour, and an enactment of paranoid suspicions is testimony to the vibrancy of the form and to Pynchon's skill, but it may be that the only important feature is the form's capacity as a relational process. The object of the paranoid search is confirmation of some controlling group or force, which, once discovered, would be a confirmation of death; the process of searching, however, is life-sustaining and at the same time a form for relating the individual to death. The paranoid search also creates a functional community in the absence of any community at all and is thus a form for relating the individual to society. The paranoid search creates a framework for structuring facts and thereby provides a mechanism for accommodating accident or fortune even if it cannot be reconciled. And the paranoid search, by relating facts, creates its own history, one that is a function of the present.

Herbert Stencil's search for V. and the facts he carefully incorporates into a V-structure are a paranoia that turns him into "clownish Stencil . . . bells ajingle, waving a wooden, toy oxgoad"(50). Nonetheless the pursuit is all there is to Stencil's life. It keeps him animate and therefore he must take it seriously; it is a necessary delusion, whose goal is "to affirm that his quarry fitted in with The Big One, the century's master cabal. . . . If she was a historical fact then she continued active today and at the moment, because the ultimate Plot Which Has No Name was as yet unrealized . . ."(210). Though he feels himself V.'s victim, Stencil recognizes that a successful search will mean that the Plot will be realized. In effect, the search aims toward his own victimization and is an individual mode of relating to death. The V-structure reorganizes and recreates a personal history. Stencil's father had been engaged in "real" intrigues and conspiracies and his theory of the Situation that has no objective reality had been a mechanism for accommodating paranoid delusions. The younger Stencil inverts history and his father's model to make suspicions actual. Although in his hands the senior Stencil's tools of spying are comic—"cloak for a laundry sack, dagger to peel potatoes" (51)—they are the same tools. The search for V. also provides Herbert Stencil with a community. His father's only legacy had been "good will in nearly every city in the western world among those of his own generation"(43) so that he was able to survive in a "population coming more and more to comprise sons and friends of the originals" (44). Stencil's inquiries also provide a reason for relating to others outside his father's descended community, people who might be useful. Without this mode of relation, "it would then be he and V. all alone, in a world that somehow had lost sight of them both" (44). Having gleaned his father's journals and contacts for facts, Stencil must rely on accident, "waiting for a coincidence"(45), to provide additional information that he can incorporate. Paranoia thus supplies the mechanism for relating chance and willful human agency in a simple form. When on Malta Stencil finds that his facts fit too well, that "events seem to be ordered into an ominous logic" (423), he confronts his paranoia for what it is. Though Fausto mocks Stencil gently with his playful comment that "thirteen of us rule the world in secret"(425), he acknowled-es that such delusions are necessary.

Stencil's paranoia is echoed in a number of minor characters: Godolphin has his Vheissu; Fairing has his parish of rats; Foppl has his 1904 uprising; and the senior Stencil has his Situation. While none of these visions rival Herbert Stencil's in complexity or pursuit, they do constitute the milieu of the novel and, like so many stencilized versions of the one paranoid preoccupation, allow Pynchon to comment on paranoia as social structure. Though Pynchon relies heavily on parody and satire in *V.*, the forms of paranoia are too important merely to be ridiculed. Even if Stencil bears the brunt of an elaborate joke played on Henry Adams and scholars of like mind, he is saved from burlesque and the novel from trumpery by Pynchon's own seriousness. The author brings his readers continually to the brink of laughter only to remind them that we all do search for structures, that there are conspiracies that have killed 60,000 Hereros and stacked Jewish corpses like rusted car bodies, that a novel can be a "mirror," and that life does go on despite the odds against it. *V.* is a self-consciously funny novel whose humor is sustained by the way in which everything in its creation seems to be related. While much of the novel's artistic success may be due to such authorial self-consciousness, its significance for Pynchon's subsequent works lies in its development of a relational form.

The efficacy of paranoia is fully established in *The Crying of Lot 49*. Pynchon no longer needs the crutch of parody or the external existence of Henry Adams's systematized thought to carry the burden of meaning. Summoned from the lethargy of Tupperware parties, suburban herb gardens, and the organized tower of her own ego by Pierce Inverarity's will, Oedipa Maas suspects that her inheritance is America but that she is an exile. The novel unfolds with her discovering the way in which facts "fitted, logically, together"(28), the way in which revelations "seemed to come crowding in exponentially, as if the more she collected the more would come to her, until everything she saw, smelled, dreamed, remembered, would somehow come to be woven into The Tristero"(58). The course of her quest parallels Stencil's in that she perceives another order of existence behind the world of appearances: "It was not an act of treason, nor possibly even of defiance. But it was a calculated withdrawal, from the life of the Republic, from its machinery. Whatever else was being denied them out of hate, indifference to the power of their vote, loopholes, simple ignorance, this withdrawal was their own, unpublicized, private. Since they could not have withdrawn into a vacuum (could they?), there had to exist the separate, silent, unsuspected world"(92). This, of course, is the world of the Tristero—its "constant theme, disinheritance"(120). Oedipa finds herself between two worlds, between inheritance and disinheritance. The clues she pieces together into the structure she comes to know as the Tristero—her paranoia—also begin to define by contrast the suspected world of appearances. Oedipa's search is not the simple construction of a conspiracy aimed at her, though that is a possibility; rather, it is evidence of the void that she must structure in the relations she establishes among facts, people, history, and her own impending death. As her former community of normal relations breaks down with the disintegration of her husband, her psychoanalyst, and her lover, she discovers a new, though hardly more stable, community of people in her clues. The difference is important because it shows her an isolation redeemable not by people but only by a form. The object of Oedipa's search is, finally, paranoia itself:

Change your name to Miles, Dean, Serge, and/or Leonard, baby, she advised her reflection in the half-light of that afternoon's vanity mirror. Either way, they'll call it paranoia. They. Either you have stumbled indeed, without the aid of LSD or other indole alkaloids, onto a secret richness and concealed density of dream; onto a network by which X number of Americans are truly communicating whilst reserving their lies, recitations of routine, arid betrayals of spiritual poverty, for the official government delivery system; maybe even onto a real alternative to the exitlessness, to the absence of surprise to life, that harrows the head of everybody American you know, and you too, sweetie. Or you are hallucinating it. Or a plot has been mounted against you, so expensive and elaborate, involving items like the forging of stamps and ancient books, constant surveillance of your movements, planting of post horn images all over San Francisco, bribing of librarians, hiring of professional actors and Pierce Inverarity only knows what-all besides, all financed out of the estate in a way either too secret or too involved for your non-legal mind to know about even though you are co-executor, so labyrinthine that it must have meaning beyond just a practical joke. Or you are fantasying some such plot, in which case you are a nut, Oedipa, out of your skull. (128)

Though there is humor in her discoveries and though Oedipa herself is capable of Stencil's style of caricature, the humor that persists is the result of irony, that which preserves in the face of incalculable odds, that which holds a mirror up to anyone who takes herself too seriously. Even as Oedipa awaits the crying of lot 49 in a room she knows to be filled with men who have pale, cruel faces, she can say to Genghis Cohen, "Your fly is open," and wonder what "she'd do when the bidder revealed himself"(137). It is perhaps this ironic self-awareness of the character (rather than of the narrator) that distances Oedipa from Stencil most, but it is also her form of paranoia. The dimensions of the conspiracy and the structure of proof have grown beyond the personal to the social in Pynchon's second novel. Stencil needs his V-structure to keep him animate; it is a singular possibility. Oedipa, however, finds herself trapped between alternatives, both of which are paranoid: "Either Oedipa in the orbiting ecstasy of a true paranoia, or a real Tristero. For there was either some Tristero beyond the appearance of the legacy America, or there was just America and if there was just America then it seemed the only way she could continue, and manage to be at all relevant to it, was as an alien, unfurrowed, assumed full circle into some paranoia" (137). With *The Crying of Lot 49* Pynchon seems to be taking the form of paranoia as far as it can go, since in Oedipa it appears to hold within its embrace all the alternatives: America, the Tristero, and Oedipa's alien existence.

If Pynchon's second novel represents an experimental perfection of the form, it is the function of *Gravity's Rainbow* to permit the form its own existence, to see what happens when paranoia is not limited by the consciousness of a single character. As already noted, a working definition of paranoia in *Gravity's Rainbow* is the discovery that everything in the creation is connected. This principle seems to hold true for Pynchon's creation itself. Ostensibly Tyrone Slothrop is the primary paranoid and the successor to Stencil and Oedipa. While Slothrop early in the novel promises to be a worthy heir—he even offers several proverbs for paranoids—he allows his carefully constructed structure of evidence to disintegrate as he has the final pieces of his puzzle within grasp. It may be only his name that betrays him since "sloth" has at its root both the meaning of "sleuth," the dogged tracker, and "sloth," the lazy dawdler. Slothrop is alternately both until he begins to disintegrate and his family's past catches up with him: "There is in his history . . . a peculiar sensitivity to what is revealed in the sky"(26). In his ancestor's case it had been the hand of God "pointing out of the secular clouds, pointing directly at him" (27). Tyrone had always thought the rocket was the hand pointing at him and he sought the special Rocket 00000 with all the reluctant fascination he could muster. The hand comes for him at a crossroad in the form of a rainbow and a remembrance of "days when in superstition and fright he could *make it all fit,* seeing clearly in each an entry in a record, a history: his own, his winter's, his country's . . ."(626). It is not possible to say what the end of Slothrop's own paranoid search may mean, but the rainbow, the crossroad, the disintegration, and the lines quoted from the last of Rilke's *Sonnets to Orpheus* suggest that Slothrop has undergone a Rilkean transformation. He and his paranoia have become one in death transfigured, a continuity of nature rather than man. With Slothrop Pynchon takes paranoia as a form to its limit; victim and conspiracy, search and discovery, isolation and community, life and death may not finally be merged, but they are brought into an ultimate relation. As he looks at the rainbow, "he stands crying, not a thing in his head, just feeling natural . . ."(626). Stencil refuses any confirmation of his paranoia. We are not permitted to see Oedipa's confirmation, if she has one. And Slothrop's end is noticeably unclimactic, despite its suggesting a sexual climax. Although Slothrop escapes conclusive classification, he does become the focus of another paranoia, the creative paranoia of the counterforce.

Slothrop's paranoia is only one of many included in *Gravity's Rainbow.* As suggested earlier, Pynchon is simply allowing the form unrestricted play. Among the more notable paranoids and paranoias are Tantivy Mucker-Maffick, who, in a variety of "operational paranoia"(25), thinks every German rocket has his name painted on it; Edward Pointsman, whose belief in Pavlovian paranoia leads him on his Slothropian experiment; Roger Mexico's paranoid vision of the White Visitation as some sort of "psychic-unity-with-the-Controlling-Agency"(124); Thomas Gwenhidwy's idea of the "City

Paranoiac"(172); Pökler's multiple paranoias concerning the Rocket and his daughter, "his dream of the perfectly victimized"(426), his "love something like the persistence of vision, for They have used it to create for him the moving image of a daughter"(422), and his vision of the Perfect Rocket that "is still up there, still descending" (426) on him; Slothrop's own feeling of "anti-paranoia, where nothing is connected to anything"(434); Greta Erdmann's paranoia about Jewish children; Närrish and von Göll's analysis of the Zone's rampant paranoias and their own respective rocket and film versions; Otto Gnahb's views on "the Mother Conspiracy"(505); Lyle Bland's involvement with "the Great Pinball Difficulty" (581); Byron The Bulb's knowledge of the "international light-bulb cartel"(649); and the other paranoias of Säure Bummer, Wimpe, Tchitcherine, Enzian, the collective crowd aboard the *Anubis,* and all the others already implied in earlier discussions. There is not a single character in *Gravity's Rainbow* who is not implicated in some paranoid fantasy, including inanimate characters such as films, rockets, drugs, trains. . . .

Paranoia itself is a character of such magnitude that it dominates the novel; finally, paranoia is all that holds *Gravity's Rainbow* together, forcing the reader to establish his own sense of plot. Of course the conspiracy is of such complexity that no one can hold all the pieces, establish relations among all the possible interlocks. It would take a computer to correlate all the facts "before we'd have a paranoid structure worthy of the name" and, as the narrator informs us just about the plot involving Lyle Bland, even the computer would not be above suspicion: "Alas, the state of the art by 1945 was nowhere near adequate to that kind of data retrieval. Even if it had been, Bland, or his successors and assigns, could've bought programmers by the truckload to come in and make sure all the information fed out was harmless"(582).

Such is Pynchon's fascination with his subject that he offers his readers a structure, a technique for interpretation, in the form of "Proverbs for Paranoids." As Kenneth Burke and others such as

Weber and Freud have noted, proverbs are stylized or strategic responses to the very situation that posed the need for them and, in a sense, function as names for shared attitudes. Although amusing, Pynchon's proverbs serve as a mechanism for reducing hysteria by naming it. They are collected here without reference to the particular Slothropian situation that called for each of them; they are provided by the narrator because "everyone has agreed to *call them other names* when Slothrop is listening . . ."(241).

Proverbs for Paranoids, 1: You may never get to touch the Master, but you can tickle his creatures. (237)

Proverbs for Paranoids, 2: The innocence of the creatures is in inverse proportion to the immorality of the Master. (241)

Proverbs for Paranoids, 3: If they can get you asking the wrong questions, they don't have to worry about answers. (251)

Proverbs for Paranoids, 4: *You* hide, they seek. (262)

Paranoids are not paranoids (Proverb 5) because they're paranoid, but because they keep putting themselves, fucking idiots, deliberately into paranoid situations. (292)

As names for Slothrop's particular terror, the Proverbs imply a structure. If situations can be recognized and named, they can be organized. Thus Slothrop's private fantasy is made public and his personal system is generalized into a principle that will take the name "counterforce." It is a principle that incidentally invites the reader both to create a plot for the novel and, more directly, to participate. Pökler's "Victim In A Vacuum!" song is addressed to the reader as well.

(All together now, all you masochists out there, specially those of you don't have a partner tonight, alone with those fantasies that don't look like they'll ever come true—want you just to join in here with your brothers and sisters, let each other know you're alive and sincere, try to break through the silences, try to reach through and connect. . . .) (415)

THE HUMAN USE OF HUMAN BEINGS

The title of this section is borrowed from Norbert Wiener's book for its suggestiveness and for its reference to Wiener's essential proposition that amid the world's increasing entropy there are local enclaves that temporarily tend toward organization. This organization, which Wiener discusses in terms of information and control, is, of course, important to many aspects of Pynchon's fiction. It is also the basis for Pynchon's specific use of control to show how a few human beings use others. In Wiener's theory the entire rationale of control is to hold back *nature's* tendency toward chaos by—as he says—adjusting society's parts to "purposive" ends; Geli Tripping makes clear what these ends are. Rathenau's instructions to ask about the real nature of synthesis and control are both the primary cause for paranoia and, possibly, a central message of *Gravity's Rainbow* if not all Pynchon's novels. Synthesis is not only a form of organization; as Kekulé's dream shows, it is nothing less than the chemical process transformed into a political, economic, and social objective: " . . . a blueprint, a basis for new compounds, new arrangements, so that there would be a field of aromatic chemistry to ally itself with secular power, and find new methods of synthesis, so there would be a German dye industry to become the IG . . ."(412). The completion of that ellipsis is paranoia's goal. Calling it an elite, a power system, temporarily, we can recognize its objective as one of Wiener's local enclaves: "Taking and not giving back, demanding that 'productivity' and 'earnings' keep on increasing with time, the System removing from the rest of the World these vast quantities of energy to keep its own tiny desperate fraction showing a profit: and not only most of humanity—most of the World, animal, vegetable and mineral, is laid waste in the process"(412). This, Pynchon suggests, is the human use of human beings. It is a suspicion that haunts his earliest stories and gradually, in the novels, takes on an increasingly definite shape until it is recognizable as the grim phoenix of *Gravity's Rainbow.*

Before considering other uses of human beings, the nature of control exposed in *Gravity's Rainbow* should perhaps be further identified as the organization toward which earlier variations tend. In addition to the exposition of Kekulé's dream, the discoveries of the nature of transformation by Webley Silvernail, Geli Tripping, and Enzian have already been discussed in the context of death transfigured. Each of these discoveries, however, carries with it the revelation —seldom sudden—that the earth and people's lives are being used to preserve the organization and energy of the elite. Such revelations belong properly to the knowledge of death, since the price of organization is waste. It is in death, freed from control, that victims can give form to their suspicions. Thus Rathenau and Bland, former architect and servant of the system, can speak without restraint. Another of these voices summoned from the beyond, who speaks in a more or less official capacity to an equally unreceptive audience, is the spirit Roland Feldspath, lately in the employ of Carroll Eventyr and the Firm. He tells the group assembled at Snoxall's of his discovery in Blicero's realm, something he had not expected in his mortality: "It's control. All these things arise from one difficulty: control. For the first time it was *inside*, do you see. The control is put inside. No more need to suffer passively under 'outside' forces . . ."(30). Feldspath refers, of course, to Rocket ooooo and Blicero's effort to consummate life and death purely on his own terms without reference to the system, or to the War, that surrounded him. Feldspath makes a crucial distinction that falls on deaf ears. He contrasts Blicero's control with that of the system, which believes in the necessity of external control—an illusion that is directed toward taking life from death and thus keeping them separate, elect from preterite, A from B:[1]

"A market needed no longer be run by the Invisible Hand, but now could *create itself*—its own logic, momentum, style, from *inside*. Putting the control inside was ratifying what de facto had happened—that you had dispensed with God. But you had taken on a greater, and more harmful, illusion. The illusion of control. That A could do B. But that

was false. Completely. No one can *do*. Things only happen, A and B
are unreal, are names for parts that ought to be inseparable. . . ."(30)

Later Feldspath takes an interest in Slothrop's paranoia, "hovering
over this Slothropian space . . . along one of the Last Parabolas"(238).
His role, it appears, is to tell new initiates into his order of being
about control:

> Well, Roland must make the best of it, that's all. If they get this far,
> he has to show them what he knows about Control. That's one of his
> death's secret missions. His cryptic utterances that night at Snoxall's
> about economic systems are merely the folksy everyday background
> chatter over here, a given condition of being. Ask the Germans espe-
> cially. Oh, it is a real sad story, how shoddily their Schwärmerei for
> Control was used by the folks in power. Paranoid Systems of History
> (PSH), a short-lived periodical of the 1920s whose plates have all
> mysteriously vanished, natch, has even suggested, in more than one
> editorial, that the whole German Inflation was created deliberately,
> simply to drive young enthusiasts of the Cybernetic Tradition into
> Control work: after all, an economy inflating, upward bound as a
> balloon, its own definition of Earth's surface drifting upward in value,
> uncontrolled, drifting with the days, the feedback system expected to
> maintain the value of the mark constant having, humiliatingly,
> failed. . . . Unity gain around the loop, unity gain, zero change, and
> hush, that way, forever, these were the secret rhymes of the childhood
> of the Discipline of Control—secret and terrible, as the scarlet histories
> say. (238)

The Discipline of Control belongs to *Gravity's Rainbow* but Pynchon
had already noted in earlier works that countless enthusiasts had
devoted themselves to control work, often without knowing it, in the
bureaucracies of waste. The grim phoenix, which creates its own
controlled holocaust and deliberate resurrection, is a symbol for all
Pynchon's novels.

From the perspective of Pynchon's last novel, *V.* can be viewed as
an exploration of the two types of control, one characterized by
Fausto's metaphor of the Virgin assailed and the other by V.'s personal synthesis of hothouse and street. While the two Stencils,

Fausto, and others look to the external control of God, nature, governments, native revolts, and conspiracies, V. embarks on a plan of "self-aggrandizement which read the conforming of events to the channels she'd set out for them as glorious testimony to her own skill"(183). She manipulates the past, as the dreams of 1904 at Foppl's villa, and the present, as the Maltese disturbances of 1919, alike to organize her one small part of creation at the expense of everyone else. V.'s use of human beings, including her own body, serves as a mirror for the outside forms of control found in colonialism, bureaucracies, automatons, jobs, cosmetic operations, and general tendencies like the drift toward inanimateness or decadence.

Control in *The Crying of Lot 49* becomes both more familiar and more sinister. Besides Mucho Maas's observations about automobiles and sound or Hilarius's various experiments, Pynchon introduces the universal industrial use of people through Mike Fallopian's bitter summary of Inverarity's corporation: "In school they got brainwashed, like all of us, into believing the Myth of the American Inventor. . . .Then when they grew up they found they had to sign over all their rights to a monster like Yoyodyne; got stuck on some 'project' or 'task force' or 'team' and started being ground into anonymity. Nobody wanted them to invent—only perform their little role in a design ritual, already set down for them in some procedures handbook"(64). Inverarity epitomizes corporate control, appearing to the anarchist Jesús Arrabal as "exactly and without flaw the thing we fight"(89). Oedipa learns that his interlocking companies are merely a reflection of the man's need "to possess, to alter the land, to bring new skylines, personal antagonisms, growth rates into being"(134); with his last will he even controls human beings from the grave.

The sinister aspect of control emerges in the seeming conflict of Inverarity's public, profit-making empire with the clandestine, anarchist Tristero. His Invisible Hand, the Puritan business principles of growth, appears to be opposed by the disinherited Other, "something blind, soulless; a brute automatism that led to eternal death"(116). Yet Oedipa finds that the two systems are inextricably and unaccountably related in the enigma of Inverarity's will. This coding and "hieroglyphic sense of concealed meaning"(13) are keys to the novel because they reveal the social equivalent of Wiener's organization based on information and control. With great skill Pynchon unobtrusively embeds Maxwell's demon in the main plot as a metaphor for Oedipa's discovery; the entire novel unfolds from this center, giving it a density and integrity camouflaged by Oedipa's detective work.

The demon as incorporated in Nefastis's machine is a model of control: "As the Demon sat and sorted his molecules into hot and cold, the system was said to lose entropy. But somehow the loss was offset by the information the Demon gained about what molecules were where"(77). He has solved the objection of modern physics that the demon requires information from outside his closed system to keep the molecules shuffled by establishing a trade-off of energy for information between the demon and a sensitive communicator. Thus the Nefastis machine works—that is, increases its organization locally—by gaining information from the outside. It maintains the illusion of a cycle while at the same time violating the cycle. As information increases, entropy decreases and life goes on. Inverarity may function as a demon in the system that is America by controlling the clues to the Tristero, which Oedipa discovers. Oedipa herself may be an unwitting demon taking information about the Tristero, organizing it into a structure, and thereby sustaining life, the paranoid form. Or the Tristero may be a demon. Oedipa recognizes that Nefastis's correlation of thermodynamic and informational entropies is one of appearance: "Yet he had made his mere coincidence respectable, with the help of Maxwell's Demon"(80). She, on the other hand, is "faced with a metaphor of God knew how many parts; more than two, anyway. With coincidences blossoming these days wherever she looked, she had nothing but a sound, a word, Trystero, to hold them together"(80). The Tristero may only be a metaphor for relating the "parts" Oedipa discovers or it may be the locus for all information control.

The social parallel to Nefastis's machine is suggested to Oedipa by Emory Bortz in a hypothetical merger of the Tristero with Thurn and Taxis: "But whoever could control the lines of communication, among all these princes, would control them. That network someday could unify the Continent. So I propose that we merge with our old enemy . . . our two systems could be invincible. We could refuse service on any but an Imperial basis. Nobody could move troops, farm produce, anything, without us. Any prince tries to start his own courier system, we suppress it. We, who have so long been disinherited, could be the heirs of Europe!"(123). Although the merger did not occur in the 1650s in the shadow of the Empire's decline, it may have happened in the 1950s after the Tristero emigrated to the country of new corporate power. Whether the systems are reconciled in Inverarity or are merely anti-systems mutually dependent on each other, they represent a structure of control that encompasses all of America. The seventeenth-century Tristero agent who proposed the merger understands that communication is control because information will permit the organization of warring princedoms, will bring order out of an increasing political and economic chaos. The agent knows that whoever controls communication controls not only the princes but the very possibility of organization. On the visible side of Inverarity's empire, organization is everywhere apparent, in Yoyo-dyne for example, where invention has been routinized in a procedures handbook. The government's postal system is also a representative of this visible organization. The Tristero, however, is the system of communication for the other world, the silent, unsuspected world of the alienated. It is a system in the service of anarchists and waste, as Oedipa observes in the people she sees using it. If the systems were somehow combined and the extremes reconciled, then control would be absolute and some minority—perhaps the Tristero's inner circle—could maintain its enclave of organization and energy at everyone else's expense. Information is the energy that keeps the system functioning; it must continually be transmitted for there to be any organization whether or not the information has any other value or meaning. In short, it is another version of the grim phoenix and the illusion of cyclical return promised by Kekulé's serpent—information for energy—but one delivered into a violation of the cycle. People get used up, as Oedipa notices in the loss of Mucho, Metzger, Driblette, and Hilarius.

While *The Crying of Lot 49* has a definite, though enigmatic, structure of control in the relationship of Inverarity and the Tristero, *Gravity's Rainbow* does not have a single metaphor to make coincidences respectable. The most comparable metaphor is the War, an environment that is an advanced entropic state for those who die and are used. At the same time it is a highly controlled and ordered plan. As with thermodynamics and information theory, the War is a matter of probabilities. In one chamber, events point to maximum probability and certain decay, disintegration, and death; but this may be all for the benefit of some elite whose "odds were never probabilities, but frequencies *already observed*"(208). It is the control of a fixed roulette wheel: "what has looked free or random, is discovered to've been under some Control, all the time . . . where only destinations are important, attention is to long-term statistics, not individuals: and where the House always does, of course, keep turning a profit . . ." (209). It is the world changed by war "with information come to be the only real medium of exchange"(258) and the only source of energy for those who control its flow. Walter Rathenau again has the clearest understanding: "He saw the war in progress as a world revolution, out of which would rise neither Red communism nor an unhindered Right, but a rational structure in which business would be the true, the rightful authority . . ."(165). There is a "terrible structure behind the appearances of diversity and enterprise"(165), one that feeds on death and depletion of energies. Katje Borgesius is used by that structure and has a working knowledge of a "real conversion factor between information and lives"(105). She may not know what the war really is, but it is recorded somewhere in the War Department's Manual:

"Don't forget the real business of the War is buying and selling. The murdering and the violence are self-policing, and can be entrusted to non-professionals. The mass nature of wartime death is useful in many ways. It serves as spectacle, as diversion from the real movements of the War. It provides raw material to be recorded into History, so that children may be taught History as sequences of violence, battle after battle, and be more prepared for the adult world. Best of all, mass death's a stimulus to just ordinary folks, little fellows, to try 'n' grab a piece of that Pie while they're still here to gobble it up. The true war is a celebration of markets. (105)

Projected against a background of horror, senseless death, and nauseating waste, the real business of war goes on with cold and precise dispassion. The power elite is never named. The closest Pynchon allows his readers to come to knowing who is really at the top of the power chart is in tickling, like Slothrop, the Master's creatures: " 'How high does it go?' is not even the right kind of question to be asking, because the organization charts have all been set up by Them, the titles and names filled in by Them . . ."(251). In one of the few glimpses of creatures who may be close to the Master, we see Clive Mossmoon talking with Sir Marcus Scammony, discussing how to dispense with their failed employee Pointsman and their uncontrollable agent Slothrop. Sir Marcus blithely observes that they will all fail but not the Operation, and Mossmoon feels himself "delivered onto the sober shore of the Operation, where all is firm underfoot, where the self is a petty indulgent animal that once cried in its mired darkness. But here there is no whining, here inside the Operation. There is no lower self. The issues are too momentous for the lower self to interfere. . . . Each of us has his place, and the tenants come and go, but the places remain . . ."(616). Even those highly placed are functionaries, human machines that perform services rather than deeds.

Although the power elite is never named, its appearance of enterprise and diversity, the facade that is supposed to be recognized, is at least partially identified: the Firm (a common euphemism for the British Special Operations Executive), AEG (German General Electric Company), Krupp, ICI (Imperial Chemicals), Shell International Petroleum, British Ministry of Supply, Bataafsche Petroleum Maatschappij, Harvard University, IG Farben, du Pont, Grössli Chemical Corporation, Sandoz, Ciba, Geigy, IG Chemie, Psychochemie AG, Shell Mex House, Siemens-Schuchert, Rheinelbe Union, Reichsbank, General Electric, the Russian, British, German, and American armies, governments and bureaucracies, Ostarzneikunde GmbH, National Research Council, Alfred Nobel's various enterprises, Anilinas Alemanas, Spottbilligfilm AG, Blohm and Voss, Standard Oil, Business Advisory Council, Chemical Foundation, Glitherius Paint and Dye, the Mafia, Masons, Chemnyco, General Aniline and Film, Ansco, Winthrop. . . . In addition to these corporate entities there are numerous individuals whom Pynchon manages to connect together in interlocking directorates, mergers, secret arrangements, and countless collusions. They are not merely named, but are related in a conspiracy that grows beyond the ability of any novel or individual to contain. This conglomerate held somehow miraculously together is the real nature of synthesis for which the benzene ring had been a blueprint. Kekulé's dream may, in fact, be the origin of the new power structure that Enzian identifies "not among firms—it was only staged to look that way—but among the different Technologies . . . and their needs which are understood only by the ruling elite . . ." (521). Regardless of whether technologies control men or men control technologies, synthesis made possible a new magnitude of control. And despite the complexity of the system, it is modeled after Pynchon's Inverarity and Tristero system in *The Crying of Lot 49*. In *Gravity's Rainbow* Maxwell's demon becomes a bureaucracy, a switching path, to make possible dreams like Kekulé's or even a parable for personnel like the chemist Liebig, who inspired Kekulé to change from architecture to chemistry. Information, of course, is the primary resource of the technological system, which knows no national boundaries and recognizes no constraint except the need for more information. In a surrealistic dream a character called Mr. Information suggests that human beings may have become expendable, or at least subservient to the needs of technology: "... the truth is that the War is keeping things alive. *Things.* The Ford is only one of them. The Germans-and-Japs story was only one, rather surrealistic version of the real War. The real War is always there"(645).

Various characters—including Enzian, Katje, Slothrop, Blicero, Silvernail, Wimpe, and Tchitcherine—know or discover that the war is merely a front for the needs of technology, but no one penetrates beneath the surface of diversity and enterprise except Blicero, who tries to substitute his own internal control. Everyone and everything is used by the meta-cartel. Slothrop—used primarily by Pointsman on behalf of his employers—claims most of the novel's attention, but Franz Pökler is an even finer portrait of the archetypal victim. Pökler's wife knows that his "fantasy, death-wish, rocket-mysticism" make him "just the type they want. They know how to use *that.* They know how to use nearly everybody"(154–55). Pökler, however, believes it is technology that is being used: "But others had the money, others gave the orders—trying to superimpose their lusts and bickerings on something that had its own vitality, on a *technologique* they'd never begin to understand"(401). Pökler will only know he has been used by another human being—just as he knows humans control technology—when Weissmann has finished with him. And his search for his daughter among the prisoners of Dora will show him how others have been used:

> The odors of shit, death, sweat, sickness, mildew, piss, the breathing of Dora, wrapped him as he crept in staring at the naked corpses being carried out now that America was so close, to be stacked in front of the crematoriums, the men's penises hanging, their toes clustering white and round as pearls . . . each face so perfect, so individual, the lips stretched back into death-grins, a whole silent audience caught at

the punch line of the joke . . . and the living, stacked ten to a straw mattress, the weakly crying, coughing, losers. . . . All his vacuums, his labyrinths, had been the other side of this. While he lived, and drew marks on paper, this invisible kingdom had kept on, in the darkness outside . . . all this time. . . . Pökler vomited. He cried some. The walls did not dissolve—no prison wall ever did, not from tears, not at this finding, on every pallet, in every cell, that the faces are ones he knows after all, and holds dear as himself, and cannot, then, let them return to that silence. . . . (432–33)

This, finally, is the human use of human beings. It makes other personalized controls such as Pointsman's or Blicero's seem almost insignificant. Yet they are all linked together in their service to the system.

In *Gravity's Rainbow* there are several identifiable instruments of control. Film, drugs, and sadomasochism are typical systems, most of which have been discussed in the context of their being used to create illusions that victimize their adherents. However, the most prominent system is the rocket, both the abstracted Rocket that seems to have a life of its own and special rockets like the 00000, 00001, or even the "Enzian." Although the control of the Rocket over individuals has been discussed in some detail already, it should be noted that despite any appearances of freedom suggested by the Rocket—even Blicero's—it is a system created and used by Them for purposes we can only imagine. Miklos Thanatz, of all people, tells Slothrop that the Rocket "really did possess a Max Weber charisma . . . some joyful —and *deeply* irrational—force the State bureaucracy could never routinize, against which it could not prevail . . . they did resist it, but they also allowed it to happen"(464). Thanatz is sophisticated in tapping Weber, but naïve in thinking the Rocket could not be routinized. Perhaps because its silent fall seems random and mysterious, the Rocket appears irrational, but it has really been under control all the time, its flight path predetermined. Control was the primary problem confronting German engineers in perfecting their system; eventually, they were able to manipulate the Rocket's apparent irrationality, its randomness, as a further psychological weapon.

Through repeated references to Weber and his sociological models, Pynchon clearly invokes the image of Weber's polarity between charisma and rationalization or bureaucratization. Though this duality persists throughout Weber's work, his ideas about charisma are ambivalent. Thanatz does not understand that the Rocket's charisma most certainly belongs to Weber's later conception, which accommodates charisma with rationalization, rather than to his earlier Dionysian, "irrational" charisma. Pynchon's use of Weber in the novel is complicated and not limited to the system of the Rocket; Slothrop, for example, also falls under Weber's charismatic framework in his evolution from a Puritan notion of grace to Bodine's more irrational grace "to keep it working" in opposition to a bureaucratized and controlled world. And the meta-cartel, in Weberian terms, represents the ultimate rationalization and bureaucratization. Near the end of *The Protestant Ethic and the Spirit of Capitalism* Weber provides a description of the Puritan calling and the world Pynchon sees:

> For when asceticism was carried out of monastic cells into everyday life, and began to dominate worldly morality, it did its part in building the tremendous cosmos of the modern economic order. This order is now bound to the technical and economic conditions of machine production which today determine the lives of all the individuals who are born into this mechanism, not only those directly concerned with economic acquisition, with irresistible force. Perhaps it will so determine them until the last ton of fossilized coal is burned.[2]

Slothrop learns that the Rocket is only the symbol of a larger system, Weber's "cosmos of the modern economic order," in which the use of everything, including Slothrop, is predetermined. He discovers that the meta-cartel has been planning its rocket system for some time and that the war is only an excuse to use it. Confronting one of the bureaucracy's creatures, he asks: ". . . doesn't it strike you as just a bit odd, you Shell chaps working on *your* liquid engine *your* side of the Channel you know, and *their* chaps firing *their* bloody things at you with your own . . . blasted . . . Shell trans*mit*ter tower, you see"(241). Tchitcherine similarly senses that the Rocket may only be the manifestation of a new state that is above politics, national interests, or conventional economics, ". . . and the Rocket is its soul"(566). It would be easy, logical even, to blame technology for the war's horrors, but as Enzian realizes, abstractions are responsible for nothing. Behind them are people, a power elite that understands the *needs* of technology: "All very well to talk about having a monster by the tail, but do you think we'd've had the Rocket if someone, some specific somebody with a name and a penis hadn't *wanted* to chuck a ton of Amatol 300 miles and blow up a block full of civilians?"(521). The Rocket, like the silent horror it brings, is merely a "spectacle, as diversion from the real movements of the War" that goes on all the time.

COUNTERFORCE

If the Rocket is a system created and used by the meta-cartel both as a business that keeps turning a profit and as a mechanism for controlling people attracted to its false charisma, then it serves Pynchon as a representation of the force of worldwide bureaucracy. The Rocket appears as an abstraction—a system, program, or force—but it is still controlled by human beings with names, people who range from the victims like Pökler to the exploiters like Pointsman to the persons in high places like Lord Scammony and the unnamed elite beyond. While insisting all the while that the meta-cartel's bureaucracy is human, Pynchon nonetheless most frequently represents it as a force. In *V.*, V. is such a representation—still human despite her prostheses, yet the symbol of a systematized force that, according to Henry Adams, had overcome the world. In *The Crying of Lot 49*, Pynchon similarly uses the potentially reconciled Inverarity empire and Tristero system, though the Tristero is certainly the more sinister and mysterious aspect of this force. V., the Tristero, and the Rocket are each the outward manifestation of a force that is identified as a conspiracy directed against the individuals Stencil, Oedipa, and Slo-throp. This paranoia is recognizable and more or less familiar. Throughout his novels Pynchon has implied a dialectic of good and evil, force and counterforce. Individuals victimized by a conspiracy hardly constitute a counterforce worthy of the name, but they are at least the point of some resistance, the isolated voice refusing to be routinized and consumed like a piece of coal. Although a few, such as Paola Maijstral, McClintic Sphere, or, briefly, Roger Mexico, seem to escape the machinations of any force, everyone else appears to be used or using, and sometimes both.

To the conscious victims, the force appears as an evil. Pynchon goes to considerable lengths to establish that any dialectic such as good and evil is reciprocal and mutually dependent, a binary system. The force needs worthy opponents if for no other reason than to keep its machinery well-oiled, its weapons operational. The victims, as noted earlier, need an enemy and the form of paranoia to maintain their own vitality amid all the waste. Used to seeing images, von Göll puts the matter simply: ". . . we define each other. Elect and preterite, we move through a cosmic design of darkness and light . . ."(495). Pynchon increasingly turns to this Puritan concept of elect and pret-erite, a system itself that is compatible with Weber's duality of cha-risma and bureaucratization. Though an analysis of Pynchon's fiction in terms of Weber's sociology, particularly as a model for social action, would undoubtedly reveal much about the complexity of Pynchon's art, it is sufficient here to observe that he incorporates Weber as a referential domain that exists outside the novels. Within the novels, the primary purpose of Puritan or Weberian dualities is to suggest a mode of action and reaction. If the meta-cartel is the epitome of the Puritan ethic as well as the ultimate form of bureacrat-ization, then opposition to the meta-cartel must belong to the vic-tims, the preterite for whom acquired grace, or charisma, may offer the only hope of escape since revolution appears impossible.

In *V.* Stencil gives little hint of opposition; rather, his mode of action is limited to accommodation and self-preservation. Fausto, by opting for delusion, chooses neither to deny nor to accept control and its opposite—accident. In *The Crying of Lot 49* Oedipa does not actually resist, nor does she seek accommodation; however, she thinks that one probable outcome of her knowledge of the Tristero will be an invitation to join it. In the meantime she can only wait, consumed by her own paranoia. It is not until *Gravity's Rainbow* that Pynchon creates a protagonist who resists. Slothrop's origins are Puritan and presumably his family was among the elect originally. Slothrop's first American ancestor, however, grew tired of the "Winthrop machine"(554–55) in 1634 or 1635 and decided to start his own ministry in the Berkshire Mountains even though he was not an ordained minister. William Slothrop became a pig farmer and, inadvertently, saw a parable in the slaughter of his pigs. He waited for "the one pig that wouldn't die, that would validate all the ones who'd had to . . ."(555). It was a matter of "action and reaction"(555); he reasoned that "without the millions who had plunged and drowned, there could have been no miracle"(554) of Christ's walking on the sea. He wrote a long tract on the subject called *On Preterition,* in which he "argued holiness for these 'second Sheep,' without whom there'd be no elect. . . . William felt that what Jesus was for the elect, Judas Iscariot was for the Preterite. Everything in the Creation has its equal and opposite counterpart. How can Jesus be an exception?" (555). Tyrone's origins were inextricably bound to the Puritan duality and centered on the issue of whether grace or election might not have equally valid counterparts. Grace has its secular counterpart in charisma as does preterition in victimization. As Slothrop discovers his paranoia and quests after the Rocket that seems to conceal his identity, he is in effect reenacting his ancestor William's inverse religion in secular terms. The elect are the elite technocrats and their grace is control. They think they have one of their own whose unique conditioning makes him the perfect tool to search out and destroy the Schwarzkommando, an alien group with no allegiance to or understanding of the Puritan system and its ethic. Shortly after discovering that there is a plot, Slothrop wonders, "Did They choose him because of all those word-smitten Puritans dangling off of Slothrop's family tree? Were They trying to seduce his brain now, his reading eye too?"(207). Perhaps They did not know about William Slothrop, only about his Puritanism. In Zürich he encounters old college friends "who got initiated at Harvard into the Puritan Mysteries: who took oaths in dead earnest to respect and to act always in the name of *Vanitas,* Emptiness, their ruler ..."(267–68) and who are already employees of the system. When he reaches the Rocket's holy center at Peenemünde he is insensitive to the stimulus " ... and likewise groweth his Preterition sure"(509). Alone in the Zone Slothrop becomes alert to trees—the resource his family exploited in the Puritan spirit—and decides their actions had been insane. Shortly thereafter, he thinks about William Slothrop and wonders: "Suppose the Slothropite heresy had had the time to consolidate and prosper? Might there have been fewer crimes in the name of Jesus, and more mercy in the name of Judas Iscariot? It seems to Tyrone Slothrop that there might be a route back ..."(556).

It is not surprising, then, that Slothrop assumes the guise of Plechazunga, the Pig-Hero who delivered a tenth-century village from the destruction of Norse invaders; his ancestor William's pigs, after all, had also found "their grace in cross-country movement"(555). Wearing his costume about the town, Slothrop discovers himself in the midst of a black market and his preterite paranoia grows: "Last of his line, and how far-fallen—no other Slothrop ever felt such fear in the presence of Commerce"(569). Later his costume saves him from certain emasculation and a control that would have ended any prospect of his finding the new order of grace, or charisma. Out of his costume and outside Cuxhaven, Slothrop undergoes the ambiguous transformation described in detail earlier. It is not simply the "Odorless and Official Death"(688) that traditional charismatic figures like Jack Kennedy and Malcolm X found waiting for them. It is perhaps a Rilkean transformation, but it may also be the kind of Dionysian charisma that Weber seems to have proposed as synonymous with *pneuma,* breath of the Holy Spirit, one that encompasses "objective" passion, the grace that comes from being one's self. Slothrop in the crossroads, "crying, not a thing in his head, just feeling natural"(626), may signify that he has found the preterite's form of grace. He may have also become the lone pig—the sacrificed animal associated with, among others, Dionysus—that William Slothrop waited for. There is no evidence of Slothrop's death in the novel, only his disintegration. One of the last to see him is Pig Bodine when he gives Tyrone the symbol of grace for those opposed to the bureaucrats' commerce. It is the dried blood of John Dillinger who was "anything but a 'common criminal'. . . . He went out and socked Them right in the toilet privacy of Their banks"(741). After this encounter, Slothrop becomes a scattered concept and "there's no telling which of the Zone's present-day population are offshoots of his original scattering"(742). Some of these offshoots organize themselves into a counterforce.

If Slothrop achieved anything like grace or a state free from the control of the worldly Puritan elite, he did so only as an individual. Regardless of his fate, he becomes a symbol for other preterite victims who have become conscious of their routinization and use. In his quest Slothrop had been identified as an ironic Wagnerian Tannhäuser for whom the Pope's staff would never bloom. After his disappearance, however, the counterforce brings news: "His orders are terse and clear, like those of the others, agents of the Pope, Pope got religion, go out 'n' find that minnesinger, he's a good guy after all . . ."(619). After organizing, the first objective of the counterforce is to find their knight, who for them has come to possess a kind of warrior-hero charisma, rather than that of just being natural. The counterforce apparently is created during a surrealistic convention of double agents. Pirate Prentice, Katje Borgesius, Sir Stephen Dodson-Truck, Jeremiah Evans, representatives of the Zone-Hereros, and others are at the convention "to trade some pain and a few truths, but all in the distracted style of the period"(545). After wandering around in amazement, Prentice "understands where he is, now. It will be possible, after all, to die in obscurity, without having helped a soul: without love, despised, never trusted, never vindicated—to stay down among the Preterite, his poor honor lost, impossible to locate or to redeem"(544). They all share Prentice's preterition, having been used by the bureaucracy meanly, as the instruments of waste and death. The theme of the conference is set by a Jesuit who acts as a Devil's Advocate. He states the truth of Rathenau that they have all come to recognize: "Death has been the source of Their power. It was easy enough for us to see that. If we are here once, only once, then clearly we are here to take what we can while we may. If They have taken much more, and taken not only from Earth but also from us —well, why begrudge Them, when they're just as doomed to die as we are?"(539). The counterforce, presumably, will take advantage of Their mortality to wage its counterwar. The Devil's Advocate, however, suggests another possibility, that death is only one of Their most carefully propagated lies and therefore it is "possible that They will not die. That it is now within the state of Their art to go on forever—though we, of course, will keep dying as we always have" (539). The Devil's Advocate does not seem to recognize the ironic accuracy of his position since he thinks in terms of people; as the reader learns from the conversation between the highly placed bureaucrats Mossmoon and Lord Scammony, "tenants come and go, but the places remain . . ."(616). In a bureaucracy, it is the office, not the person, that continues, and offices do not know death. Despite his official role, the Devil's Advocate sounds the theme for the counterforce: "But rather than make that leap of faith, perhaps we will choose instead to turn, to fight: to demand, from those for whom we die, our own immortality. They may not be dying in bed anymore, but maybe They can still die from violence. If not, at least we can learn to withhold from Them our fear of Death. For every kind of vampire, there is a kind of cross. And at least the physical things They have taken, from Earth and from us, can be dismantled, demolished—returned to where it all came from"(540).

The counterforce is augmented by Roger Mexico when he realizes that not only has he been used, but he has been used through Jessica, whom he loved. He joins the counterforce in a ceremonial rite of entering the temple of commerce and pissing on the bureaucrats, including Pointsman, assembled to discuss how they will use the Earth's oil. Prentice explains the counterforce to a novice Mexico: "Of course a well-developed They-system is necessary—but it's only half the story. For every They there ought to be a We. In our case there is. Creative paranoia means developing at least as thorough a We-system as a They-system—"(638). Adept at probabilities, Mexico is suspicious and presses Prentice who says: "I mean what They and Their hired psychiatrists call 'delusional systems.' Needless to say, 'delusions' are always officially defined. We don't have to worry about questions of real or unreal. They only talk out of expediency. It's the *system* that matters. How the data arrange themselves inside it"(638). The We-They system begins to look like the Elect-Preterite system of the Puritans. The only difference between We's and They's is who defines the delusions—which to Mexico means, "well, you're playing Their game, then"(638). This fact ensures that the counterforce will never win; even if it should miraculously overthrow Them, it will eventually substitute its own delusions—such is the role of any elite. It may also be the only thing that distinguishes Slothrop from his seekers since he is an individual and not a system. In the meantime there is no victory and the counterforce is the only alternative, the only spark of irrationality and the closest thing to charisma in the Zone. As Osbie Feel says, "*They're* the rational ones. We piss on Their rational arrangements. Don't we . . . Mexico?"(639).

    Beyond Katje's interview with Enzian, in which he tells her she is free and meant to survive—"a life-sentence"(662)—and the Gross Suckling Conference, which passes the resolution that "the dearest nation of all is one that will survive no longer than you and I, a common movement at the mercy of death and time: the ad hoc adventure"(706), the counterforce's only engagement with the enemy is at a dinner of former Krupp executives and friends. Mexico and Bodine (aided by the presence of Brigadier Pudding) disrupt the dinner, but Mexico knows that the counterforce is a failure: "They will use us. We will help legitimize Them, though They don't need it really, it's another dividend for Them, nice but not critical . . ." (713). The duality of We-They has doomed the counterforce by making it part of the system: "They are as schizoid, as double-minded in the massive presence of money, as any of the rest of us, and that's the hard fact. The Man has a branch office in each of our brains, his corporate emblem is a white albatross, each local rep has a cover known as the Ego, and their mission in this world is Bad Shit. We do know what's going on, and we let it go on"(712–13). Rationality, like entropy, is inevitable. Charisma, if found at all, is only a temporary interruption. The single choice for the counterforce is between life and death: "Letting it sit for a while is no compromise, but a decision to live, on Their terms . . ."(713). Toward the end of the novel a spokesman for the latter-day counterforce admits that Slothrop was only a "pretext"(738) and that the counterforce committed the same mortal sin as their enemy had in its illusion of control, that A could do B, that life and death are separable: "The true sin was yours: to interdict that union. To draw that line. To keep us worse than enemies, who are after all caught in the same fields of shit —to keep us strangers"(739). It is the same lesson Oedipa Maas learned about excluded middles. For most of us there is no union, no transfiguration even within the individual self; only our bodies are transfigured with other of the Earth's accumulated wastes.

The counterforce is an inherent failure, then. The closest anyone can come to escape is possibly the natural charisma of a Slothrop— though he is undoubtedly unique—or the temporary moments of caring that Leni Pökler imagined and Mexico found during the distraction of the war. If the novel contains any sign of hope at all, it is a scientific modernization of God's promise to Noah. It is gravity's rainbow, which Pynchon offers as a token of the covenant made with the earth rather than with man, just as God's covenant had been with the earth and the rainbow a sign to man. The rainbow is both the parabola of the Rocket's flight, the arc of ascent and falling, and the rainbow of Rilkean transformation. Before it became a biblical sign, the rainbow had been the bow of the hero hung as a sign of victory and a warning. It was also a ring, only half of which was visible. In the novel it is a promise that the bureaucracy's system, its Rocket, "sooner or later must crash to its death, when its addiction to energy has become more than the rest of the World can supply, dragging with it innocent souls all along the chain of life"(412). It is gravity that transfigures death: ". . . Gravity, taken so for granted, is really something eerie, Messianic, extrasensory in Earth's mindbody . . . having hugged to its holy center the wastes of dead species, gathered, packed, transmuted, realigned, and rewoven molecules . . ."(590). Nora Dodson-Truck, one of the most mysterious characters in *Gravity's Rainbow,* speaks what may be the covenant. Part of the psychic team at the White Visitation, she had never really been one of them —she had already receded so far from anything merely human that she left a vacuum. When she looked increasingly to the Outer Radiance, she only took "more of the Zero into herself"(150), for she saw nothing there. She speaks across memory, from the void: "*I am Gravity, I am That against which the Rocket must struggle, to which the prehistoric wastes submit and are transmuted to the very substance of History . . ."* (639). The covenant with earth is a promise not of redemption or resurrection, but of death transfigured. The control is inside the mass of accumulated waste. The Earth will reclaim its own, regardless of what rational and intricate systems man might build. They will all fall. It is a promise. If there is a lament, it may be such as that which ends Rilke's "Tenth Elegy:"

> And we, who have always counted
> on joy as *ascending,* would suffer
> the emotion that almost alarms us
> when a joyful thing falls.[3]

A SCREAMING

From Los Angeles at the turn of the century pentacostalism erupted into a modern mass movement that, in a curious way, is another preterite front against venerated order. Acquired grace, being filled with the holy spirit, distinguishes the movement, particularly the charismatic form of speaking in tongues—emphatic expression without semantic reference—the language of angels. Glossolalia is a fundamental form, one that exemplifies a dichotomy that haunts Pynchon's stories and novels: the mass of so much myth, structure, plot, order, and meaning destroyed over and over again by something irrational. In Pynchon's fiction there comes a screaming—a rocket perhaps, or a "Word, spoken with no warning into your ear, and then silence forever"(25). Not unlike Rilke, Pynchon seems to ask who, if he cried, would hear him from among the Qlippoth. Only when you hear it do you know for certain that you are not dead.

Pynchon is conscious—self-conscious—of the fact that his novels are local enclaves of organization taken from the chaos of infinite possibilities. It is perhaps surprising, then, that Pynchon would give his fantasy such definite and precise shapes when the dangers of entropy, routinization, analysis, and consumption are so great. Certainly one of paranoia's freedoms is precisely the capacity to create elaborately detailed structures from an irrational, even false, premise and then to abandon them. But we must assume that Pynchon's shapes are deliberate since the act of publishing his stories and novels is one that implies a response or reaction. He is providing information —a commodity of exchange—in what can only be viewed as an effort to increase organization, concentrate energy. Because it incorporates Pynchon's own act and because it is one of the most recurrent themes of his fiction, communication may provide the framework for discovering how various things come together.

Although Pynchon's first and second stories touch lightly on themes of communication, manipulation, control, and failure, "Entropy" introduces the all-purpose metaphor of the closed system, of which communication is one manifestation. The two communication situations of the story, which have already been discussed in relation to social entropy, constitute a dialectic related to all the other dualities that structure Pynchon's fiction: the hothouse and the street, Inverarity and the Tristero, and the multiple dualities of *Gravity's*

Rainbow. Implying the similarities among closed social, thermodynamic, and communication systems, Pynchon suggests Mulligan's party and Callisto's hothouse as alternative representations of the effects of increasing world entropy. Without going into the technical complexities of information theory, it is possible to reconstruct in a schematic way the communication situation that intrigues Pynchon.

Among many possible referents for the information theories displayed in Pynchon's texts, Abraham Moles's *Information Theory and Esthetic Perception* is at least representative. While other books may be more readily identifiable as sources, Moles's theme of communication from art to the human being and his structuralist approach more nearly coincide with Pynchon's ideas than the more familiar works of Wiener, Cherry, Shannon, or Weaver. Moles suggests a number of oppositions such as banality and originality, redundancy and information, intelligible form and informative output, order and disorder, predictability and unpredictability. These correspond approximately to the respective situations of Callisto and Mulligan, both of which occur against a background of increasing world disorder and are defined by their relationships with it. In information theory, this background is noise, which appears to be disorder since the messages of communication are the orderly, organized opposite. However, the only thing that distinguishes noise from messages is intent; noise is what one does not wish to transmit or receive. The perfect noise, by analogy with light, is white noise, in which all " 'frequencies' have the same probability of occurrence," according to Moles, who describes it as "the expression of perfect disorder."[4] A message occurs in ordering, imposing a structure, which creates expectation and implies intent. At a minimum it is band noise (one within a given frequency range) and implies some order hidden beneath the amorphous white noise. In Mulligan's situation, band noise, such as the instrument-less music of the quartet, implies some structure. Later, in *The Crying of Lot 49,* Oedipa's circuit-card image of San Narciso similarly has a "hieroglyphic sense of concealed meaning, of an intent to communicate"(13).

Messages have a temporal form, a spectrum in which amplitude is a function of frequency. Einstein showed that noise is the result of agitation of electrons and "is thus inherent in the nature of things and proportional to the absolute temperature"(84). Callisto fears a heat death due to entropy's reaching an absolute temperature and pure noise, noise that emanates from the apartment below him. The only way to counteract noise is to reduce the "pass band," or range of frequencies that a channel will transmit, and thereby particularize the message in advance. In short, "the nature of things" limits perception by an uncertainty principle analogous to the Heisenberg situation: "What is gained in sensitivity is lost in the variety of elements" (84). By increasing sensitivity and decreasing the disorder he perceives outside his apartment, Callisto consciously attempts to reduce communication to its most limited possibilities and ironically minimizes the potential for information at the same time. Moles summarizes this analysis in a manner that is particularly relevant to Pynchon:

> *Noise* thus appears as the *backdrop of the universe,* due to the nature of things. The signal must stand out from noise. There is no signal without noise, no matter how little. Noise is the factor of disorder contingent on the intent of the message, which is characterized by some kind of order. It introduces a dialectic, figure-ground, connected with the dialectic, order-disorder, which constitutes the second law of thermodynamics. The general theorem about entropy, "disorder can only increase in an isolated system," amounts to saying that noise can only degrade the orderliness of the message; it cannot increase the particularized information; it *destroys intent.* (85–86)

Noise can be filtered by selecting a sensitivity band from the range of frequencies. The narrower the band, the less noise but also the more selective the message that can be received. Such a filter increases the response time so that the narrower the band, the more time is required, until finally so much time is required that the message will have changed—another aspect of the uncertainty principle. The human being, however, seldom feels these limitations since he is already selective about the messages he receives, and in this sense perception is selection. Information is typically reduced in a message to a more selective level by a reduction in the elements used in the message or by increasing redundancy by increasing probability. The behavior of a human being who receives messages is governed by his *a priori* knowledge about the message and its symbols. In the human, as in the computer, memory determines a message's structure, its organization, its originality, and its redundancy, and this structuring is effected by education. The intermediary of past experience, or education, is inscribed in the memory; a person's past history, through memory, effects his present and thus constitutes his symbolizing code and the *a priori* structuring of messages—a reduction in uncertainty. Memory summarizes all the past messages an individual has received and thus embodies a learning system that is modified by each succeeding message.

In the dualities established by Moles, Mulligan's party is ground, an approximation of white noise in which all possible components exist within the same probability; it is a scene of disorganization, accident, and failure to apply a filter. The party is distinguished only slightly from the background noise of the world's increasing entropy, in which maximum entropy is maximum (equiprobable) information. It is open, people come and leave, but it opens only to the background of the world's chaos; while not strictly a closed system itself, it is part of one. However, because the party is at least partially distinguished from the larger background, it seems to have some intent to order, band noise, concealed within it. Mulligan does make some attempt to restore order among his guests but the party continues to merge into background as the noise "reached a sustained, ungodly crescendo"(291). Despite the general implications of the party, it at least does not exclude the possibility of originality and irrationality, which, in the context of Weber, can be viewed as positive values. Mulligan makes his attempt at order by one-to-one communication with guests such as Saul, who complains about "Ambiguity. Redundance. Irrelevance, even. Leakage. All this is noise. Noise screws up your signal, makes for disorganization in the circuit"(285). Saul's comparison of human behavior to a machine only underscores Mulligan's human efforts; men are not machines though it is often hard to distinguish between them. Individual efforts within the world's increasing entropy and against the background noise may be all that is possible.

Callisto makes another kind of individual effort. His apartment is intended to be all figure in contrast to the party and the world outside, even though noise from the street and the party penetrates his environment. Callisto has made a deliberate choice to use as many filters as possible to organize and structure his private domain. The band width of the messages he will receive is so narrow that he is able to integrate all his ideas about Adams, Boltzmann, Gibbs, and Clausius because with the passing of time, their originality and information are lost. His is a weighted perception constructed of redundancy and endlessly repeated themes, discriminated from all background noise and any possibility of originality. Callisto can receive only one message, particularized and structured in advance. Thus he lives in his memory—which structures messages—and is "helpless in the past"(292). He has no viable present. His learning system has stopped evolving with *The Education of Henry Adams.* Callisto has created the closed system within his own apartment that he fears in the world's culture, "in which ideas, like heat-energy, would no longer be transferred, since each point in it would ultimately have the same quantity of energy; and intellectual motion would, accordingly, cease"(284). While Callisto is paralyzed, Aubade takes the only possible action. She smashes the window, allowing an equilibrium to be established between the apartment and the world outside. Though it means an eventual heat-death when the world's entropy increases sufficiently, it introduces noise, disorder, uncertainty, and information into a system that had become a self-fulfilling prophecy.

The situations of Mulligan and Callisto do not define the extent of Pynchon's interest in communication generally, but they do pose a central, recurrent problem: how is significant communication possible against a background of increasing disorder and noise if the alternative is redundancy, banality, and a predetermined structure? This question is an issue for Pynchon as well as his characters. In terms of the paranoia metaphor, the connecting structure tends toward the easily recognizable and banal while the impulse that this structure protects is original. Meaning, in information theory, exists in the author and the reader apart from the novel; what is communicated is complexity and unpredictability. Thus the more intelligible the form, the more banal and predictable it is. Information theory partially resolves the dilemma by proposing the existence of two kinds of information: semantic and aesthetic. It is the former that has been discussed thus far since it is the one that is the substance of recognizable, discussable forms. Aesthetic information is personal and untranslatable since it refers to knowledge shared only between the sender and receiver. While semantic information relates to the external world and has a goal of eliciting a response or action, aesthetic information does not have an intent or a goal, but refers only to internal states. Any message has both types of information, one of which is general and tends more toward the intelligible while the other—aesthetic information—is particularized and tends more toward the unpredictable. Though connected, the two types of information are not proportional. Hence in the same message semantic information may tend toward recognizable forms without affecting aesthetic information. The distinction explains in part how Pynchon can write such original works using rather conventional and banal forms. Within his novels, this distinction similarly suggests how characters who exist in a world characterized by increasing social disorder and semantic banality can, on occasion, appear to transcend their milieu.

In subsequent stories Pynchon deals with communication and the problem of living in such a world. In his article on Watts he takes particular note of the role of mass media in imposing an illusory, white-oriented image of majority reality on an alien culture. Communication is control. In *V.* Pynchon gives ample evidence of a rising noise level and general banality. Stencil, as the embodiment of form, comes immediately to mind. Like Callisto, he is an admirer of Henry Adams, speaks of himself in the third person, and seeks a hermetic existence in the comfort of his search as proof against the forces of chaos that V. represents for him. He reduces all communication to the predictable, to what he knows in advance. When, on Malta, he is surprised by unexpected information and the possibility that accident has entered into his system, he nearly panics. His only recourse is retreat into the safety of his form and the pursuit of a redundant clue. Profane's schlemihlhood is also a form but one that tends to reduce communication to zero. He is characterized by an impassiveness and silence. Profane may also be viewed as apparatus, a channel for messages that have little relevance to his inanimate instrumentality. He is even identified, through Kilroy, with a band-pass filter. When he receives messages—honest attempts at communication— from Rachel, Fina, and Paola, Profane invariably filters out anything human. The most stimulating conversation he has is with a machine whose message he does not understand. The Whole Sick Crew, of course, provides much of the noise of the novel. Slab, for example, refers to himself as "a Catatonic Expressionist and his work as 'the ultimate in non-communication' "(45). The Crew is an emblem of modern decadence and pure redundancy: "For it was the unhappy fact that most of them worked for a living and obtained the substance of their conversation from the pages of Time magazine and like publications"(46).

Pynchon's most interesting comment in V. on the potential for meaningful communication in such a world comes from Fausto Maijstral. Because he is a poet he is at least intuitively aware of the possibilities of aesthetic communication as a means of counteracting the banality of semantic communication. Writing his confessions to Paola, Fausto describes himself as having three possible modes of existence: a relationship, a given name, or an occupant of his room. These are reducible either to his being a name in someone else's conversation or to his speaking to himself, as he does in his confessional. It is solipsism, personal communication for which redundancy is merely a vehicle. He goes on to say that "the room simply is. To occupy it, and find a metaphor there for memory, is our own fault" (284). In taking up his position in the room, Fausto appears to be another Callisto or Stencil who uses memory as a filter. Fausto, however, has been on the street and knows about social and linguistic entropy. He has gone through a process he calls "a successive rejection of personalities"(286), which is only another way of stating a principle of communication theory formulated by George Herbert Mead that the self emerges in the act of communication by becoming an object to itself. Fausto says that he sold his soul "to history in little installments. It isn't so much to pay for eyes clear enough to see past the fiction of continuity, the fiction of cause and effect, the fiction of a humanized history endowed with 'reason' "(286).

With Fausto, Pynchon adds communication theory to information theory, thus taking into account the social as well as the statistical situation. Fausto's progressive emergence of self also demonstrates that communication is a mode of action, an establishment of the possibility of future action, and a way of creating at least a personalized social order. Fausto progresses from the level of "undergraduate sentiment" and "rhetoric-for-its-own-sake"(287) to a "retreat into abstractions"(289) to a "retreat from retreat" and a "sensitivity to decadence", at which point he decides that "poetry is not communication with angels or with the 'subconscious.' It is communication with the guts, genitals and five portals of sense. Nothing more" (297). In his last stage of evolution, he comes to realize that communication is necessary for his own survival as well as that of the community even if the outcome is a predictable banality, redundancy, and noise. Fausto is an artist and returns to metaphor as a compromise between the extremes of decadence, chaos, and noise on the one hand, and structure, order, and predetermined form on the other. Metaphor permits the use of intelligible forms without the obligation to believe them or to deny the fundamental irrationality of the world beneath appearances:

> Living as he does much of the time in a world of metaphor, the poet is always acutely conscious that metaphor has no value apart from its

function, that it is a device, an artifice. So that while others may look on the laws of physics as legislation and God as a human form with beard measured in light-years and nebulae for sandals, Fausto's kind are alone with the task of living in a universe of things which simply are, and cloaking that innate mindlessness with comfortable and pious metaphor so that the "practical" half of humanity may continue in the Great Lie, confident that their machines, dwellings, streets and weather share the same human motives, personal traits and fits of contrariness as they.

Poets have been at this for centuries. It is the only useful purpose they do serve in society: and if every poet were to vanish tomorrow, society would live no longer than the quick memories and dead books of their poetry.

It is the "role" of the poet, this 20th Century. To lie. (305)

Metaphor permits the poet a mode of existence that is a self-conscious delusion, almost like the paranoid's structure, without the obligation to believe it. Although it may only reflect his role as an artist, Fausto articulates a viable compromise between redundancy and noise. Metaphor can be widely recognized and its semantic information be quite intelligible while concealing and carrying a high degree of personalized aesthetic information.

In *The Crying of Lot 49* communication becomes a subject as well as a theme. Oedipa Maas finds herself between two systems: one is the official system—the hermetic tower like Fausto's room with the banal conversations of suburban routine and the redundant, exhausted forms of life as it appears to be, including "lies, recitations of routine, arid betrayals of spiritual poverty"; the other is the secret, mysterious system for the alienated and unassimilated people of the streets—"a real alternative to the existlessness, to the absence of surprise to life"(128). Inverarity's ostensibly conventional will, like the noise of Mulligan's party, seems to conceal some intent to communicate just as his town appears to be typical of Southern California and yet has a hieroglyphic meaning: "As if, on some other frequency, or out of the eye of some whirlwind rotating too slow for her heated skin even to feel the centrifugal coolness of, words were being spoken"(13). From one perspective, Oedipa's task is discovering a compromise, a way to communicate between the two alternatives. She is repeatedly reminded that her quest is one of communication: her paranoia depends on a word; Driblette tells her she is like a Puritan, "so hung up with words, words"(56); she realizes that her education has prepared her to be a "whiz at pursuing strange words" (76); and Bortz tells her that the Jacobean play had been altered as a way of dooming it: "What better way . . . than to change the actual words. Remember that Puritans were utterly devoted, like literary critics, to the Word"(116–17). As she learns more about the Tristero, she discovers that it is a channel of communication for the alienated, withdrawn, and irrational; its messages tend toward noise and disorder, *'now reduced to handling anarchist correspondence'*(129–30). By contrast, however, the Tristero makes the official channels appear redundant and encapsulated.

She confronts her dilemma in Nefastis's machine:

> "Communication is the key," cried Nefastis. "The Demon passes his data on to the sensitive, and the sensitive must reply in kind. There are untold billions of molecules in that box. The Demon collects data on each and every one. At some deep psychic level he must get through. The sensitive must receive that staggering set of energies, and feed back something like the same quantity of information. To keep it all cycling. On the secular level all we can see is one piston, hopefully moving. One little movement, against all that massive complex of information, destroyed over and over with each power stroke."(77)

As already noted, the demon allows Pynchon to relate thermodynamic and social entropy with information entropy, a correspondence that contains or influences all the important themes of his novel. However, in the limited area of communication, the important feature of Nefastis's machine is that it requires a "sensitive" person to effect communication. In information theory increasing sensitivity necessitates an increase in selectivity and a reduction in the variety of elements that can be transmitted. Communication obviously cannot occur on the semantic or social levels, but it might be possible on the personal, even idiosyncratic, level if Oedipa were sensitive enough. Nefastis himself demonstrates the distinction and indicates that his machine is directed only at the semantic level. He is devoted to another communication machine, the television, whose banal cartoon shows and news programs energize him; he wants to have intercourse with Oedipa during news about China and "all those Chinese. Teeming. That profusion of life. It makes it sexier, right?" (79). Nefastis's machine can never work because he wants to get something for nothing, mistakenly assuming that information is nothing. In tracking down clues, Oedipa knows that information—or at least the more valuable, concealed information—is something and is the result of hard work.

She also knows that information is not the same as meaning. Even as information about the Tristero accumulates, her understanding of its meaning for her and of the reason she was supposed to discover it grows more ambiguous. She begins to wonder "if the gemlike 'clues' were only some kind of compensation. To make up for her having lost the direct, epileptic Word, the cry that might abolish the night"(87). Oedipa recognizes that what held the thermodynamic and informational entropies of Nefastis's machine together was a metaphor; she also recognizes the Tristero as a "metaphor of God knew how many parts"(80). Like Fausto, she begins to sense that the metaphor is both a lie and a necessary illusion for living with things that simply are, the concealed meaning behind the outward appearances of order and reason. It may be the cry that succeeds on the aesthetic level. Oedipa's encounter with the old sailor reveals to her the secret of how the sensitive can communicate:

> She remembered John Nefastis, talking about his Machine, and massive destructions of information. So when this mattress flared up around the sailor, in his Viking's funeral: the stored, coded years of uselessness, early death, self-harrowing, the sure decay of hope, the set of all men who had slept on it, whatever their lives had been, would truly cease to be, forever, when the mattress burned. She stared at it in wonder. It was as if she had just discovered the irreversible process. It astonished her to think that so much could be lost, even the quantity

of hallucination belonging just to the sailor that the world would bear no further trace of. She knew, because she had held him, that he suffered DT's. Behind the initials was a metaphor, a delirium tremens, a trembling unfurrowing of the mind's plowshare. The saint whose water can light lamps, the clairvoyant whose lapse in recall is the breath of God, the true paranoid for whom all is organized in spheres joyful or threatening about the central pulse of himself, the dreamer whose puns probe ancient fetid shafts and tunnels of truth all act in the same special relevance to the word, or whatever it is the word is there, buffering, to protect us from.(95)

The mattress is a metaphor for memory, that which structures all communications and gives them their originality and redundance. Memory is unique to each individual even if all memories include the same standardized histories, the same shared symbols, and the same limited forms for expression. The saint, the clairvoyant, the true paranoid, and the dreamer all depend on metaphor as the relational form that can hold the original, the true, the cry that might abolish the night in its intelligible redundancy: "The act of metaphor then was a thrust at truth and a lie, depending where you were: inside, safe, or outside, lost. Oedipa did not know where she was"(95). Communication is a mode of action—the establishment of a future —and in metaphor Oedipa at least sees the possibility for continuing in, even being relevant to, the America she discovers through Inverarity's will. Paranoia functions on the social level like metaphor in the communication act. In the end, her paranoia can save her from nothing, but it does permit her a private vision in a public world: "She knew that the sailor had seen worlds no other man had seen if only because there was that high magic to low puns, because DT's must give access to dt's of spectra beyond the known sun, music made purely of Antarctic loneliness and fright. But nothing she knew of would preserve them, or him"(96). His world, like Oedipa's, is unique to his memory's ability to structure and organize it. We walk among crowds but are always alone; we talk with many but speak only to ourselves.

The importance of Oedipa's self-discovery is stressed by the contrast that Mucho Maas provides. Everyone and every message, whether original or redundant, intelligible or not, is reduced to the same thing. As he explains to Oedipa, "Listen to anything and take it apart again. Spectrum analysis, in my head. I can break down chords, and timbres, and words too into all the basic frequencies and harmonics, with all their different loudnesses, and listen to them, each pure tone, but all at once"(105–106). The process of filtering and increasing sensitivity is the same for Oedipa as for Mucho, but he claims "a separate channel for each one . . . and if I need more I just expand"(106). Mucho's procedure is similar to the process of inversion in information theory but he goes much further: "Everybody who says the same words is the same person if the spectra are the same only they happen differently in time, you dig? But time is arbitrary. You pick your zero point anywhere you want, that way you can shuffle each person's time line sideways till they all coincide"(106). His colleagues say, "he's losing his identity . . . He's a walking assembly of man"(104). Mucho is the antithesis of Fausto, who tells Stencil, "We do not walk ganged . . . all our separate selves, like Siamese quintuplets or more"(424–25). Despite their facing essentially the same dilemma regarding communication, Oedipa and Mucho come to opposite conclusions. Whereas Oedipa concludes that the vehicle is unimportant and only conceals the intent to communicate, Mucho is interested only in sound: "The songs, it's not just that they say something, they *are* something, in the pure sound. Something new"(107). While Oedipa becomes isolated, Mucho merges with an undifferentiated mass of humanity in "his vision of consensus"(106).

The Crying of Lot 49 contains an aesthetically dense and dynamic model of communication. The Tristero, Inverarity's will, the Nefastis machine, Mucho's spectrum analysis, and Oedipa's metaphor are all complex and overlapping manifestations of information theory and the social theory of communication. Though Pynchon differentiates among various possibilities, he wryly leaves his readers with a riddle. It is only Oedipa's central role in the novel that relates all the parts and holds them together in her paranoia. There is a clear implication that metaphor as a thrust at truth and a lie offers Oedipa, at least, a viable mode of endurance for her particular circumstances, for the symmetry of two systems of communication. However, it is an alternative based on faith and transcendence, both of which are ephemeral qualities. Even if she is not quite Puritanical in her pursuit of the word, she is somewhat mystical. To the extent that she resembles Slothrop in his search for preterite grace, Oedipa searches for charisma—the breath of the Holy Spirit, the gift of tongues, glossolalia, the epileptic Word—rather than the secular word of semantics. At the novel's end, she walks along railroad tracks and thinks about what the Tristero was supposed to have inherited. Above her is "a web of telephone wires . . . the very copper rigging and secular miracle of communication"(135), and that may be all that is left—a secular rather than inspired or divine communication: ". . . Americans speaking their language carefully, scholarly, as if they were in exile from somewhere else invisible yet congruent with the cheered land she lived in"(135). The America Inverarity has left behind is routinized and bureaucratized, but the invisible world may exist. At least some people still try to communicate, keep trying to find the sensitive other who will understand the truth behind the lie:

> And the voices before and after the dead man's that had phoned at random during the darkest, slowest hours, searching ceaseless among the dial's ten million possibilities for that magical Other who would reveal herself out of the roar of relays, monotone litanies of insult, filth, fantasy, love whose brute repetition must someday call into being the trigger for the unnamable act, the recognition, the Word. (135–36)

Oedipa knows that there are only two alternatives: "Behind the hieroglyphic streets there would either be a transcendent meaning, or only the earth"(136). But her paranoia holds both possibilities. She ends the novel seated in the presence of "the priesthood of some remote culture" or a "descending angel" to await the "crying of lot 49"(138). It may be a cry that will abolish the night.

Crying gives way to screaming in *Gravity's Rainbow*. The novel begins and ends with a rocket: "A screaming comes across the sky. It has happened before, but there is nothing to compare it to now" (3). The rocket is also called "the Word, the one Word that rips apart the day"(25). The epileptic Word, a cry to abolish the night, and the Word, a screaming that rips apart the day, claim the same basic form. In a sense, *Gravity's Rainbow* has happened before in *V.* and *The Crying of Lot 49*, but Pynchon's latest novel is beyond comparison. If novels can be compared with messages, *Gravity's Rainbow* has such complexity and diversity that it cannot be apprehended at once, only serially, and so much is lost in the process that the message has changed before it can ever be assimilated. If we acknowledge that every attempt at understanding is doomed to frustration, at least we can take comfort in metaphor. The central metaphor of *Gravity's Rainbow* is, of course, the Rocket, which can be viewed as a communication system with sender, message, receiver, and circuit defined by the Rocket's parabolic path. It is this metaphor more than any other that conceals an intent to communicate and confronts the reader: "But the Rocket has to be many things, it must answer to a number of different shapes in the dreams of those who touch it . . ."(727). As the metaphorical center of the novel, the Rocket system incorporates the reader, places him at the receiving end of all Pynchon's information: "after all you're used to asking 'how much,' used to measuring, to comparing measurements, putting them into equations to find out how much more, how much of, how much when . . ."(726).

Almost every character in the novel is affected by the Rocket's system. Pointsman sees in it the possibility of "the true mechanical explanation"(89). For Enzian it is a "Text, to be picked to pieces, annotated, explicated . . ."(520). It is transcendence for Pökler and the edge of revelation for Tchitcherine. Mexico sees music in the Poisson distribution of the rocket falls, and Katje Borgesius believes that the Rocket's trajectory is a circuit. As already noted, the Rocket is also a symbol of control for the bureaucracy; it is a system of information that relates all of the cartels together in their exchange and coordination of technology.

Slothrop, of course, is the central character of the novel and he pursues the Rocket as a Puritan after the holy Word. It is Slothrop's Puritan past and his family's business of paper-making—"a medium or ground for shit, money, and the Word"(28)—that causes him to be selected by the meta-cartel to seek out and destroy Enzian. Like his ancestors, he is assumed to be good at interpreting texts, the "Puritan reflex of seeking other orders behind the visible . . ."(188). Slothrop, however, is not one of the elect and the Word, finally, has a different meaning for him. There is a difference between "Slothrop's own Puritan hopes for the Word, the Word made printer's ink, dwelling along with antibodies and iron-bound breath in a good man's blood . . ."(571) and the elect's view of the Word made flesh. The importance of the word to the elect is reinforced by Frans Van der Groov, one of the people "trapped among frequencies of their own voices and words"(110). He thinks the tragedy of the Dodoes he exterminates is that they lack speech: "*only in His Word is eternal life to be found*"(111). However, the narrator points out that it is with the Word that the elect would establish their hegemony of control: "No language meant no chance of co-opting them in to what their round and flaxen invaders were calling Salvation"(110).

Slothrop is among the preterite whom the Puritans thought would be damned because they were not meant to be saved; they were passed over. But preterition also means an affinity for the past, a backward-looking, "learning to cherish what was lost"(693). For Slothrop, the Rocket is one more "entry in a record, a history . . . instructing him, dunce and drifter, in ways deeper than he can explain . . ."(626). Slothrop finds a "state of minimum grace"(603) in his preterition, his being passed over. While the elect have the illusion of a continuous past and future, a salvation that precedes life and succeeds death, the preterite are more tenuous. At Peenemünde his "personal density" begins to decrease proportionately to his "temporal bandwidth"(509) as his preterition grows and the control of the Rocket's Text over him diminishes: " . . . is it, then, really never to find you again? Not even in your worst times of night, with pencil words on your page only Δt from the things they stand for? And inside the victim is twitching, fingering beads, touching wood, avoiding any Operational Word. Will it really never come to take you, now?"(510). Among the preterite there is a sense that the Revelation has already occurred sometime in the past. So it may be for Slothrop as the Rocket's Operational Word ceases to haunt him and the Rocket itself becomes the cross in a circle, a symbol of transcendence, and, perhaps, a screaming. When Slothrop ceases to search for the Rocket, communication is no longer a mechanism for control.

Slothrop had sought information about Blicero's Rocket 00000. When he appeared as Weissmann in *V.*, Blicero ironically decoded Mondaugen's sferics, atmospheric noise from outside the world, into Wittgenstein's opening proposition of the *Tractatus* in an extreme example of filtering information and of exercising control. The full significance of Weissmann's interest in Wittgenstein's picture theory of language is not revealed until *Gravity's Rainbow* when he literally tries to situate himself—or more accurately his substitute and his transmitted words—outside the world, outside the correspondence of language with reality. With the aid of his special Rocket, he intends to transcend language and throw Wittgenstein's ladder—with its logical supports—away after him. Blicero's program of putting control inside has already been discussed; in addition to the objective of consummating life in death, however, Blicero seeks to expand the limits of his world, to exert his will on reality, and to speak in the realm of Wittgenstein's silence. Blicero's interest in language is reaffirmed when we learn of his infatuation with Rilke, whose poetry replaces the *Tractatus* as his inspiration. Blicero can accommodate both the philosopher and the poet, however. When he names Enzian after Rilke's gentian, he feels that "words are only an eye-twitch away from the things they stand for"(100). Blicero remakes reality to conform with his words, not only by naming but by enacting games under his control. He uses language to structure the reality he wants and to destroy any competing reality that others under him might have: " . . . every true god must be both organizer and destroyer"(99). As the war progresses and Blicero retreats more into his own private world, he becomes less a person and more a presence "with the same reach toward another shape as words trying to make their way through dreams"(666). By the war's end, "he never leaves the single dream, there are no more differences between the worlds: they have become one for him"(721).

The instruments of Blicero's final attempt at transcendence of reality through language are the Rocket and Gottfried, to whom he talks for hours. After months of forcing Gottfried into stock roles and redundant forms for which his lines are all well known in advance, Blicero suddenly addresses him differently and leaves him without a set role: "This is so more-than-real . . . he feels he must keep every word, that none must be lost. Blicero's words have become precious to him"(721). Gottfried listens while Blicero unfolds his dream of going beyond the limits of language-determined reality, a linguistic gravity: "I dream of a great glass sphere, hollow and very high and far away . . . the colonists have learned to do without air, it's vacuum inside and out . . . it's understood the men won't ever return . . . they are all men. There are ways for getting back, but so complicated, so at the mercy of language, that presence back on Earth is only temporary, and never 'real' . . . passages out there are dangerous, chances of falling so shining and deep"(723). In Gottfried's ear "a tiny speaker has been surgically implanted. . . . The data link runs through the radio-guidance system, and the words of Weissmann are to be, for a while, multiplexed with the error-corrections sent out to the Rocket"(751). Gottfried will carry Blicero's words beyond the limits of reality and language into the vacuum, and the Rocket will become a literal message addressed, presumably, to Rilke's angels. The content of the message matters less to Blicero than his having opened a new channel of communication. In *V.* he received a message from the stars; in *Gravity's Rainbow* he returns his own: " . . . a Word, spoken with no warning into your ear, and then silence forever"(25). Blicero knows that the Rocket will eventually fall and his message will be lost, but it is an attempt to exert control over Wittgenstein's world for a moment. It may also be a cry the angels can hear: "This ascent will be betrayed to Gravity. But the Rocket engine, the deep cry of combustion that jars the soul, promises escape. The victim, in bondage to falling, rises on a promise, a prophecy, of Escape . . ."(758). For a moment the Rocket hangs over a curve of the Earth along which people who look to the sky can wish upon the evening's first star, but a star that falls, "a bright angel of death"(760) that hangs over us all, heretics and believers alike.

Pynchon permits Blicero's Rocket to retain its mystery even as he transforms it into the abstraction of the last section of the novel. Rocket 00000 loses its identity to the Rocket system, which can be interpreted in a variety of ways. As a metaphor for communication, the abstracted Rocket corresponds loosely to the sonic object of information theory since it is this concept that helps explain how aesthetic information exists simultaneously with redundancy and intelligibility. If sound, such as music, is regarded as a temporal phenomenon, having direction in time, time can be mapped into space by recording. Thus time can share the characteristics of space; it can be reversed, for example, or its formerly indivisible continuity can be divided infinitely, like the delta-t of the Rocket's fall. These divisions of sound-space are called sonic objects, entities that can be regarded as the microstructures of the original sound and, when combined, as the carriers of energy and information. They can be recombined or considered separately, each with its own evolution in time (attack, body, decay) corresponding to the Rocket's ascent, Brennschluss, and descent. They constitute a perceptual form, a way of isolating sound between silences so that it might be apprehended. Although unnecessary, it may be useful to regard the Rocket as such a perceptual form for the novel; it incorporates time and space in the Rocket's parabola and it complements the Rocket as film object: "Imagine a missile one hears approaching only *after* it explodes. The reversal! A piece of time neatly snipped out . . . a few feet of film run backwards . . . the blast of the rocket, fallen faster than sound—then growing *out of it* the roar of its own fall, catching up to what's already death and burning . . . a ghost in the sky . . ."(48).